Precious
PERVERSIONS

SOUTHERN LITERARY STUDIES

Scott Romine, Series Editor

Precious PERVERSIONS

Humor, Homosexuality, and the Southern Literary Canon

TISON PUGH

Louisiana State University Press
Baton Rouge

Published by Louisiana State University Press

Manufactured in the United States of America
First printing

Designer: Barbara Neely Bourgoyne
Typefaces: Thirsty Soft and Trade Gothic, display; Ingeborg, text
Printer and binder: Maple Press (digital)

Library of Congress Cataloging-in-Publication Data

Names: Pugh, Tison, author.
Title: Precious perversions : humor, homosexuality, and the Southern literary canon / Tison Pugh.
Description: Baton Rouge : Louisiana State University Press, 2016. | Series: Southern literary studies | Includes bibliographical references and index.
Identifiers: LCCN 2015035735| ISBN 978-0-8071-6269-9 (cloth : alk. paper) | ISBN 978-0-8071-6270-5 (pdf) | ISBN 978-0-8071-6271-2 (epub) | ISBN 978-0-8071-6272-9 (mobi)
Subjects: LCSH: American literature—Southern states—History and criticism. | Humor in literature. | Homosexuality in literature. | Southern states—In literature.
Classification: LCC PS261 .P83 2016 | DDC 810.9/975—dc23 LC record available at http://lccn.loc.gov/2015035735

The paper in this book meets the guidelines for permanence and durability of the Committee on Production Guidelines for Book Longevity of the Council on Library Resources. ♾

To Gregory Edward Dole, Daren Glenn Hill, and Robert Ellis Sanford

Thanks for the laughs.

Contents

Acknowledgments

I appreciate the support of the University of Central Florida College of Arts and Humanities, under the leadership of Dean José Fernández, for a sabbatical that allowed me the necessary time to finish this manuscript. UCF's Learning Institute for Elders provided a timely grant that assisted this project, for which I am deeply grateful. The chapter "Camp Sadomasochism in Tennessee Williams's Plays" was published previously in *Texas Studies in Literature and Language*, under the editorship of Kurt Heinzelman; the chapter "Florence King's Queer Conservatism and the Gender Politics of Southern Humor" was published previously in *Mississippi Quarterly,* under the editorship of Ted Atkinson. I appreciate their permission to republish these essays here.

Precious PERVERSIONS

INTRODUCTION

PRECIOUS PERVERSIONS

An oldie but a goodie: the southern belle returns home from her grand European tour, and her friends eagerly ask her what she learned during her travels. "Well, over there they have men who make love to other men, and they're called *gay*!" Shocked beyond measure, her inquisitive friends press for more scandalous revelations. "Well, over there they have women who make love to other women, and they're called *lesbians*!" Titillated beyond belief, the belle's friends plead for even more such perverse disclosures. "Well, over there they have men who lick women's most private parts!" Her friends cry out in horror, "What do you call a man who would do such a filthy thing?" The belle coolly drawls, "Well, I'm not sure, but I called mine *Precious*."

As an example of queer southern humor, this joke plays on the invisibility of homosexuality in the U.S. South, in which the belle's naive friends lack any understanding of eroticism outside the strictest parameters of heteronormativity: homosexuality can only be imagined "over there," in a foreign landscape marked by Continental decadence. Coupled with their ignorance of homosexuality, the friends' comprehension of heterosexuality appears to extend only to the missionary position (if it extends even that far), and the belle's phrasings, laden with the honeyed sweetness of debutante delicacy, likewise cast her as an innocent abroad—until the punchline brings together that most clichéd of southern appellations, *Precious,* with the revelation of her daring sexual sophistication during her travels. What could not have happened in this comic version of the South—its inhabitants literally have no words for the acts and identities described—now infiltrates the land, with this belle (one can only assume, given the abbreviated nature of this and most such anecdotes) insisting on such pleasures in her future. At the same time, this joke reinforces the marginalization of homosexuality in the South, where its straight citizens, or so we are to believe, simply do not know that some men love men, that some women love women, and that gay people express these affections physically. While not an overtly homophobic joke, this chestnut relies on the marginalization of southern queerness for its humor to function, yet it also renders visible, if only momentarily, this most precious perversion of same-sex desire and love—precious to its practitioners, perverse to its detractors, and integral to the construction of southern sexuality in the wrangling between these poles.

Of course, one should not indict the South as homophobic because of a single comic tale of precious perversity—anti-queer humor is not unique to the states below the Mason-Dixon line—but, all jokes aside, the South has proved itself demographically and, one might even add, determinedly more homophobic than other regions of the United States. For example, prior to the U.S. Supreme Court's 26 June 2013 decisions in the cases of *Hollingsworth v. Perry* and *United States v. Windsor*, which unleashed a series of successful challenges to laws prohibiting gay marriage, northernmost Maryland was the only southern state that allowed gay marriage, with the Deep South uniformly hostile to extending marital rights. Not until the Court's decision in *Obergefell v. Hodges* on 26 June 2015 did the South's holdouts—Louisiana, Mississippi, Georgia, Arkansas, Missouri, Tennessee, Kentucky, and Texas—finally accept gay marriage.[1] In his critique of southern culture, Carlos Dews suggests that if "an attribute of the South thought of as characteristically southern" is analyzed, one will "find . . . beneath it either misogyny, homophobia, racism, or classism."[2] The myth of the South as a land of friendly faces and boundless hospitality clashes with the reality experienced by many of its citizens as they face daily discrimination due to core aspects of their identities. Historical and sociological studies of southern gay life—including such works as John Howard's *Men Like That: A Southern Queer History*, E. Patrick Johnson's *Sweet Tea: Black Gay Men of the South*, and Bernadette Barton's *Pray the Gay Away: The Extraordinary Lives of Bible Belt Gays*—attest to the discrimination, often accompanied by physical, mental, and spiritual violence, that queer men and women have faced.[3] The work of these scholars testifies to the challenges of queer southern life, where the dominant culture has historically prized a blanket construction of sexual and racial heteronormativity as one of its defining virtues—no matter the blinders necessary to endorse such a view.

Nonetheless, as James T. Sears wryly notes, "Southern history is never simple and seldom straight,"[4] for despite its overarching homophobia, the South must grapple with the repercussions of marginalizing its many gay citizens. This paradox shines forth in the South's rich literary legacy, which includes the flourishing throughout the twentieth century and into the twenty-first of a striking array of gay, lesbian, and bisexual authors, among them such leading figures of the southern renaissance as Tennessee Williams, Carson McCullers, and Truman Capote. In the wake of the South's reemergence as a literary powerhouse, talents such as Florence King, John Kennedy Toole, Bertha Harris, Alice Walker, Rita Mae Brown, Howard Cruse, Fannie Flagg, John Waters, Allan Gurganus, Dorothy Allison, Kevin Sessums, David Sedaris, and Del Shores collectively attest to the vibrancy of queer experiences throughout the region as a source of inspiration.

Gay southern authors face the conundrum of living in and writing about a land that refuses to acknowledge their full humanity, for throughout much of the twentieth century, normative southern ideology demanded the closeting, if not the erasure, of homosexuality. The South relies on its mythologies to whitewash its truths, and part of the social construction of southern identity denies the possibility of homosexuality and other such ostensible "perversions." Indeed, in many ways the South is itself a myth, a collective American vision of the region, its people, and its folkways. As Jennifer Rae Greeson explains, "Wherever U.S. citizens were born, wherever we presently live, whatever our personal experiences of the southeastern states—for all of us knowing about our South is part of knowing what it means to be an American. This South that we hold collectively in our minds is not—could not possibly be—a fixed or real place."[5] An imaginative reconstruction of a land, a looking glass through which the United States sees its interior Other, the South flutters on the borders between reality and fantasy while retaining the ability to conscript and construct its citizenry into their appropriate roles for this regional and national fantasia.

Greeson is surely correct in her contention that the South could not possibly be real, yet this fantasy and its inevitable self-contradictions harshly affect many of its inhabitants. Pondering the South's history of racism, Stephen A. Smith unpacks the ways that southern mythology dismisses the humanity of vast segments of its population: "The old mythology of the South and the society it depicted were 'for whites only.' There were no black planters living in the fabled white-columned mansions, there were no black belles in hooped skirts on verandahs, there were no black cavalry officers in uniforms of gray, and there were no black industrialists smiling at their millhands and balance sheets. The old myth had absolutely no meaning for blacks, and it held meaning for very few whites when blacks began to have the opportunity to participate in the 'Southern way of life.'"[6] Comparing the discrimination that African Americans and homosexuals have faced is not without its risks, yet Smith's picture of the "for whites only" South highlights the vagaries of bigotry. Transgressions of racial lines would not have been countenanced in the old South, yet as much as homosexuality is denigrated in so many southern traditions, it is quite possible to imagine gay planters, lesbian belles, a cavalry officer in love with another soldier, and a prosperous industrialist buggering one of his millhands on the sly—but only if one envisions these hypothetical queer southerners as hiding their sexual orientations and closeting their liaisons under a veneer of normative whiteness. Unlike race, one's sexuality can be denied, cloaked, or otherwise camouflaged, as well as confessed or revealed. As Richard Dyer aptly remarks, "the problem with queers is you can't tell who is and who isn't—except that, maybe, if you know the tell-tale signs, you can."[7]

Historically, the South has compelled many of its queer citizens to deny the truth of their desires to survive in such hostile terrain. As Howard documents, this problem is compounded by individuals who engage in same-sex acts yet renounce or otherwise deny homosexual identities or even the same-sex desires that they have acted on: in contrast to "men who identify as gay or otherwise see same-sex desire as central to their being," some men "who experienced or acted on male-male desire . . . didn't identify as gay." Howard also hypothesizes, "These men probably predominated, though no one will ever be able to say with certainty."[8] Even when queer southerners refuse to conform to the region's insistence on sexual normativity, other southerners often hide their queerness for them. James Keller provides a rich example of this hypocrisy in how Columbus, Mississippi, celebrates its identity as Tennessee Williams's birthplace while obfuscating his homosexuality from public view. Celebrate the town that gave birth to this great American literary treasure, the town pronounces in its plaques and memorials to Williams, but please overlook his perversion of southern sexual normativity.[9] If one cannot see evidence of gay lives, the marginalization and vilification of queer people continues apace, with sexually normative southerners never compelled to acknowledge their shared humanity with people of various sexual orientations.

Certainly, a good deal of twentieth-century southern literature belittles homosexuality, and a few examples will suffice to demonstrate the virulence of this tradition. In Walker Percy's *Love in the Ruins,* the protagonist Thomas

More ironically muses over the sad state of the American literary arts due to the popularity of gay novels: "The Southern gothic novel yielded to the Jewish masturbatory novel, which in turn gave way to the WASP homosexual novel, which has nearly run its course"; he then sighs, thereby to accentuate Percy's ruefully satiric point: "Gore Vidal is the grand old man of American letters."[10] Beyond such snide aspersions, other authors depict gay sex as a traumatic experience of violation. Flannery O'Connor, in *The Violent Bear It Away,* paints the sodomitical rape of Marion Francis Tarwater as the ultimate degradation that catalyzes his spiritual mission, but more so, the perpetrator of this violent act assumes monstrous, vampiric, and subhuman qualities after sating his criminal lust: "His delicate skin had acquired a faint pink tint as if he had refreshed himself on blood."[11] Indeed, O'Connor identifies this character as the devil himself, aligning homosexuality with the ultimate avatar of evil.[12] James Dickey's *Deliverance* derives its narrative power from the possibility of rural southern men sodomizing strangers they encounter in the woods, as the protagonist Ed narrates the events culminating in his friend Bobby's rape: "The white-bearded man was suddenly also naked up to the waist. There was no need to justify or rationalize anything; they were going to do what they wanted to. I struggled for life in the air, and Bobby's body was still and pink in an obscene posture that no one could help. The tall man restored the gun to Bobby's head, and the other one knelt behind him."[13] The brutality of this encounter surfaces in its apparent randomness, in which homosexual violation occurs without the need for its perpetrators "to justify or rationalize anything." But one could well turn this formulation on Dickey himself: how does he "justify or rationalize" using sodomy as an apparently transcendental signifier of inhuman degradation that rural southern men—"rednecks" in common parlance—engage in as expressions of violence rather than affection?[14] Such are the mechanisms of homophobia, in which various writers have denigrated homosexuality and homosexual intercourse without querying the roots of their depictions. More common than outright derision, however, are queer depictions relegated to the margins of the text, and William Faulkner's shadowy treatment of gay themes exemplifies the occlusion of homosexuality such that for many readers it simply fails to register.[15] Sometimes even the chance that a character could be gay, as arises in William Styron's depiction of his protagonist in *The Confessions of Nat Turner,* engenders outrage and controversy, as Michael Bibler documents in his study of readers' reactions to the novel.[16]

Beyond such derogatory treatments of homosexuality reigns an extensive silence, in which many narratives simply do not acknowledge the likelihood of queer lives, queer loves, and other such precious perversions of southern sexual gentility. In some ways such silence is even more deadening: one can argue against biased depictions of gay life, but it is harder to resist the virulent miasma of nothingness. Furthermore, many literary scholars unwittingly contribute to this prevailing history of literary homophobia by focusing more on the disturbing consequences of homosexuality in southern fiction than on its pleasures. Jaime Harker notes that the "tone of much of this scholarship . . . is somber, an investigation of tortured racial and sexual politics," and concludes, in a pithy yet powerful formulation, that the sexual traumas depicted in narratives of the South receive unduly sustained attention from literary critics: "Corncobs and castration have haunted the scholarly psyche."[17] And so this study takes as its foundational questions: Against this backdrop of prejudice and exclusion, what do southern queers find funny about the South, and how do they create laughter in response to its stifling traditions? How do these authors reformulate the southern literary canon in light of queer desire and humor, and how does the southern literary canon resist or facilitate its reconstitution? Certainly, as seminal comic theorists including Francis Hutcheson, Henri Bergson, and Sigmund Freud have argued, humor reveals deep truths—often latent truths—about jokers and the cultures from which they emerge, as well as how the butts of their jokes are constructed within discourses both private and public.[18] "Humour is not resigned; it is rebellious. It signifies the triumph not only of the ego, but also of the pleasure principle, which is strong enough to assert itself here in the face of adverse real circumstances," Freud avows, pointing both to the cultural work of humor in contesting a society's prevailing order and to the power of such resistance for the comic who skewers the dominant social order.[19]

For both gays and straights, the South is a land of contrast and ironies, arising in large part from the reversals engendered by the Civil War. This conflict, undertaken by the South to defend slavery and white privilege, ended with these ambitions unfulfilled. While a war that cost approximately 750,000 human lives is hardly a laughing matter, such inversions, in terms of the structural tropes of humor, invite ironic reassessments of prevailing views.[20] Much humor is based on ironies and incongruities, with the humorist taking advantage of these disruptions of social expectations to elicit laughter. According to Quintilian, at its core irony consists simply of circumstances when "we understand something which is the opposite of what is actually said."[21] Søren Kierkegaard observes, with a muted levity in his analogy, that "Irony is a disciplinarian feared only by those who do not know it, but cherished by those who do. He who does not understand irony and has no ear of its whisperings lacks *eo ipso* what might be called the absolute beginning of the personal life."[22] C. Vann Woodward, the South's preeminent twentieth-century historian, explains that many southerners could not perceive the ironies of their daily lives: "In the nature of things the participants in an ironic situation are rarely conscious of the irony: else they would not become its victims. Awareness must ordinarily be contributed by an observer, a nonparticipant. And the observer must have an unusual combination of detachment and sympathy. He must be able to appreciate both elements in the incongruity that go to make up the ironic situation, both the virtue and the vice to which pretensions of virtue lead."[23] So many southerners cannot, or do not bother, to perceive the ironies of their culture, and so they steep in its prejudices and biases, which consequently seep further into the land's fabric.

Woodward correctly proposes that observers and nonparticipants typically view the irony of a situation more clearly than those embroiled in it, yet it is critical to stipulate that many observers and nonparticipants of a culture live within its very borders but are precluded from the privileges that its normative members enjoy. Shut out from the party, these Others can look through the windows to note the disparities between mythology and reality. Mab Segrest, explaining the traditions of southern laughter and their ironic sensibility in relation to gay identity, posits that:

> Southern humor . . . plays with irony, with several levels of truth and lies. That's because truth, like justice, has been pretty besmirched by white Southern culture, a culture built on a great lie: that Native Americans and Africans were less than human and therefore could be killed or enslaved. A complimentary lie is the lie of normalcy (taught so well in Southern Sunday schools and churches): Jesus (fairskinned and blond) loves me, so I am normal and good (white, straight, Christian), better than those deviants from the norm (Blacks, queers, Jews, for instance). This notion of normalcy is really quite unnatural—a lie—since everyone is a bit peculiar. People lie to protect each other and themselves from what is falsely established as truth. This habit of white lies is the heart of Southern manners and civility and the great gentleness that exists, along with the great violence, in Southern people.[24]

Within Segrest's formulation, the South serves up civility and violence in roughly equal measure, with manners and etiquette forming a veneer to camouflage the violence. Florence King echoes this view when pondering the region's "exquisite balance between hatred and hospitality."[25] Such disparities between appearance and reality allow fertile conditions for irony to flourish, which fosters the South's unique styles of humor, another constituent part of its overarching mythology.

For, in contrast to the cultural construction of flinty, stoic, and passionless Yankees stands the image of joking, playful, and merry southerners, whose humor defines their land. Robert Higgs affirms that "Humor is as much a product of the South as cotton, coal, timber, music, and fundamental religion,"[26] and the South's vibrant legacy of humor testifies to the importance of the comic in defining its regional character—as a brief overview of its comic sensibilities attests. Throughout much of the antebellum and post–Civil War periods of American history, the South was characterized as fundamentally unserious because of its affection for humor and amusements. Consider C. G. Parsons's 1855 broadside: "The slave States are proverbial for their amusements. The families of wealthy slaveholders are seldom taught to labor, or to engage in any kind of business. Life is to them but a play-day, and the question of every morning is—how to kill time?"[27] Such stereotypes of the indolent yet mirthful South contribute to its mythology, for these visions became an integral part of various southerners' sense of cultural identity. Nevertheless, as much as humor flows throughout the South in its past and its present, its valences shift in reaction to various cultural conditions. Wade Hall sees a heightened emotionality as key to southern humor during the years of Reconstruction: "Since so much of post-Civil-War Southern humor was retrospectively oriented, it naturally tended to pathos. Pathos was implicit in much prewar writing . . . but it was not until after the war that it became an almost indispensable ingredient."[28] Much southern humor contains a dark streak as well, as Andrew Silver demonstrates in his *Minstrelsy and Murder: The Crisis of Southern Humor, 1835–1925,* which offers detailed analysis of the writings of Augustus Baldwin Longstreet, George Washington Harris, Charles Chesnutt, and Mark Twain: "It is this jarring failure of humor—this bold generic inconsistency, this darkness at the heart of the comic—that defines southern humor as it emerges from the nineteenth century, marking its radical departure from nineteenth-century norms of good humor."[29] Again, the Civil War's place in a history of southern laughter cannot be overlooked, for it is a primary source of this darker vision of the comic. In a final example of the South's construction through humor, Arthur Palmer Hudson, in his 1936 study *Humor of the Old Deep*

South, could see only a thoroughly unified culture: "Our stage is the heart of the old deep South—a region geographically unified, naturally homogenous; historically one-storied or sharing many stories of the same kind, inhabited by people of the same racial and social background, subjected to similar outside influences, bound up in the same destiny."[30] Within Hudson's analysis of southern humor, the landscape brooks no variations in race, sexual orientation, or other markers of personal identity, suggesting that laughter permeates the land and defines its people uniformly, as he pays little attention to its fluctuations in spirit and sensibility over its history and among its subpopulations. As this abridged account of southern humor illustrates, to study the region's humor is to study its identity in relationship to itself, to the rest of the United States, and to its history, whether recent or long past. In this light, any characterization of the South's regional humor—as mirthful, as retrospective, as dark, as unitary—reflects to some degree the conditions that one establishes as its parameters.

Notwithstanding their differing perspectives and premises, these various studies of southern humor highlight the ways in which, in Simon Critchley's terms, a region's people build a communal identity through their shared comic sensibility: "A sense of humour is often what connects us most strongly to a specific place and leads us to predicate characteristics of that place, assigning certain dispositions and customs to its inhabitants."[31] While names such as Mark Twain, Joel Chandler Harris, and Flannery O'Connor stand atop the canon of southern literary humor, Roy Blount Jr. theorizes that a comic sensibility enlivens all native southerners: "Being humorous in the South is like being motorized in Los Angeles or argumentative in New York—humorous is not generally a whole calling in and of itself, it's just something that you're in trouble if you aren't."[32] Thus, even southern writers not primarily known for a mirthful style—including Edgar Allan Poe, Zora Neale Hurston, and Robert Penn Warren—on occasion employ a lighter tone in their fiction and verse.[33] Of course, not all southern writers, whether straight or gay, strive for humorous effects in their writings, but as Blount suggests, they all live in a land that values humor, with this sensibility frequently finding an outlet, even if muted, in their fiction.

Similar to its role in defining southern culture, humor assists in establishing community in gay and lesbian subcultures. Throughout much of the twentieth century, when many queer people closeted themselves and faced difficulty finding allies and lovers, a transgressively ironic, often mordant, comic sensibility served as a subcultural shibboleth to distinguish friends from foes. As Joseph Goodwin explains in his folkloric study of queer humor, "Humor allows us to express ideas that are normally socially inexpressible, and in doing so we give our listeners quite a bit of insight into our thoughts and values. To function as secret communication among gays, jokes must contain a highly esoteric referent. Recognition of the humor suggests that the listener is probably homosexual."[34] Queer humor assists gays in identifying kindred spirits: if one's interlocutor understands and reacts positively to one's comic sensibility, the odds improve that she or he is a fellow traveler in gay circles. It must be noted, however, that these rhetorical circumstances shift when queer southern authors write to wider audiences: as members of a sexual minority seeking readers throughout the United States and beyond, these writers must choose whether to encode queer humor into their writings, to overlook gay issues in favor of ostensibly more universal themes, or to write openly about desires deemed taboo within their culture.

As the following chapters demonstrate, gay southern authors frequently employ humor when depicting their native soil, yet should such humor be labeled "subversive"? Many humor theorists highlight its subversive valence, its propensity, in Rod Martin's words, "to push the boundaries of social propriety, attack 'sacred cows,' and rebel against social norms.'"[35] Charles Flowers, in his anthology of queer humor, states that humor can be "truly progressive, in the sense of creating change, both personal and collective,"[36] and Gloria Kaufman opens her anthology of feminist humor by proclaiming, "Humor is empowering. Oppressed peoples deliberately use humor to lighten the burdens of daily life so that they can survive."[37] While the humorous possibilities of attacking "sacred cows," of voicing a progressive political agenda, and of empowering the disenfranchised may serve as necessary steps in resisting prejudice and discrimination, they do not in themselves correlate with eradicating injustice or achieving the desired ends of social integration, and it is prudent to consider the limits of the comic in advancing social reforms: Aristophanes's *Lysistrata* ended neither war nor sexism in fifth-century B.C.E. Athens, nor did it prove the efficacy of sex strikes as a persuasive tactic for resolving marital disputes. Similarly, as much as some queer southern humorists mercilessly satirize the region's mores, it is insufficient simply to theorize that their humor "subverts" these traditions. Even with gay men's camp humor, which often involves over-the-top parodies of gender and normative culture, caution is warranted against excessively optimistic assumptions about humor's seditious force.

Camp humor reimagines possibilities of gender and culture, yet, as Andrew Britton contends, "Camp is individualistic and apolitical, and even at its most disturbing asks for little more than living-room."[38] A man putting on a dress and a tiara does not a revolution spark.

Beyond simply asserting the subversive nature of queer southern humor, this book examines how various authors employ unique strands of comedy in their writings that, while they may indeed reconceive the prevailing southern social order, also expand the parameters, themes, and tropes of southern literature. For while humor has rarely, if ever, operated as a panacea for social ills, it hones individuals' understanding of their cultural landscapes, as Ralph Ellison perceived: "For by allowing us to laugh at that which is normally *un*laughable, comedy provides an otherwise unavailable clarification of vision that calms the clammy trembling which ensues whenever we pierce the veil of conventions that guard us from the basic absurdity of the human condition."[39] Laughter helps individuals and societies to see the familiar anew and, consequently, to confront the duplicities, paradoxes, and core resilience of humanity—a view that never ceases to astound, if also to frustrate, and when we are lucky, to amuse. Queer southern authors turned to their comic muses frequently and, in so doing, rewrote the paradigms of southern literature in revolutionary ways. The southern literary canon, quite simply, was never the same after these queer authors, yet the southern literary canon simultaneously has appeared united against some of these authors gaining entry into its ranks. The varying careers and reception histories of the six primary authors examined in this study—Tennessee Williams, Truman Capote, Florence King, Rita Mae Brown, Dorothy Allison, and David Sedaris—testify to the marginalized status of much queer humor yet also to how these writers managed to have their voices heard.

Chapter 1 explores the ways in which camp humor infiltrates Tennessee Williams's otherwise "straight" dramas. Few critics would classify such works as *A Streetcar Named Desire* and *Cat on a Hot Tin Roof* as comedies, yet Williams's subtle camp style opens up readings and performances of his plays that extend their sensibility to the comic. For Williams, camp becomes a mode of life in the South, with the necessary double posturing of humor camouflaging desires taboo for his time. Furthermore, he frequently imbues depictions of sexual relationships with a subtext of sadomasochistic desire that, because of the exaggerated posturings of such sex roles, further encourages ironic stagings of his plays. Iconic characters including Blanche

Dubois in *Streetcar* and Margaret in *Cat* stand as archetypally campy figures despite the searing nature of Williams's dramas, and this chapter unlocks how camp sadomasochism contributes to their latent humor, which can build to the point of parody.

While celebrated as one of the defining wits of his day, who proved his tongue's sharp edge with his withering assessment of Jack Kerouac and the Beats' literature—"What they do . . . isn't writing at all—*it's typing*"[40]—Truman Capote built his reputation primarily on his serious literary endeavors, particularly his gothic bildungsroman *Other Voices, Other Rooms,* his innovative nonfiction novel *In Cold Blood,* and his short stories of psychological depth and texture (e.g., "Miriam," "Shut a Final Door," "The Headless Hawk"). Beginning with a brief overview of the relative dearth of comic moments and modes in Capote's literature, Chapter 2 analyzes Capote's most extended comic venture: his screenplay for John Huston's caper film *Beat the Devil.* This movie, which is typically overlooked in assessments of his literary career, gave Capote free rein to indulge his comic sensibility through camp stylings. From this vantage point, the chapter then looks for camp humor in other milestone texts of Capote's career, suggesting the possibility that Capote's archly comic voice, in satirizing the tropes of southern gothicism, elevates *Other Voices, Other Rooms* into a foundational text of the southern renaissance. In contrast, Capote's unfinished novel *Answered Prayers* highlights his failure to maintain a camp voice in his fiction, as his parroting of other celebrities' punch lines overshadows his unique comic sensibility.

While gay men and lesbians have been jointly construed as the Other in southern culture, men and women experience this prejudice differently, and this difference fosters distinct relationships to and deployments of humor. The next chapters address two of the preeminent queer, southern, comic female writers of the later twentieth century—Florence King and Rita Mae Brown—and align their humor with their experiences with second-wave feminism as it swept through the United States, both North and South, in the 1960s and 1970s. Chapter 3 examines the question of women's wit and feminist politics in the patriarchal South. King flagrantly defied southern norms of women's sexual decorum, such as in her brazen defense of the erotically transgressive female: "There is no such thing as a fallen woman; when she steps out of her place, she always steps up."[41] While many readers assumed that such an unapologetically feminist voice expressed a politically left sensibility, King brusquely rejected such an identification: "In my 1985 memoir *Confessions of a Failed Southern Lady,* I related a Lesbian affair I had in graduate school at the University of Mississippi in 1958. It made me the darling of radical left-wing females who assumed that I shared their political views merely because I had gone to bed with a woman," she begins, as she then outs herself politically: "*It's time you know I'm a Republican.*"[42] King's rapier-sharp wit highlights the variability of humor as a means for reassessing culture, and this chapter also explores her disidentifications with various aspects of her identity, including her gender, sexuality, southernness, and political affiliation, which she employs to unsettle readers' understanding of the comic and its constructions of southern gender.

In Chapter 4, the analysis turns to *Rubyfruit Jungle,* Brown's thinly veiled memoir of her lesbian life in the South, as well as other novels in her extensive corpus, such as *In Her Day, Southern Discomfort, Sudden Death, Venus Envy, Riding Shotgun, Alma Mater, Six of One, Bingo, Loose Lips,* and *The Sand Castle. Rubyfruit Jungle* uproariously claims southern women's right to free themselves from regional codes of heteronormative desire, and in this and her other works Brown reimagines the comic as a distinctly female genre—one that spurns what she sees as the masculinist biases of wit in favor of a woman's style of zany humor. The South serves as a conservative foil for Brown's progressive vision, yet she troubles a ready endorsement of American feminism by considering the ways in which northern feminists, reflecting their blind belief in America's construction of the South as its internal Other, undercut the movement's purported message of sororal unity. Roughly contemporary in age—King was born in 1936, Brown in 1944—these women respond in starkly different terms to the shifting social and sexual mores in the South, yet their turns to humor illustrate the necessity of reimagining gender roles in the U.S. South, as well as the limits of such perspectives within an increasingly feminist landscape.

Dorothy Allison soared into the southern literary canon with her instant classic *Bastard Out of Carolina,* and Chapter 5 explores her rich humor, a facet of her writing largely overlooked in scholarly considerations of her work. While many readers focus on the traumatic aspects of her fiction, particularly its plotlines of child abuse, incest, and poverty, she embeds strong threads of defiant humor in her narratives that enlighten her stark treatment of southern lives mired in poverty. Still, Allison approaches comedy with caution, for, as she has discussed frequently in interviews and essays, she recognized and resisted her early tendency to use humor to deflect attention away from the truths of poverty, discrimination, and abuse. Through a voice of comic bravado, Allison does not palliate her traumatic themes yet allows her characters the possibility of resistance to their constructions as the Other within their own homes. Thus, as much as traumatic themes are key to Allison's authorial agenda, her works also delineate the necessity of coupling trauma with humor—not to laugh at such physical and emotional violence but to trace out the limits of trauma as the defining force of its victims' lives.

Chapter 6 engages with David Sedaris's comic memoirs to ponder whether southern humor is moving into what might be termed its postsouthern phase. As the South (and the Sun Belt as a whole) becomes more homogenous and loses its sharply demarcated sense of regional identity through increased migrations, the contours of southern humor and southern literature are changing as well. Sedaris foregrounds his homosexuality in his public persona, speaking openly of his long-term relationship with his partner Hugh Hamrick and thereby modeling, in many ways, the core normativity of same-sex desire. In several passages throughout his many essays, Sedaris questions the conjoined nature of social constructions of race and homosexuality in the South, both pointing to the ways in which discrimination unites marginalized peoples and overwriting key distinctions in how race and homosexuality are experienced. Sedaris further models a postsouthern identity in his mixed stances toward the South—sometimes expressing sentiments reflective of its mores, and other times denouncing them—and through these variations in voice he demonstrates the ways in which geography defines his humor not monolithically but kaleidoscopically.

The conclusion ponders the role of the comic in building the southern literary canon and the contradictions inherent in defining certain texts as representative of the highest cultural ideals. Of the queer authors analyzed in this monograph, Tennessee Williams rests atop the heights of the southern literary canon, yet he is known for his poignant dramas that probe the heart of the human condition—less so for the wicked humor bubbling underneath. Capote's reputation still stands at a crossroads: embraced by some, overlooked by others, and celebrated more in popular culture than in literary circles. Despite their respective blockbuster successes with *Confessions of a Failed Southern Lady* and *Rubyfruit Jungle,* along with their extensive other writings, Florence King and Rita Mae Brown are mostly overlooked in scholarly studies of southern literature. Noting this discrepancy between their achievements and the critical reception of their works, the conclusion questions the denigration of women's comic voices in building the southern literary canon. Despite the relative paucity of her corpus to date—two novels, a short-story collection, a poetry collection, and a book of essays—Allison's critical reputation is noticeably—indeed, measurably—firmer than King's and Brown's, which indicates the tendency of scholars to praise trauma over laughter. As a Yankee-born belles-lettrist, Sedaris may be deemed insufficiently literary, insufficiently southern, and excessively comic for inclusion in the canon, although it is perhaps too early to draw firm conclusions about his status. The southern literary canon shifts as new names enter while others quietly exit, and through this intervention into canon formation, this book queries the place of queer southern comic authors in the literary tradition and the varying receptions these authors have faced, arguing forcefully for a reassessment of its construction.

In evaluating the contradictory meanings of voices comic, queer, and southern, this book focuses on a multiply marginalized field: a subsection of comic literary works by a subsection of gay authors within the overarching subfield of southern literature—a branch of writing distinctly American yet simultaneously fenced in by the markers of regionalism. While these chapters illuminate dominant styles and concerns of gay southern humor in the mid-twentieth to the early twenty-first centuries, it is not their objective to catalog and assess all queer southern humorists, along with their unique styles.[43] Foremost, this book examines primary modes and interests of queer southern humor: camp for Williams and Capote in the mid-century South, a converging yet disparate treatment of second-wave feminism for King and Brown in the later twentieth century, the potential for humor to emerge from sexual and social trauma for Allison, and the vagaries of geography for determining Sedaris's sense of himself as a citizen of the postsouthern South. Taken together, these chapters then allow the conclusion to offer insights about the southern literary canon in relation to its formation and its reformation as the decades pass. The tragic vision of southern literature holds primacy in the popular and the scholarly imagination, yet shifting this focus from the tragic to the comic unsettles its very foundations, forcing readers to consider the various premises that elevate William Faulkner and diminish Florence King, that esteem Walker Percy yet marginalize David Sedaris, and so on.

At the same time, it is necessary to query the very meaning of the term *queer southern author,* for it implies a coherent identity through which to read these writers' corpuses. As Donna Jo Smith cautions, "One of the dangers for specifically southern lesbian/gay studies projects is that we will privilege an oversimplified visibility and stability in both *queer* and *southern* identity,"[44] and along these lines, many queer southern authors have rejected either or both of these adjectives preceding *author*. Tennessee Williams refused the constraints of being labeled a gay writer, for he saw himself as writing on universally human themes: "I don't want to be identified as a writer of such-and-such a sexual inclination. I think gay writers have to cease to be known simply as gay writers; they must be admitted into the totality of writers, without any special label attached to us, if *Time* magazine and news publications will allow it."[45] Likewise, Truman Capote repudiated the label of a southern writer: "I haven't any milieu. . . . When people say Truman Capote is a Southern writer, I merely find it irritating."[46] Florence King's frustration with queer identity politics led her to reject lesbianism—"Above all, I avoid lesbians. It's impossible to enjoy a martini when someone keeps saying, 'I'm tired of being invisible'"[47]—and instead to embrace a single lifestyle, which she endorsed as a way to enhance one's productivity: "The reason I can 'do what I do' is because I've never married. He travels fastest who travels alone, and that goes double for she. Real feminism is spinsterhood."[48] Rita Mae Brown bristled at efforts to delimit her purview and audience to an exclusively lesbian one, pointing out how such terms cordon off minority writers from the wider realm of literature: "Look, calling me a lesbian writer is like calling Baldwin a black writer. I say no; he is not: he is a great writer and that is that."[49] David Sedaris criticized the tendency of bookstores to sort works by gay authors into literary ghettos: "In terms of the gay and lesbian section, whenever I see one in a bookstore, I think, 'What's that doing there? What's that *section* doing there? Why are these books segregated? . . . I use the word 'boyfriend,' so I go next to the fisting manual?"[50] Of the six primary authors explored in this monograph, only Dorothy Allison delineates her sexual orientation as integral to her vocation as a writer: "I am and always have been completely matter-of-fact about being a lesbian," as she contrasts her authorial ethos with "gay writers who defensively insist that they wish to be seen as writers first and gay or lesbian secondarily."[51] Given the resistance of Williams, Capote, King, Brown, and Sedaris to the very concept of gay authorship, I must concede that, on a certain level, the book's foundational premise constructs authorial identities that would likely be questioned by the writers themselves. It is nonetheless worthwhile to examine these authors together in order to elucidate how gay southerners have found comic voices in a hostile landscape and how this humor expands an understanding of the South's celebrated literary traditions.

For precious perversions matter: the social construction of a sexual act or identity as perverse bears brutal repercussions for countless human beings. The counteridentification of a "perversion" as precious—as essential to a fully realized existence—establishes the thrust of the modern queer rights movement, which is grounded in the freedom of individuals to decide for themselves the nature of their intimate lives. Within the representations of desire in literary texts with comic themes, the precious perversions of queer love face the additional task of elevating the comic to a genre deemed equal to such modes as epic, tragic, and realist—the ones that win the laurels. The comic itself is denigrated as a perverse form when its greatest practitioners find themselves locked out of the canon because of longstanding aesthetic prejudices against humor. Thus, the comic itself is in many ways as much a precious perversion of literary form as homosexuality is to longstanding constructions of southern sexual decorum. This book, in sum, argues for a reevaluation of queer love and queer humor within the southern literary canon, for this dual marginalization bleaches this rich regional field into an unnecessarily arid one.

A final note: it is, of course, a fool's endeavor to analyze humor. E. B. White despairs of such imprudent efforts: "Analysts have had their go at humor, and I have read some of this interpretive literature, but without being greatly instructed. Humor can be dissected, as a frog can, but the thing dies in the process and the innards are discouraging to any but the pure scientific mind."[52] Along these lines, Roy Blount Jr. gives an even bleaker assessment of the potential outcomes when he argues that such an effort exposes a basic misunderstanding of southern culture: "At the bottom of Southern humor lies this fundamental truth: that nothing is less humorous, or less Southern, than making a genuine, good-faith effort to define and explain humor, particularly Southern humor."[53] Humor motivated this study, yet the genre of a scholarly monograph requires a purpose beyond sheer amusement, and, to this end, an analysis of southern humor cannot promise as much pleasure as its source texts. If we fail to analyze humor, however, we overlook how particular comic voices reveal, create, and probe the cultures in which they lived. The old axiom "It's just a joke" deflects attention from humor's meaning, but comic texts and genres encode deep questions of whom and what a particular society values. If we are to comprehend both how southern culture has historically found homosexuality to be laughable and how southern queers have managed to laugh in the face of their marginalization, we must take these precious perversions seriously and simultaneously recognize that the pleasures of humor carry cultural weight well beyond their immediate audiences. Those who laugh last, laugh best, the old adage proclaims, but perhaps more importantly, those who laugh last might finally understand what the joke is really about.

1

CAMP SADOMASOCHISM IN TENNESSEE WILLIAMS'S PLAYS

I have always depended on the kindness of strangers.

I am Maggie the Cat!

Don't you understand? I was PROCURING for him!

In the mouths of distinguished actresses, these memorable lines from Tennessee Williams's dramas ring with searing pathos, but when gay men or others seek to deflate tragedy into comedy through arch delivery and gendered antics, Williams's words dwindle readily into camp. These characters—Blanche Dubois, clinging to her exaggerated world of southern pretense in *A Streetcar Named Desire;* Margaret, ravenously pursuing her husband's love and her father-in-law's fortune in *Cat on a Hot Tin Roof;* and Catherine, fending off the memories of her cousin Sebastian's gruesomely cannibalistic demise in *Suddenly, Last Summer*—can move from high drama to camp hilarity in the blink of a drag queen's eye. To declare that these characters and others from Williams's vast corpus can be camped, however, reveals little about the playwright's comic instincts, for many cultural artifacts that were not created with humorous intentions can be recruited for camp stagings. Because of camp's many, often contradictory, points of construction, defining and analyzing it sparks a multitude of interpretive difficulties: "To talk about Camp is therefore to betray it," as Susan Sontag warns.[1] The crux of camp as an aesthetic form arises in its protean nature; an artist may create a camp work, a performer may transform another artist's creation into camp, or an audience may perceive camp in an artifact or performance even—and sometimes especially—when unintended by its creator or performer. My camp sensibility need not align with those of my readers, and it need not align with any particular camp sympathy—or antipathy—on the part of Williams, who frequently decried its banality. That Williams's plays can be camped thus is an issue separate from whether his construction of them invites camp performances. Nonetheless, I contend that, despite Williams's hesitations over such humor, camp circulates surreptitiously throughout many of his greatest works and opens them to interpretations and performances that undermine their dramatic core.

Along with the propensity for camp latent throughout his corpus, Williams imbues many of his works with traces of sadomasochistic desire. As David Savran points out, "sadomasochistic logic . . . unconsciously structures so many of William's most troublingly erotic texts."[2] Numerous passages from various plays support Savran's observation. Heavenly confesses to Dick her fantasies of sexual debasement in *Spring Storm:* "I'd been reading *The Sheik*—I wanted to be pursued an' captured an' made a slave to passion!" (1:7). *Summer and Smoke* features John commenting to Rosa on the violent physicality of their lovemaking: "You never make love without scratching or biting or something. Whenever I leave you I have a little blood on me" (1:618). In *Camino Real,* Baron de Charlus, discussing his need for a room at the "Ritz Men Only" with its manager, A. Ratt, adumbrates the masochist play he anticipates later in the evening: "You know the requirements. An iron bed with no mattress and a considerable length of stout knotted rope. Chains this evening, metal chains. I've been very bad, I have a lot to atone for" (1:770). In *Sweet Bird of Youth,* Chance hopes to turn the tables on the Princess and assert his authority over her by forcing her to assume a submissive position:

> CHANCE: You like to give orders, don't you?
> PRINCESS: It's something I seem to be used to.
> CHANCE: How would you like to *take* them? To be a slave? (2:167)

With lovers seeking punishment and administering it to each other, with characters negotiating their respective positions as masters and slaves, Williams's dramas contemplate the physical pains that accompany erotic pleasures within a sadomasochistic matrix.

From these brief examples, it is clear that Williams's plays can be camped and that sadomasochistic desires surface in various characters' descriptions of their erotic pastimes. In this overlap the congruencies of camp and sadomasochism come to the fore. Foremost, both are performative modes: a performer camps to bring to the surface a text's latent humor, and a sadomasochist assumes the role either of sadist or masochist in an ensuing sexual act. Also, both involve the construction and destruction of social hierarchies—of taste and aesthetics in camp, and of the dominator and the dominated in sadomasochism. In this chapter my objective is not to provide an overarching reading of one of Williams's plays through the joint lens of camp and sadomasochism but to explore how these contrasting dynamics intersect in various moments throughout his work. A lens of camp sadomasochism creates a deeper perspective on the submerged humor of one of America's greatest dramatists, who is better known for his characters' tragic downfalls than for their comic subtones. As Charles Brooks concedes of Williams's humorous touches, "Although his vision of the world is not primarily comic, comedy contributes to his success,"[3] and, in this light, camp sadomasochism illuminates a key aspect of the playwright's dark humor.

Camp

Its mercurial qualities encompass a range of forms and pleasures, yet at its heart, much camp consists of affectionate, knowing, and humorously exaggerated reinterpretations of respected cultural texts. Credited as the first to define *camp* in *The World in the Evening,* Christopher Isherwood proposes, "You can't camp about something you don't take seriously. You're not making fun of it; you're making fun out of it."[4] Among the fifty-eight theses that follow her admonition on the futility of defining camp, Sontag hypothesizes, "Camp is a vision of the world in terms of style—but a particular kind of style. It is the love of the exaggerated, the 'off,' of things-being-what-they-are-not."[5] She further suggests, "Camp is art that proposes itself seriously, but cannot be taken altogether seriously because it is 'too much,'" citing Shakespeare's *Titus Andronicus* and Eugene O'Neill's *Strange Interlude* as examples of this species.[6] Mark Booth pinpoints the gendered dynamics of camp, suggesting that the "primary type of the marginal in society is the traditionally feminine, which camp parodies in an exhibition of stylised effeminacy."[7] By highlighting the arbitrary correlation between sexed bodies and stereotypical traits, camp foregrounds the artificiality of gender as a social construction and then dismantles these conjunctions of body and gender so that comic pleasures can unfold. Moe Meyer observes camp's intersection with gay and queer cultures, defining it as "the total body of performative practices and strategies used to enact a queer identity, with enactment defined as the production of social visibility," for an affinity for camp marks the gay community's unique sensibility vis-à-vis the hegemonic culture.[8] Kathryn Conrad defines camp simply as "a politics of affection, even when the satiric knife may cut a bit deeply."[9] From these multiple viewpoints emerges a sense of camp as a purposeful, pleasureful travesty, in which excess and parody unite in performances and cultural artifacts that simultaneously exalt and debase other forms through an outré comic style. Its tone is sharp, with its affections nonetheless evident.

In his *Memoirs* (1972), Williams registered his strong distaste for camp. Recalling New York City's gay scene in the mid-twentieth century, he notes its relative dearth of a camp sensibility and approvingly comments: "They have cast off, I notice, much of the swish and camp that made them, when assembled in such numbers, unattractive to me. I enjoyed the company of the 'camps' at one time when I was young and lived at the 'Y.' But my closest friends, though as capable of camp as I was, then, were not the 'obvious' types."[10] Conceding his capacity for camp, as well as his former enjoyment of campy companionship, Williams instead praises gay men who abstain from this archly performative style of humor. Indeed, Williams perceived camp as a stigma placed on gays by the wider culture, commenting further in his *Memoirs:* "'[S]wish' and 'camp' are products of self-mockery, imposed upon homosexuals by our society. The obnoxious forms of it will rapidly disappear as Gay Lib begins to succeed in its serious crusade to assert, for its genuinely misunderstood and persecuted minority, a free position in society which will permit them to respect themselves, at least to the extent that, individually, they deserve respect—and I think that degree is likely to be much higher than commonly supposed."[11] Here Williams limns camp as a defense mechanism with which gay men protect themselves from society's bigotry through the humor of gender play. Disliking its many "obnoxious forms," he rejects camp for its detrimental effect on queer liberation, hypothesizing that, because it is a subculturally idiosyncratic, and thus possibly alienating and isolating, mode of humor, it would perpetually marginalize homosexuals from mainstream society. In a 1977 interview with George Whitmore published in Winston Leyland's San Francisco–based journal *Gay Sunshine,* Williams reiterates his distaste for camp, conjuring a particularly acerbic vision of a prototypically campy queen: "I wish that the gays would get away from riding around in Cadillac convertibles, especially the fat ones that look like travesties of Mae West, and just camping it up on the streets in public view."[12]

Despite Williams's sharp disparagement of camp in these 1970s recollections, in other instances he enjoyed such humor. William Jay Smith, a college friend of Williams, reminisced over Williams's campy performance in Molière's *Scapin,* which was staged by Washington University's Department of French: "he gave a performance that a more sophisticated audience would have taken as deliberate high camp. As it was our local audience had not the remotest idea of when to laugh since [they] had not a clue as to what was going on."[13] One camp performance during his college years does not metamorphose Williams into a latent camp humorist, yet in the same interview in which he pillories fat gay men driving Cadillacs and "camping it up on the streets in public view," he also avows camp's pleasures: "Camp is fun though, I enjoy camp. I think it's an important element of American humor. It's an outlet for us. We can't be serious all the time. We need the . . . diversion of camp."[14] He also acknowledges in his *Memoirs* that, despite his reputation for penning searing tragedies, a comic sensibility infiltrates his work: "I am not really a misanthrope or a gloom-poet. In fact, I am much more of a clown, an almost compulsive comedian in my social behavior. The humor sometimes may be black, but it is still humor."[15] Williams blurs comic modes in this statement, as the mordant sensibility of black humor does not typically assume a clownish tone. In this intermingling of the genres of comedy, Williams's clowning with a subtext of black humor parallels camp's tonality, for, in Meyer's words, camp encodes "a suppressed and denied oppositional critique embodied in signifying practices."[16] This formulation applies well to Williams's plays in that they signify clearly as dramas yet latently communicate a ready potential for alternate modes of performance to excavate their humorous undertones.

Williams's rejection of swishy gay men and camp parallels his rejection of queer theater, for he saw himself as transcending the social prejudices that might pigeonhole him as an exclusively homosexual writer. He sought respect as a writer without any modifiers to delimit the scope of his art and declared that, if he were so constrained, "I would be narrowing my audience a great deal. I wish to have a broad audience because the major thrust of my work is not sexual orientation, it's social. I'm not about to limit myself to writing about gay people."[17] Realizing that openly gay works would not likely be commercially viable for midcentury American theater, Williams designed his plays to avoid such categorization. (He nonetheless received several disparaging reviews focused more on his sexuality than on his dramas—as evidenced by critic George Jean Nathan's flippant assessment of him as "a Southern genital man."[18]) Reacting to an allegorical interpretation of his work, Williams explains to Whitmore: "I picked up a copy of *Gay Sunshine* [issue 29/30] saying that plays such as *Streetcar,* and virtually all of my plays, were really lies because they were about homosexuals disguised as women, which is a preposterous allegation and a very dangerous one. It's dangerous to the whole art, to all the written arts."[19] Still, Williams himself notes congruencies between his life and his plays, with these similarities becoming allegorized through the plays' construction of a metareality in which queer experiences are transformed into universal ones. To this end, he admits: "I draw all my characters from myself. I can't draw a character unless I know it within myself."[20] Further along these lines, he affirms in his introductory essay to *Small Craft Warnings,* "Is it or is it not right or wrong for a playwright to put his persona into his work? My answer is: 'What else can he do?'—I mean the very root-necessity of all creative work is to express those things most involved in his experience" (2:710). Refusing to be categorized as a gay playwright for much of his career, in one of his final works, *Vieux Carré,* Williams depicted several gay characters, including its protagonist, the Writer, who represents Williams in a colorful reimagination of his past. Thus, while Williams snubbed camp and denied writing gay plays, these apparent rejections of queer culture require caveats that recognize their influence on his work. Furthermore, given that he had such a wide-ranging career, it is hardly surprising that he modulated his viewpoints as cultural circumstances changed and as his artistic interests shifted.

Certainly, in his extensive cast of characters, Williams codes most of them as heterosexual, yet Queen in *Not about Nightingales* illustrates his deployment of a camp figure to disrupt the play's presentation of normative masculinity. As the protagonist Jim commences a love affair with Eva, Queen models alternate paradigms of masculinity untethered from heterosexual desire. By naming this figure "Queen," Williams communicates the character's sexuality to viewers, as is also apparent through Queen's archly performative and campy declarations. "All my life I've been persecuted by people because I'm refined" (1:114), Queen pouts, then exclaims in exasperation, "Oh, for the love of nasturtiums!" (1:126). In a similar vein, *The Mutilated* features a character referred to as Pious Queen. In *Small Craft Warnings,* as Leona seeks a new life free from the baggage of her past, she voices one of Williams's strongest endorsements of camp amusements:

"What I think I'll do is turn back to a faggot's moll when I haul up to Sausalito or San Francisco. You always find one in the gay bars that needs a big sister with him, to camp with and laugh and cry with, and I hope I'll find one soon" (2:763). With these queeny characters and a thematic endorsement of companionship based on a shared appreciation of camp, Williams lightly alludes to camp traditions in otherwise "straight" works.

Few other characters in Williams's plays read so blatantly as camp figures as Queen and Pious Queen, or as hungry for queer amusements as Leona, but camp's power as a subversive form arises in its ability to seep into otherwise "straight" narratives, those not primarily concerned with gay themes and issues. In her reading of Charles Ludlam's *Camille: A Travesty on "La Dame aux Camélias,"* Kate Davy uncovers the camp sensibility of a narrative that cloaks its queer edges: "the play is not gay inasmuch as its address is not exclusively homosexual, but within the dynamics of the production the machinations of homosexuality surface, 'come out,' and are rendered visible in the pockets, gaps, and fissures of an ultimately less-than-monolithic heterosexual configuration."[21] Many of Williams's plays invite similar readings: a heterosexual storyline can be interpreted as masking a homosexual one, but even more, the polyvalent sexualities of these storylines connect them to their latent camp sensibility. *Cat on a Hot Tin Roof* exemplifies this distinction: Brick's sexuality remains a point of contention in analyses of the play, for it stands within the realm of reasonable interpretations that, as Brick claims, his love for Skipper was purely fraternal, in contrast to Skipper's love for him. Indeed, at one point Williams insisted that "Brick is definitely not a homosexual."[22] The "pockets, gaps, and fissures" of the play nevertheless offer avenues for queer readings—most obviously those that view Brick as a closeted homosexual but also, in this instance, those that interpret Maggie as a campy cat.

Sadomasochism

Sadomasochism is not typically viewed in a humorous light, primarily because it belongs to the purview of the erotic, where laughter would fatally puncture desire. Nonetheless, many sadomasochistic fictions, including such foundational texts as Marquis de Sade's *Justine* and Leopold von Sacher-Masoch's *Venus in Furs,* generate humor in their unrelenting focus on sexual degradation. At least, such laughter surfaces as a possibility for readers who do not puritanically deny themselves the pleasure of enjoying literary accounts of abjection and cruelty rendered ridiculous through their excess. In his provocative reading of Sade's rich narratives, Philippe Sollers argues, "Tout ce qu'ecrit Sade est humour" (Everything that Sade writes is funny).[23] Likewise, Sacher-Masoch encourages his readers to enjoy the pitiful comedy of his protagonist Severin's humiliations in love. In one encounter with his cruel beloved Wanda, Severin recalls, "She flung down the whip and burst into a loud peal of laughter. I imagine my theatrical attitude must have seemed the height of comedy." In the novel's climax, when Wanda arranges for another man to whip him, Severin realizes, "My situation was dreadfully comic and I should have laughed at it myself had it not also been so desperately humiliating."[24] If readers choose not to laugh at the litany of excessive horrors inflicted upon Justine in *Justine,* if they withhold their chuckles at the depravities of love that Wanda perpetrates against Severin in *Venus in Furs,* narrative pleasures are unnecessarily foreclosed, and these narratives' surface significations of pain and degradation overwrite their complementary investment in the savage comedy of human sexual relationships. Furthermore, as Gilles Deleuze argues, sadomasochism invites strategic deployments of humor, for the roles that masochists and sadists play spark a plenitude of contradictions and reversals: "The masochist is insolent in his obsequiousness, rebellious in his submission; in short, he is a humorist, a logician of consequences, just as the ironic sadist is a logician of principles."[25] Perceiving the possibilities of a masochist liberated from submission and of a sadist embracing the irony of sexual power dynamics, which stand not as fixed poles but as oscillating positions, Deleuze locates a latent humor in sadomasochism that opens up possibilities of camp performances. In assuming the role of either the sadist or the masochist in a sexual act, a person accesses sadomasochism's performativity, which invites mocking enactments that undercut its purported eroticism. Thus, while nothing can be more deflating to sexual passion than ill-timed humor, sadomasochism registers the ways in which contrasting performances elicit alternate energies—and thus wherein camp potential lurks.

As the brief examples from *Spring Storm, Summer and Smoke, Camino Real,* and *Sweet Bird of Youth* indicate, threads of sadomasochism can be found throughout Williams's corpus, but his short story "Desire and the Black Masseur" explicitly explores this dynamic. This narrative details the desires of the appropriately named Anthony Burns, a white man who embraces masochistic pleasures from the hands of an African American man employed at a local massage parlor. Williams foreshadows the story's conclusion in its opening description of Burns—"Everything absorbed him and swallowed him up, and still he did not feel secure" (205)—which reaches its culmination when the masseur consumes him: "The giant began to devour the body of Burns. It took him twenty-four hours to eat the splintered bones clean" (211).[26] Such a brief summary makes the story sound more horrific than humorous, and most critical commentary focuses on its conflicted depiction of racial and sexual relations. Nathan Tipton uncovers "the story's more sinister subject matter," which he sees "in the undercurrent of explicitly racial violence both accompanying and as a consequence of the interracial homosexual desire shared between Burns and the Black Masseur."[27] Annette Saddik argues of the story's conclusion that "the incorporation of the body in the cannibalistic act signifies a yearning for wholeness—a oneness—which will put an end to fragmentation through, on the one hand, the ultimate 'union' with the other, and, on the other hand, an eradication of desire . . . in the annihilation and death of the 'self.'"[28] From these perspectives, Williams's admittedly troubling tale explores two queer men's quest for love, with their transgression of southern racial codes complicating their search for mutual fulfillment.

While Tipton's and Saddik's readings, as well as others in a similar vein, tease out significant thematic threads in the narrative, they overlook its dark and campy humor that builds through its Grand-Guignol excesses.[29] Simply put, this story is hilarious. Its exaggerations—Burns's discovery of his masochistic rapture, the masseur's willing participation in these pleasures, their discovery in *flagrante delicto* by the massage parlor's manager—impart an off-kilter romantic patina to these star-crossed lovers whose affections subvert cultural norms. Rewriting the typical scripts of romance, their relationship begins not with the standard rituals of courtship but with Burns's erection and an acknowledgment of the latent humor of sexuality, with the protagonist succumbing to the masseur's violent ministrations: "Immediately after the passing of the first shock, a feeling of pleasure went through him. It swept as a liquid from either end of his body and into the tingling hollow of his groin. He dared not look, but he knew what the Negro must see. The black giant was grinning" (208).[30] In this revision of the romantic comedy, Burns transgresses expected protocols of courtship by readily sporting his erection before even the first date, and the Black Masseur responds with a grin, admitting both his erotic interest and his delight in finding a kindred spirit. In another comic scene, Burns's employer notices his pained movements and inquires about his health; Burns mentions his frequent massages to convince him that he is recuperating. In indirect discourse, the boss observes, "It don't seem to do you any good," to which Burns enthusiastically replies, "Oh, yes, . . . I am showing lots of improvement!" (210). Literally crippled by love yet ecstatic in his pain, Burns speaks his truth that undercuts prevailing social codes of love. A gay, interracial, and sadomasochistic twist on *Romeo and Juliet* with Mutt-and-Jeff leads, Burns and his masseur love despite society's strictures against homosexuality, violence, and cannibalism. In effect, the story is sweet yet terrifying, as its sadomasochistic plotline limns a romance that transgresses the line even between one's lover and one's dinner. Sontag's identification of Shakespeare's *Titus Andronicus* as camp illuminates the sort of horrific yet ready humor in "Desire and the Black Masseur." One might not laugh at the litany of torments Shakespeare unleashes in this narrative—Lavinia suffering rape and mutilation, Tamora eating her sons in the cannibalistic feast Titus sets for her—but what else can one do with a play that includes the barbaric excess of the stage direction, "*Enter a Messenger, with two heads and a hand*"?[31] Likewise, laughing at "Desire and the Black Masseur" depends in large part on readers' willingness to view sadomasochism as at least potentially campy, with its excesses reaching, in this instance, to the black masseur's alimentary canal.

Staging Camp Sadomasochism in Williams's Plays

Camp and sadomasochism unite in various moments throughout Williams's corpus, but it is important to stress that he employs these themes subtly, and their resulting union need not create farce as much as mediate between comedy and tragedy. In Edward Gordon Craig's justly famous formulation of the theater's power, he observes its roots in farce: "Farce is the essential Theatre. Farce refined becomes high comedy: farce brutalized becomes tragedy."[32] Williams blurs the apparent opposition of comedy and tragedy with his camp sadomasochism, submerging a brutal humor in the painful pleasures and disavowals of various characters. Furthermore, while sadomasochism suggests a rigid demarcation of sexual identity—the sadist torments, the masochist endures—such overdetermined roles would strip the theater of its power if they were too rigidly held. As in David Ives's loose theatrical adaptation of Sacher-Masoch's *Venus in Furs,* titled *Venus in Fur* (2010), much of the humor arises in the oscillating uncertainty of sadomasochistic relationships unmoored from their ostensible anchors. Furthermore, much of William's play with sadomasochism relies on women's presumed passivity in midcentury America, aligning the southern belle figure with a model of feminine passivity that devolves into a caricature of masochism when filtered through the exaggerated lens of camp. The antiquated gender mores of the American midcentury—famously idealized in self-abnegating television mothers like June Cleaver, Donna Reed, and Harriet Nelson—promoted a model of womanhood based upon the evacuation of internal desires in favor of service to others. As Carol Warren outlines, the vision of the American family at that time endorsed masculine networks at the expense of feminine autonomy and privileged "male domination and female (and child) submission," which was manifested through "the division of labor in the family and in the society as a whole."[33] At what point, then, does feminine passivity metamorphose into masochism? For Williams's female protagonists, the treacherous terrains of southern gender and sexuality constrain their range of personal options and identities, with masochistic—and thus often farcical—potential lurking in their attempts to navigate their sexual and social relationships.

In *27 Wagons Full of Cotton,* Williams employs the narrative structure of the erotic triangle, in which two men's struggle against each other for dominance is mediated through the woman for whom they share an erotic attraction.[34] Jake Meighan and Silva Vicarro express their desire for Jake's wife Flora through sadomasochistic gestures. Jake worries that he could be arrested for setting ablaze the cotton gin at Silva's Syndicate Plantation, so he coaches Flora to confirm his alibi, threatening her with violence if she does not vouch for his whereabouts. Flora cries in pain, "Lemme go! Christ, Jake! Let loose! Quit twisting, you'll break my wrist!" Despite the violence of this encounter, Williams's stage directions indicate that Flora and Jake equally enjoy its eroticism: "*She whimpers and rubs her wrist but the impression is that the experience was not without pleasure for both parties*" (1:310). Their subsequent dialogue, with Flora's moaning and monosyllabic exclamations, resonates with an erotic subtext:

FLORA: (*whimpering*) Mmmm-hmmmm! Mmmm! Mmmm!
JAKE: (*huskily*) Tha's my swee' baby girl.
FLORA: Mmmmm! Hurt! Hurt!
JAKE: Hurt?
FLORA: Mmmm! Hurt!
JAKE: Kiss?
FLORA: Mmmm!

JAKE: Good?
FLORA: Mmmm . . . (1:310–11)

Evoking his desire to consume his beloved, Jack asks, "What would I do if you was a big piece of cake?," and soon answers his question: "Gobble! Gobble!" (1:311). Within Williams's cannibalistic thematics, the desire to consume the beloved represents the sadist's ultimate fantasy to control and possess, yet the voicing of this desire as "Gobble! Gobble!" during a moment of eroticism jolts its tenors, introducing an undercurrent of humor to Jake and Flora's violently sexual play.

Williams gave *27 Wagons Full of Cotton* the subtitle *A Mississippi Delta Comedy* (1:307), and so it is clear that the story's violence can be played for laughter. Structurally, the play's comedy hinges on a reversal, as Silva avenges himself on Jake by applying the same sadistic yet seductive techniques on his enemy's wife. Although Flora denies her masochistic impulses, Silva sees through this pretense, telling her, "I think you like to be switched." Flora replies, "I don't. I wish you'd quit," but Silva refuses her refusal: "You'd like to be switched harder" (1:321). As scene 3 begins, after Silva has followed Flora into her house despite her insistence that he remain outside, Williams stresses the savagery of their encounter: "*Dark streaks are visible on the bare shoulders and arms and there is a large discoloration along one check. A dark trickle, now congealed, descends from one corner of her mouth*" (1:325). The violence of their erotic liaison results in Flora's bruises and bleeding, but in her ensuing dialogue with Jake, she laughs repeatedly ("*Flora utters a breathless laugh*"; "*She laughs again, like water spilling out of her mouth*"; "*She laughs again*"; "*Her laughter spills out again*"; "*Flora laughs*"; "*She laughs*"; "*She laughs again*"; "*She laughs weakly*"; "*laughing helplessly*"; "*She giggles*"; "*Flora laughs weakly*"; "*She goes off into another spasm of laughter*"; "*She has another fit of giggles*"; "*Flora laughs to herself*" [1:325–28]). Sadomasochism breeds the comic excess of the play's conclusion, creating conditions for stagings that honor, extend, and heighten this humor that borders on hysteria. Moreover, Flora's brand of southern womanhood—a cultural role that, in its embroidered femininity, stands perpetually ripe for exaggerated performances—also imbues the play with camp potential. As Silva begins seducing Flora, raising his shirt to display his skin tone, she modestly proclaims, "You don't have to show me! I'm not from Missouri!" (1:317), with her assumption of feminine decorum ironically highlighting her lack thereof.

"Now what the Sam Hill is so funny?" asks Archie Lee Meighan (Karl Malden) to the unnamed bystanders, who laugh at his wife Baby Doll's emasculating treatment of him.

In *27 Wagons Full of Cotton,* Williams portrays Jake and Silva as sadists, yet the play's film adaption, *Baby Doll* (dir. Elia Kazan, 1956, with Williams's screenplay), demonstrates the potential for the camp roles of sadist and masochist to be reimagined and reassigned. In Karl Malden's performance of Archie Lee Meighan as an ineffectual and powerless man, he laments of his virginal wife, "There's no torture on Earth to equal the torture a cold woman inflicts on a man." As he speaks, Carroll Baker, in the title role, coolly licks her ice-cream cone. Feminine coldness is a standard trope of heteroerotic masochism (as in Sacher-Masoch's *Venus in Furs)*—and, Baby Doll's enjoyment of her frozen treat ironically parallels her pleasure in denying Meighan sexual access to her. Williams thought that the film did not pursue its humor far enough: "the script . . . has a wanton hilarity to it, in my opinion, a quality which was never fully or rightly used in the film."[35] *Baby Doll* nonetheless stands as a camp classic in the excesses of its staging, particularly in the bizarre mise-en-scène of Baby Doll's bedroom, where she sleeps in a crib, and in the mad hide-and-seek game she plays with Silva, in which the scene's erotics are corrupted through Baby Doll's grotesquely virginal innocence. Bad-taste auteur John Waters praises the film's camp, recounting its influence on his childhood aspirations: "Hoping to one day own a dirty movie theater, I planned to show *Baby Doll* for the rest of my life, attracting the wrath of the Pope and causing a scandal in my parents' neighborhood."[36] Waters's shtick relies on hyperbole and thus stands as a form of camp humor unto itself, yet his paean to *Baby Doll* also captures how its treatment of sexual desire not merely flouts social norms but exposes the erotic as a children's game played by adults—in body if not in mind.

In another instance of camp sadomasochism, Williams dramatizes the lurid desires of elderly Miss Collins for their seriocomic effect in *Portrait of a Madonna.* The title satirizes its protagonist, an aged southern belle wracked by the emotional torment of her virginity, as well as compares her sexual desires to the presumably nonexistent ones of the Virgin Mary. The play begins as Miss Collins telephones Mr. Abrams, the apartment manager, to report her repeated rapes: "I'm not responsible for it, but night after night after night this man has been coming into my apartment and—indulging his senses!" (1:347). In this play, rape remains within the realm of masochistic fantasy for Miss Collins, whereas in *Streetcar,* Blanche Dubois suffers its real, traumatic force. For Miss Collins, masochistic fantasies allow her to envision violation as the painful bliss of submission, while she remains safely within the realm of the imaginary. As Nick Mansfield explains, fantasy structures much masochistic pleasure: "the actual masochistic behavior does not realize or achieve the pleasure that the masochist dreams of. It is a mere rehearsal, a representation."[37] Similarly, Walter Braun concludes that women's masochistic fantasies, within a heterosexual matrix, allow them to ponder the freedom of the self through degradation: "When a man possesses them they submit to it as one of the many ways in which they can be debased and humiliated to the point of annihilation. Their only desire is that their personality and individuality shall be submerged and obliterated."[38] As an object of satire because of her antiquated southern femininity, Miss Collins desires rape—or, more to the point, she *thinks* she desires rape—to effect such an obliteration of her self. She fixates over the lost boyfriend from her youth who would have transformed her life and given her the identity of wife and mother, and thus saved her from her lonely fate as a spinster. Denied this possibility in the present, she fantasizes that her former beau is now the rapist who nightly forces this metamorphosis upon her. She speaks in comically archaic language and breathlessly bewails that her phantom lover has been "indulging his senses" through her violation.

Miss Collins serves simultaneously as a tragic and as a comic figure, and the Porter's and the Elevator Boy's reactions to her establish these oppositional perspectives. The Elevator Boy dismissively states, "An ole woman like her is disgusting, though, imaginin' somebody's raped her," but the Porter is more sympathetic. He replies that she is "Pitiful, not disgusting," then redirects the Elevator Boy's attention to their jobs: "Watch out for them cigarette ashes" (1:349). While the Porter voices compassion for a woman so plagued by loneliness that she envisions rape, no matter its horrors, as a means to human connection, the Elevator Boy imagines her violation and constructs an outlandish scenario for its execution, not as an act of depravity but of humor: "I seen a guy that could do that once. He crawled straight up the side of the building. They called him The Human Fly! Gosh, that's a wonderful publicity angle, Miss Collins—'Beautiful Young Society Lady Raped by The Human Fly!'" (1:351). With these words, the Elevator Boy translates rape into farce, yet at the same time, his version is only slightly more ridiculous than Miss Collins's fantasy as she herself tells it.

Throughout the play's dramatic action, Williams paints Miss Collins as an excessive figure ripe for camping. Foremost, her body and demeanor establish a richly grotesque disjunction between her vision of herself and her actual appearance, as the stage directions indicate: "*Self-consciously she touches her ridiculous corkscrew curls with the faded pink ribbon tied through them. Her manner becomes that of a slightly coquettish but prim little Southern belle*" (1:350). One need only think of Lady Wishfort in William Congreve's *The Way of the World* (1700) or of Bette Davis's over-the-top camp performance in *What Ever Happened to Baby Jane?* (dir. Robert Aldrich, 1962) to visualize the longstanding comic convention of an elderly woman adopting the mannerisms of a young girl. Miss Collin's assumption of the style and fashions of a child renders her humorously pathetic. (Indeed, the Elevator Boy declares, "Okay. She's Shoiley Temple" [1:352].) Furthermore, this patrician spinster pronounces with comic hypocrisy her judgment against women who have suffered the true horror of rape: "When men take advantage of common white-trash women who smoke in public there is probably some excuse for it, but when it occurs to a lady who is single and always com-*pletely* above reproach in her moral behavior, there's really nothing to do but call for police protection" (1:353). In these lines Williams's play echoes a comedy of manners in the style of Richard Brinsley Sheridan or Oscar Wilde, with Miss Collins's aristocratic voice mocking her own position through the ludicrousness of her words, as well as in their stylized delivery ("com-*pletely*"). As the play concludes, she eagerly anticipates her arrest for the phantom rapes, mistaking the doctor, who has come to escort her to the state asylum, for an avenging priest: "I know! (*excitedly*) You've come from the Holy Communion to place me under arrest! On moral charges!" (1:357). With Miss Collins's longing for the debased pleasures of masochism underscoring her every word, her lines invite camp restagings by those who perceive the humorous undercurrents beneath her tragic exterior and realize the camp potential to be found in Williams's satirizing of the sort of southern womanhood that she models.

Through the camp sadomasochism of their storylines, Williams encourages his audience to laugh *with* Flora, as she giggles merrily, if not hysterically, throughout the denouement of *27 Wagons Full of Cotton,* and *at* Miss Collins, as she fantasizes over her imminent arrest "on moral charges." Sadomasochism invites such humor, and, in these instances, Williams welcomes it. Still, in line with his prevailing distaste for camp, he explicitly directs his directors and audiences not to laugh at other characters who could potentially be seen as parodic figures of southern femininity. Of Vee in *Battle of Angels,* he writes, "*Although a religious fanatic, a mystic, she should not be made ridiculous. Her portrayal will contain certain incidents of humor, but not be devoid of all dignity or pathos*" (1:198). Likewise, he constructs Alma in *Summer and Smoke* as potentially inviting laughter through her exaggerated mannerisms even as he discourages this response: "*In Alma's voice and manner there is a delicacy and elegance, a kind of 'airiness,' which is really natural to her as it is, in a less marked degree, to many Southern girls. . . . The characterization must never be stressed to the point of making her at all ludicrous in a less than sympathetic way*" (1:579–80). In this play's revision as *Eccentricities of a Nightingale,* Reverend Winemiller explains to Alma that her peers mock her stylized behavior:

REV. WINEMILLER: What they imitated was your singing, I think, at a wedding.
ALMA: My voice? They imitated my voice?
REV. WINEMILLER: Not your voice but your gestures and facial expressions.
ALMA: Ohh . . . This leaves me quite speechless!
REV. WINEMILLER: You're inclined to—dramatize your songs a—bit too much! You, you get carried away by the, the emotion of it! (2:445)

As Flora and Miss Collins demonstrate, southern femininity, with its artifice and exaggeration, invites camp stagings, which Williams confirms with his admonitions for audiences not to laugh at Vee and Alma. Southern womanhood, then, stands as a ready target of camp humor. In *A Lovely Sunday at Creve Coeur,* Helena diagnoses Dorothea with a "Southern belle complex" (2:950), a phrase that pathologizes southern women as psychologically agitated because of their conscription into this archaic yet archetypal gender role. Kathryn Lee Seidel notes in this regard that the southern belle fascinates readers because "she represents a human ideal, now regarded as antique, but at once eliciting a paradoxical nostalgia and serving as a warning for the present."[39] The southern belle is thus a readily campable figure, and so even when the sadomasochistic themes are not as clearly drawn as they are in *27 Wagons Full of Cotton* and *Portrait of a Madonna,* camp potential simmers in Williams's plays featuring southern women in lead roles. For Williams, sadomasochism connotes more a sexual energy circulating among his characters than their fixed erotic identities, yet it imbues his female protagonists with the hyperbolic posturings of desire that allow them to be so readily mocked.

In *Portrait of a Madonna,* Williams created source materials and inspiration for the play widely acclaimed as his masterpiece: *A Streetcar Named Desire.*[40] With her desire to access the glories of her past through sexual encounters in the present, Miss Collins serves as a precursor to Blanche Dubois, yet the two differ in their relationship to stagings and parodies of sadomasochistic desire. It is Stella who best models the abnegations of the self at masochism's core. She freely admits her raw desire for her husband Stanley—"When he's away for a week I nearly go wild!" (1:478)—and their frequent fights expose the violent underbelly of their marriage. Williams writes in the stage directions, "*Stanley gives a loud whack of his hand on [Stella's] thigh*" (1:494), and Stella disapproves: "It makes me so mad when he does that in front of people" (1:495). On the surface, Stella's words communicate her anger and embarrassment about her abusive marriage and concomitantly reveal her to be trapped by the cultural mores of the midcentury American South. At the same time, however, her words direct attention not exclusively to Stanley's sexually aggressive act but to the public nature of its display—"when he does that *in front of people*" (my italics)—hinting that she welcomes such actions within the privacy of their bedroom. Stanley and Stella's raucous argument shocks the neighbors, and Eunice fails to comprehend the passion behind their conflict when she incorrectly predicts, "You can't beat on a woman an' then call 'er back! She won't come" (1:502). Stella soon explains to Blanche, "He was as good as a lamb when I came back and he's really very, very ashamed of himself." She also admits the pleasure she found in his brutality: “I was—sort of—thrilled by it” (1:505). Although Williams colors her marriage with these traces of sadomasochism, Stella does not stand as a target for camp restagings as much as her sister does. If one camps *A Streetcar Named Desire,* one camps with Blanche—and her interactions with Stanley—as the primary target.

Much of *Streetcar*’s camp potential arises from Blanche’s and Stanley’s genders, for, even when these roles are played “straight,” the actors must perform versions of femininity and masculinity that border on the cartoonish. As William Free notes, “Blanche is feminine helplessness and cultivation taken to absurd extremes. Stanley opens beer bottles with his teeth; Blanche soaks for hours in her bath.” He also cites Sontag’s analysis of camp’s genders, in which she focuses on “the corny flamboyant femaleness of Jayne Mansfield, Gina Lollobrigida, Jane Russell, Virginia Mayo; the exaggerated he-man-ness of Steve Reeves, Victor Mature.”[41] Sontag mentions stars, not roles, in these lines, but the flamboyant femaleness of Blanche and the exaggerated he-man-ness of Stanley must shine through performances of these characters if the play is to succeed. Blanche comments on Stanley, “there he is—Stanley Kowalski—survivor of the stone age! Bearing the raw meat home from the kill in the jungle!” (1:510), a feat depicted in the play’s opening scene as he totes a “*red-stained package from the butcher’s*” (1:470). In recognizing Stanley’s hypermasculinity while overlooking her hyperfemininity, Blanche foregrounds gender’s power to define men, women, and their social roles, even as it also elicits excessive performances that deviate from ostensible norms.

In his interactions with Blanche, Stanley relies on sadomasochism’s legalistic posturing in his attempts to ensure that she will submit to his authority. As Slavoj Žižek explains, the law is conscripted to define the parameters of many such relationships: “Sadism follows the logic of institutions, of institutional power tormenting its victim and taking pleasure in the victim’s helpless resistance. More precisely, sadism is at work in the obscene, superego underside that necessarily redoubles and accompanies, as its shadow, the ‘public’ Law.”[42] To this end, Stanley cites legal statutes to coerce Blanche to accede to his desires. “In the state of Louisiana we have the Napoleonic code according to which what belongs to the wife belongs to the husband and vice versa” (1:484), he first declares to Stella, and he soon repeats this passage virtually verbatim to Blanche in an attempt to cement his authority over her (1:489). In his efforts to control Blanche—and thus to gain access to her supposed fortune—Stanley employs sadomasochistic strategies similar to those he uses with his wife as the play moves inevitably to its sexually violent showdown.

It would be challenging (although by no means impossible) to stage Blanche's rape as camp, for to do so would sabotage the spirit and themes of Williams's masterpiece. Here the primary difference between Miss Collins and Blanche as potential camp figures emerges: whereas Miss Collins masochistically fantasizes about rape yet never feels its brutality, Blanche is actually raped and thus becomes a tragic heroine. As this climactic scene approaches, Blanche denies the possibility that she could enjoy sadism—"Deliberate cruelty is not forgivable. It is the one unforgivable thing in my opinion and it is the one thing of which I have never, never been guilty" (1:552)—yet she is trapped within Stanley's erotic worldview, in which, as is evident in his relationship with Stella, sadomasochism establishes an erotic negotiation of power and forgiveness. When Stanley ominously intones to Blanche, "We've had this date with each other from the beginning" (1:555), the audience must confront the fact that Stanley's excessive performance of gender extends beyond sexual play with his wife to sexual violence against his sister-in-law. When Stella denies the possibility that the erotic wrangling she enjoys with Stanley could have a darker, crueler edge—"I couldn't believe her story and go on living with Stanley" (1:556)—she abandons Blanche to her tragic end.

Viewing Williams's plays through a lens of camp sadomasochism does not overwrite this standard vision of Blanche as a tragic heroine. Rather, it explains why she serves as a figure suitable for camping in performances seeking to expose the play's latent humor. Williams's depictions of female protagonists suffering from the "Southern belle complex" frequently evince their masochistic tendencies, even when this masochism is not expressed as a manifestation of their erotic desires. Thus, Williams draws Blanche on the masochistic borderline of suffering. She teeters on the edge of sanity; he describes her "*faintly hysterical humor*" (1:471), as well as her sardonic assessment of how her family lost its former affluence because of their predilection for erotic pleasures: "The four-letter word deprived us of our plantation" (1:490). Echoing Williams's stage directions admonishing audiences not to laugh at certain characters, Blanche wants to ensure that she does not serve as an object of ridicule. While writing a letter to her former boyfriend Shep Huntleigh, she pleads, "Don't, don't laugh at me, Stella!" (1:508). The core paradox of Blanche's desire emerges in her conflicting desire to dominate and to be dominated. Certainly, in several scenes she aggressively pursues her sexual desires, most notably in her attempted seduction of the paperboy—"I want to kiss you, just once, softly and sweetly on your mouth" (1:520). In a gendered role reversal of Stanley and Stella's relationship, Mitch hopes Blanche will punish him for any perceived transgressions: "Just give me a slap whenever I step out of bounds" (1:524). He aligns himself with the type of masochistic subservience that would establish Blanche as his "Venus in fur." When the play reaches its conclusion, as Blanche proclaims her most famous line, "Whoever you are—I have always depended on the kindness of strangers" (1:563), the countercurrents of Stanley's sadism, Blanche's masochistic suffering, and the oscillations of desire that potentially destabilize Williams's construction of tragedy depend upon the director's fidelity to Williams's vision of his play as a tragedy. The director can adhere to that vision or cut the narrative loose from these generic moorings to revel in its sexual artifice of desires denied yet unvanquishable.

With this in mind, Chicken's words in *Kingdom of Earth* enlighten how Williams's characters speak lines potentially interpreted as humorous while nonetheless contemplating violence against women: "They's two ways to stop hysterics in a woman. One way is to give her a slap and the other way is to lay her. Sometimes you got to do both" (2:675). The latent camp of *A Streetcar Named Desire* surfaces in the realization that, within a camp perspective, Chicken's words could well apply to Blanche. By reimagining rape as the curative Blanche seeks to jolt her out of her complacency, *A Streetcar Named Desire* could indeed be a camp comedy—or at least a dark and violent one, along the lines of a Flannery O'Connor short story. Whereas rape and spousal abuse do not lend themselves well to humor, and their theatrical depiction would likely alienate audiences both of yesterday and today, one need only recall Ralph Kramden's repeated threat to his wife Alice in the hit 1950s television program *The Honeymooners*—"One of these days . . . Pow! Right in the kisser!"—to contextualize the ways in which violence against women was played for laughs in midcentury America and thus to see how camp performances would simply exaggerate Williams's deployment of similar tropes.

In *Cat on a Hot Tin Roof,* Williams suggests in a stage direction that Margaret's sexual relationship with Brick has negatively affected her disposition: "*It is constant rejection that makes her humor 'bitchy'*" (1:888). As much as Williams denies that his plays masquerade gay men under his female protagonists, this bitchy humor aligns Margaret with queer figures, no matter their biological sex. In her forceful yet resistant performance of femininity, the bitch stands as a camp archetype—alluring and attractive, yet willful and imperious, and perpetually ready with a sarcastic barb to deflate the pretensions of those in her company. Female performers renowned for their camp appeal, including Mae West, Joan Crawford, Tallulah Bankhead, Bette Davis, and Madonna, play with bitchiness in their roles and in their public personas, rejecting masculinist constructions of their celebrity in favor of flagrant performances of their unique desires, sexual or otherwise. In this light, Margaret's union of the "Southern belle complex" with bitchiness aligns her with a camp sensibility, for she lays bare the artifice of this cultural fantasy of domesticated femininity.

Margaret's masochistic desire for Brick further imbues this character with camp potential, as evident in her paean to his sexual prowess:

> "Such a wonderful person to go to bed with, and I think mostly because you were really indifferent to it. Isn't that right? Never had any anxiety about it, did it naturally, easily, slowly, with absolute confidence and perfect calm, more like opening a door for a lady or seating her at a table, than giving expression of any longing for her. Your indifference made you wonderful at lovemaking—*strange?*—but true.
>
> You know, if I thought you would never, never, *never* make love to me again—I would go downstairs to the kitchen and pick up the longest and sharpest knife I could find and stick it straight into my heart, I swear that I would!" (1:892)

Because these lines stress Brick's reluctance to engage in intercourse with his wife, many critics see them as evidence of his repressed homosexuality—a reading with which I do not disagree.[43] Their ambiguity, however, extends beyond the realm of latent homosexuality to include traces of sadomasochistic desires. Margaret's words underscore that Brick measures the effect of his sexual acts and dispenses them coolly and calculatingly; he appears reluctant to give pleasure through intercourse, despite the fact that Margaret enjoys his prowess. Furthermore, Margaret confesses the utmost masochist fantasy: to sacrifice herself on the altar of sexual devotion to the beloved. If she cannot please her beloved, she will kill herself, and she returns to this theme in the play's concluding lines while consoling Brick: "Oh, you weak, beautiful people who give up with such grace. What you need is someone to take hold of you—gently, with love, and hand your life back to you, like something gold you let go of—and I can! I'm determined to do it—and nothing's more determined than a cat on a hot tin roof—is there? Is there, baby?" (1:1005). Reiterating the metaphor of a cat jumping on a hot tin roof, Margaret embraces the masochistic suffering of loving Brick.

She pledges her ability to endure past the point of pain, and while these lines concentrate on her tender concern for Brick, one should not overlook the bitchy core of the character speaking them. With bitchiness percolating underneath the character's exterior, Margaret's campiness waits ready to burst through the façade of southern decorum that audiences realize just barely holds her in check.

With its lurid plotline of a gay man devoured by young boys, *Suddenly, Last Summer* has long generated controversy, as evident in Alan Sinfield's damning assessment of it as "Williams' most homophobic play."[44] Surely, though, it bears ample potential to be staged as Williams's most darkly comic, for, similar to "Desire and the Black Masseur," it thematizes cannibalism as an excessive enactment of masochistic passivity gone awry. Although Sebastian Venable has been devoured prior to the play's dramatic action, the spectral traces of his sadomasochistic orchestrations of desire continue to resonate for his mother and cousin in the narrative present. Also, Mrs. Venable's grotesque quest to maintain her family's social honor by having her niece Catherine lobotomized (so that she may never divulge the lurid circumstances of Sebastian's death) allows Williams to embellish the figure of the southern matriarch to ludicrous extremes—Mrs. Venable's camp potential is barely containable. Similar to Margaret, her version of southern femininity hums with bitchiness, such as in her withering assessment of Catherine's debutante ball: "I went to the expense and humiliation, yes, public humiliation of giving this girl a debut which was a fiasco. Nobody liked her when I brought her out" (2:128). Refusing to acknowledge her son's homosexuality yet insisting upon his desirability, Mrs. Venable prudishly yet aristocratically proclaims, "My son, Sebastian, was chaste. Not c-h-a-s-e-d! Oh, he was chased in that way of spelling it, too, we had to be very fleet-footed I can tell you, with his looks and his charm, to keep ahead of pursuers, every kind of pursuer!" (2:110). With these words Williams foreshadows the play's conclusion, as the audience learns that Sebastian was not chaste during his lifetime but rather chased to death by a swarm of young cannibals. By including herself in these lines, declaring that both of them needed to be fleet-footed to escape "every kind of pursuer," Mrs. Venable, like Miss Collins in *Portrait of a Madonna,* refuses to admit that age has laid waste to her beauty, thereby succumbing to the pathology of her "Southern belle complex."

In contrast to Mrs. Venable, who lives in a world of denial, Catherine sees her cousin Sebastian clearly, recognizing his rapacious sexual appetite: "We were *going* to blonds, blonds were next on the menu. . . . Cousin Sebastian said he was famished for blonds, he was fed up with the dark ones and was famished for blonds" (2:118). Returning to his theme of cannibalism—which Kevin Ohi reads in the narrative as "a figure for gay male sex acts, whether that means anal sex or, perhaps more to the point . . . analingus or fellatio"[45]—Williams prepares his audience for the ironic reversal of the predator becoming the prey. Ironic reversals need not carry comic subtones, but they frequently imbue a narrative with humor by toppling previously established expectations. Catherine, caught within her cousin's web of sadomasochistic pursuits, now lives in a world severed from believability, as she cries: "this you won't believe, nobody *has* believed it, nobody *could* believe it, nobody, nobody on earth could possibly believe it, and I don't *blame* them!—They had *devoured* parts of him" (2:147). Williams's thematic deployment of cannibalism as the logical conclusion of sadomasochistic desires can be played straight—or for melodrama, to which the film version mostly aspires—but these lines fall into humor readily, for this shocking revelation is, quite simply, too much. Sadomasochistic desires function like a virus in *Suddenly, Last Summer,* infecting the surviving characters with camp potential as they grapple with the repercussions of Sebastian's sexual appetite that ultimately consumed him.

"Desire and the Black Masseur," *27 Wagons Full of Cotton, Portrait of a Madonna, A Streetcar Named Desire, Cat on a Hot Tin Roof,* and *Suddenly, Last Summer* jointly testify to Williams's interest in the intersection of camp humor and sadomasochism, and these dynamics imbue many of his other works with a similar undercurrent of transgression and latent humor. This is not, however, to suggest that his corpus should be pressed through an interpretive cookie cutter; to argue simply that Blanche and Stanley, or other pairings in other plays, engage in a sadomasochistic relationship would overlook the complexities of characters that refuse easy categorization as victim or victimizer, and of the submerged comic potential that, in line with camp stagings and interpretations, springs to the surface. Under the light of camp sadomasochism, much of Williams's corpus challenges the grand and comforting illusion of human sexuality as a spiritually uplifting union of two souls. Indeed, such perfect harmony stands as a chimerical illusion in his plays, for in many instances their tragic force is derived from how they uncover the emotional devastation wreaked by the failures of lovers to love.

But sexuality also invites laughter, and at the heart of much laughter is discomfort with humanity's erotic, and thus animal, nature. As Italo Calvino explains, "For laughter is also a defense of our human trepidation in the face of the revelation of sex. . . . The cheerful state of mind that accompanies talk about sex may therefore be understood not only as impatient anticipation of the hoped-for happiness, but also as a recognition of the boundary that is about to be crossed, of entry into a space that is different, paradoxical, and 'sacred.' Or else, simply, as the modesty of words in the face of what is too far beyond words."[46] Transgressing boundaries can elicit a range of responses, but a comic and camp sensibility responds to Calvino's "modesty of words" with hearty laughter—often even when such modesty registers from a searing tragedy or from the otherwise unlaughable force of rape, despair, cannibalism, and other such horrors to the human condition. Williams's genius throughout so many of his plays demands audiences to confront the inherent pain of loneliness and the ever-present possibility that sexual congress will not transcend individual suffering. In southern landscapes populated by women afflicted by the belle complex, who seek but cannot hold on to the simple creature comforts of affection and love, a mordant humor reminds audiences of the facades of southern culture and its pretenses of sexual normativity. Through these traces of camp sadomasochism, Williams allows—even if he does not invite—his audiences and those who stage his works to consider a latent humor as well, despite his aversion for those campy queens who turn simply everything into a joke.

2

LAUGHING WITH TRUMAN CAPOTE

Insult, Camp, and Gothic Excess

Despite their mixed critical reception, Truman Capote's literary achievements should assure him enduring acclaim as one of the preeminent figures of the southern renaissance. Notable accomplishments include his prize-winning debut with the short story "Miriam," breakout success with the gothic bildungsroman *Other Voices, Other Rooms,* popular recognition with *Breakfast at Tiffany's,* and critical and commercial triumph with *In Cold Blood.* His range was wide, as shown by *Observations,* a coffee-table book collaboration with photographer Richard Avedon, and *Indiscretion of an American Wife,* his first Hollywood screenplay. While mostly withholding his humor from his literary efforts, Capote unleashed his sharp wit in his personal life and through his public persona. As an acerbic commentator on celebrity culture, he brashly insulted those whom he perceived to be pretenders, charlatans, or outright enemies. Most funny people recognize the need to temper their wits according to the rhetorical circumstances at hand, and various comics have lamented the expectations of their fans, and sometimes of their friends as well, that they should be perpetually amusing—no matter how taxing the creation of such endless levity might be. Capote staked his reputation as a serious literary artist, and the overarching gravity of his corpus reflects this ambition. As E. B. White explains, "The world likes humor, but treats it patronizingly. It decorates its serious artists with laurel, and its wags with Brussels sprouts."[1] In Capote's quest for respect as a literary artist, an excessively comic voice might have undercut his efforts.

Against the currents of his serious literary efforts, however, run countercurrents of camp, excess, and submerged levity. Whereas his witty, acerbic public persona places him in the company of such figures as Oscar Wilde and Dorothy Parker, Capote's literary work appears markedly dissimilar from theirs in breadth and tone. Capote vented his sense of humor most flagrantly in his screenplay of John Huston's 1953 film *Beat the Devil*—a cinematic camp classic often celebrated as the first of its genre but mostly overlooked in critical assessments of Capote's literary career.[2] Capote's camp humor infiltrates Huston's otherwise "straight" caper flick, sneaking a queer sensibility into the film's plotline of winsome adulterers outwitting four nefarious criminals. Given Capote's appreciation of humor in his life and in this film, it is not surprising that his comic sensibility would flavor his more serious works. The submerged camp humor of *Other Voices, Other Rooms* illuminates his unique voice as a member of the southern renaissance, for its outré qualities, which contemporary critics found appalling, evince his interest in reformulating the codes of gothicism to depict the trials and pleasures of gay southern life. In complementary contrast, the failures of camp in his unfinished novel *Answered Prayers* testify to the limits of the comic for his authorial agenda.

Capote's camp humor aligns with many of his queer themes, and through his comic sensibility he reassesses cultural codes of sexuality and finds them laughable. As Cynthia Morrill explains of camp's resistant stance vis-à-vis normative culture, "What becomes manifest, what initiates the Camp condition, is the queer's position in a representational economy invested in the Platonic parameters of Being. Camp results from the uncanny experience of looking into a nonreflective mirror and falling outside of the essentialized ontology of heterosexuality."[3] For Capote the disjunction between society's mirror and his unique experiences as a gay southerner sparked numerous opportunities for creating literature and laughter, and his cagy play with comic and camp voices needs to be seen as an integral aspect of his literary voice to appreciate fully his contributions to the southern renaissance.

Capote's Public Insults and Literary Comic Style

In various accounts of his life, Capote's sharp humor and moxie shine through, revealing him as a fearless, exuberant, and defiantly queer wit. Donald Windham, a longtime friend and collaborator with Tennessee Williams, recounts an episode from Capote's life that exemplifies his cheeky insolence: "Once, on a New York street, when [Capote] was telling me an anecdote in a high voice accompanied by expansive gestures and saw a burly truck driver glowering at him, he sassed: 'What are you looking at? I wouldn't kiss you for a dollar,' and cowed the man completely."[4] Turning the tables on this man by positing and immediately rejecting his phantom desires, and thus by constructing him as a sexually unfulfilled closet queen, Capote plays with a brashly comic voice despite the potential for homophobic violence to erupt. In a similar vein, Tennessee Williams, recalling in his *Memoirs* their travels together, warmly compliments Capote on his humor: "Truman was about the best companion you could want. He had not turned bitchy. Well, he had not turned *maliciously* bitchy. But he was full of fantasies and mischief. We used to go along the first class corridors of the *Mary* and pick up the gentlemen's shoes, set outside their staterooms for shining—and we would mix them all up, set them doors away from their proper place."[5] Along with such pranks, Williams recalls Capote's suggestive banter with an importuning Episcopal bishop who outwore his welcome:

> "You know," he drawled sweetly to the Bishop, "I've always wanted to have a Bishop's ring."
>
> The Bishop chuckled indulgently.
>
> "A bishop's ring is only available to a bishop." . . .
>
> "Oh, I don't know," countered Truman, "it occurred to me that maybe I might find one in a pawnshop. You know, one that had been hocked by a defrocked bishop."
>
> He drawled out "defrocked bishop" in a way that left no doubt of his implication. The bishop turned redder than usual and excused himself from the table and we were not disturbed by his persistent approaches for the rest of the voyage.[6]

Embarrassing this unwelcome suitor through his humor, Capote simultaneously performs with a comic sensibility for his companions on this trip. Brazenly queer and scrappily confrontational, Capote earned his nickname of the "Tiny Terror" for his sharp, biting, and devastatingly funny tongue, which he wielded like a weapon to strike his adversaries down to size.[7]

Williams proposes that in his youth Capote had not yet turned "*maliciously* bitchy," but his humor frequently was laced with venomous insult. Capote's comments about his longstanding nemesis Gore Vidal range from critical assessment of his literature—"There's nothing original in him. His books wobble like a ball trying to find the hole in a pinball machine. He has style in his essays and in his person, but not as a writer of prose fiction"[8] —to a flat-out attack: "I'm always sad about Gore—very sad that he has to breathe every day."[9] Others he publically taunted include Jacqueline Susann ("a truck driver in drag"),[10] Meryl Streep ("she looks like a chicken"),[11]

Ernest Hemingway ("old closet queen"), Mary McCarthy ("If there's anyone in American literature who knows what a whore would see when she looks at the ceiling, it's Mary McCarthy"),[12] and Marlon Brando ("A deity, yes; but more than that, really, just a young man sitting on a pile of candy").[13] Aware that some of the general public found his litany of insults off-putting, Capote breezily suggested that they should admire him for his brutal honesty: "Well, they could say, 'You may not like him, but you must admit he's very candid.'"[14]

In the creation of his public persona, which in many ways required as much attention as one of his literary works, Capote's sharp wit appears as one of his defining characteristics, yet few of his narratives readily evince this daring comic sensibility. One of the few exceptions, the short story "Children on Their Birthdays," features Capote's primary foray into black humor, which he couples with cartoonish violence as he invites readers to laugh at Miss Lily Jane Bobbit's untimely demise: "You could see what was going to happen; and we called out, our voices like lightning in the rain, but Miss Bobbit, running toward those moons of roses, did not seem to hear. That is when the six o'clock bus ran over her" (135).[15] A devastating irony emerges: this bus was to facilitate Miss Bobbit's escape from the South, thus allowing her to pursue her aspirations to Hollywood stardom. Another short story collected in *A Tree of Night,* "My Side of the Matter," features a southern family dispute, with its narcissistic narrator facing the justified outrage of his in-laws:

> "God will punish him," says Eunice.
> "Oh, Sister," says Olivia-Ann, "let us not wait for God." (203)

A madcap melee ensues—the narrator attacks the maid Bluebell with an umbrella, his wife gives birth to their child, and Olivia-Ann threatens him with a fourteen-inch hog knife, as the narrator barricades himself, quickly yet languidly, in the parlor, to enjoy a "five-pound box of Sweet Love candy" (205). "Children on Their Birthdays" and "My Side of the Matter" testify to Capote's ability to fashion effective comic fiction, but, given the relative paucity of such texts in his corpus, it appears that he seldom answered the call of his comic muse.

Some of Capote's works can be labeled as generically comic in their sensibility, if not particularly humorous in their effects. The novellas *The Grass Harp* and *Breakfast at Tiffany's* are comic in the broadly Dantean sense of a narrative that concludes optimistically. (The *Divine Comedy* models this form; its narrative journey results in the protagonist's deeper comprehension of the world's spiritual mysteries but without moments of laugh-aloud humor.) Surely in *The Grass Harp* the vision of Collin and his friends escaping from their southern town's straitjacket of conformity to live in a tree house springs from a comic imagination, yet the novella balances its comedy with tragic undertones, most notably in Dolly Talbo's death. Through his experiences Collin comes to a deeper understanding of life's challenges and beauty—"A waterfall of color flowed across the dry and strumming leaves; and I wanted then for the Judge to hear what Dolly had told me: that it was a grass harp, telling, a harp of voices remembering a story" (97)—and so readers witness an ultimately uplifting narrative, if one without many richly funny moments. So, too, with *Breakfast at Tiffany's,* in which Holly Golightly learns that she cannot continually run away from her difficulties. She confesses to the narrator: "But what about me? . . . I'm very scared, Buster. Yes, at last. Because it could go on forever. Not knowing what's yours until you've thrown it away" (109).[16] With *The Grass Harp* and *Breakfast at Tiffany's,* Capote's comic sensibility matches generically with Northrop Frye's observation that much comic literature focuses on events in which "the hero does not transform a humorous society but simply escapes or runs away from it, leaving its structure as it was before."[17] Collin's and Holly's narrative journeys—sweet and sentimental for the former, sophisticated yet heartfelt for the latter—play out in a broadly comic mode without particularly humorous events. Had Capote desired for them to be riotously funny as well as generically comic, along the lines of "Children on Their Birthdays" and "My Side of the Matter," he surely could have achieved that effect. Rather, in these literary works, Capote mostly resisted the allure of humor, a pattern he freed himself from in his campy script for John Huston's *Beat the Devil.*

Capote's Camp in *Beat the Devil*

Heeding the advice of producer David O. Selznick, who hired Capote to pen the screenplay for Vittorio de Sica's *Indiscretion of an American Wife* (1953), John Huston engaged Capote as the scriptwriter for his caper film *Beat the Devil.* Huston had rejected earlier scripts by James Helvick and the team of Tony Veiller and Peter Viertel.[18] Considering the film's plot and Huston and Humphrey Bogart's prior work together—most notably, the classics *The Maltese Falcon* (1941), *The Treasure of the Sierra Madre* (1948), and

The African Queen (1951)—Capote envisioned taking a satiric perspective on the material:

> I thought that instead of a straight melodrama, it should be a sort of satire or takeoff on all those movies Bogart and Sidney Greenstreet used to make. When we got to the shooting stage, I would write the next day's script the night before. It was typed the next morning by the secretaries, and nobody, literally, knew what was going on. Sometimes, not even me. I did it that way because I didn't think they'd like my ideas or go along with them.
>
> There were times when Bogey almost resented being put on, or being made fun of, but when it was over, all of us got a big laugh.[19]

The dissolute shenanigans that went on during the shooting of *Beat the Devil* have become Hollywood legend, with descriptions of raucous parties, excessive drinking, and Capote and Bogart's infamous arm-wrestling match—which Capote won.[20] Despite its big stars, acclaimed director, and talented scriptwriter, however, *Beat the Devil* flopped upon its release. No one, it seems, got the joke.

Such disastrous openings have greeted many camp films, including those now esteemed as classics of the genre, including Russ Meyer's *Faster, Pussycat! Kill! Kill!* (1965), Jim Sharman's *The Rocky Horror Picture Show* (1975), Sam Raimi's *The Evil Dead* (1981), Paul Verhoeven's *Showgirls* (1995), and Tommy Wiseau's *The Room* (2003). After such films fizzle upon their initial release, a subculture of viewers grows to appreciate the excess and exaggerations of their aesthetic lapses and cherishes them as guilty pleasures. Having found an audience attuned to their unique sensibilities, these films' reputations grow despite—or rather, because of—their obvious flaws. Roger Ebert said of Huston's film: "*Beat the Devil* went straight from box office flop to cult classic and has been called the first camp movie."[21] Quite simply, many people do not recognize, understand, or appreciate camp, and so it is not surprising that many of *Beat the Devil*'s contemporary reviewers condemned it as a notable stinker. Peter Barnes disparaged its "witless inanities" and concluded, "Actors of the caliber of Bogart, Morley, and Lorre can do nothing with dialogue (Truman Capote) which lacks wit and meaning. Except for some bizarre close-ups, this is two hours of unrelieved tedium."[22] (Barnes must have truly despised *Beat the Devil,* for it runs a mere eighty-nine minutes.) B. G. Marple conceded the film's value as light entertainment while lamenting that it would sabotage Huston's career: "*Beat the Devil* will not increase John Huston's reputation. But because of his ability, and an excellent cast, and Italian scenery, we are entertained by, rather than made censorious of, human nastiness."[23] Registering similar dismay over Huston's squandered abilities, Lindsay Anderson asserted that the film proved Huston's "talent [is] going sadly and seriously astray," yet he also seemed to sense, if not fully appreciate, its camp sensibility: "*Beat the Devil* has the air of an expensive house-party joke, a charade which enormously entertained its participants at the time of playing, but which is too private and insufficiently brilliant to justify public performance."[24] Over a decade later the critical tides turned, and in a 1966 essay for *Film Society Review,* an anonymous critic pointed "to the talented collection of actors and film personalities in the cast, to Huston who was then at the summit of his skill, and to Truman Capote's inspired script," concluding that these "are the ingredients which fell together by some chance or happy design to form a masterpiece of absurdity."[25] In the years between its release and its rediscovery, a new audience learned to love what previous viewers rejected, finding in the film an off-kilter storytelling delightful in its disjunctive style.

The plot of *Beat the Devil* does not readily reveal its camp affinities, for it adheres to the foundational premises of the caper genre. Billy Dannreuther (Humphrey Bogart) serves as the agent for a gang of four criminals—Peterson (Robert Morley), Julius O'Hara (Peter Lorre), Jack Ross (Ivor Bernard), and Ravello (Marco Tulli)—determined to finagle ownership of uranium rights in Africa. While stranded in Italy waiting for their boat to depart, they encounter Gwendolen and Harry Chelm (Jennifer Jones and Edward Underdown). Gwendolen quickly determines to pursue Billy, as Billy's wife Maria (Gina Lollobrigida) sets her sights on Harry. As a consequence of Gwendolen's active imagination and frequent lies, Peterson and his comrades become convinced that she and Harry are attempting to outwit them in their pursuit of the ill-gotten gains and thus decide to eliminate Harry, who has threatened to report them to the authorities. After a brief, misbegotten foray into Africa, the group returns to Italy, where the criminals are soon arrested and the marriages surprisingly restored.

Camp invokes style over substance, a privileging of social facades rather than philosophical foundations, and, as Ebert suggests, "There are times during the movie when you can sense Capote chuckling to himself as he supplies improbable dialogue for his characters."[26] To this end, Capote's script endorses a breezy and insouciant sensibility as the film's preeminent value. When Maria reminds Billy of a past confederate, she comments, "He killed a lot of people, didn't he?" Billy's reply focuses not on the man's immoral actions but on his flair in carrying them out: "Ah, but he had a better style—besides, he was out for a kingdom." As this conversation ends, Billy adds ruefully, "Naturally, it doesn't do to be fussy." Camp also values pretense and imagination over sincerity and perception, an emphasis that guides Capote's characterization of Gwendolen. Her reaction to the jouncing jalopy that drives them to dinner—"What a wonderful car! It looks as if it had won the Gran Prix D'elegance many years ago"—reveals her ability to perceive reality as she chooses to do so, without being constrained by the truth of the circumstances surrounding her. Later Peterson asks in wonder, "You mean Mrs. Chelm is an unqualified liar?," to which Billy replies, "Well, let's say she uses her imagination rather than her memory." With artifice as the film's chief virtue, Capote weaves together a distinctly amoral tale, infusing a Wildean sensibility into a tale of international intrigue.

Gwendolen and Harry appear to be a marvelously mismatched couple, with her flights of fancy set in contrast to his buttoned-down British decorum, yet they ultimately model the humor of artifice in marital relationships. After winning their chess game, to which she seemed to be paying scant attention, Gwendolen airily dismisses her husband's intellect: "Harry's been all out of sorts today. Usually he's a wonderful loser." Harry appears to find tedious his wife's extravagances and apologizes to Billy: "You must excuse my wife; she has a very lively imagination." Harry's staid demeanor counterbalances Gwendolen's hyperbolic flair, yet it is soon revealed that he merely assumes the role of the British squire, as Gwendolen explains to Billy: "It's just that he sees himself in a place in the west country with trout streams and horses, leading the life of a country squire. It's not his fault if people take it for granted that he has a place like that. He's never once said that he had." Following Susan Sontag's famously succinct definition of camp—"Camp sees everything in quotation marks. It's not a lamp, but a 'lamp'; not a woman, but a 'woman'"[27]—even Harry is not who he appears to be, not an English squire but an "English squire" who assumes the role that he desires despite the mismatch between reality and appearance.

While many theorists of queer humor posit that camp relies on an excess of emotion (in such performances as drag queens lip-synching torch songs), it can also shift the expected tenor of a scenario to expose the artificiality of human relationships. While viewers might expect a wife's frank admission of her erotic interest in another man to catalyze an encounter fraught with passion, in *Beat the Devil* a startling lack of emotion builds this scene's understated humor. When Maria candidly tells Billy, "You know, if

Dreaming of an English escape from her Italian paradise, Maria (Gina Lollobrigida) ponders leaving her husband Billy (Humphrey Bogart)—news that he accepts stoically, even genially.

I ever leave you, it will be for someone of the type of Harry Chelm," Billy replies, "Bully for you." His lackluster response to her confession suggests that he does not love her, yet despite his interest in an adulterous affair with Gwendolen, he never gives any sign that he would abandon Maria for a new lover. Playing this scene for its emotional depth, however, would restore the coherent paradigms of desire and identity that Capote campily reframes, and so the denial of affection ironically becomes its most convincing enactment. The film's concluding punch line, in which Harry telegrams Gwendolen to inform her that he has won the African mineral rights and will forgive her if she returns with his hot-water bottle in hand, lacks any convincing expression of marital affection, while still providing a happy ending. Comedies typically rely on marriages and implied fecundity to carry their conclusions, as in Shakespeare's multiple marriages concluding *As You Like It* and *Twelfth Night.* Capote's resolution to this caper adheres to this formula while tweaking it with a campy, queer edge, in which a hot-water bottle is esteemed more highly than the woman who delivers it.

Part of the play of cinematic camp involves the construction of audiences, both in a film's storyline and in its reception, who are and who are not attuned to its humor: just as some audience members do not enjoy a film's camp artifice and reject it, some characters do not understand the jokes surrounding them and fail to see the comedy of life as it unfolds. In light of this comic logic, Capote's characterization of the criminals stresses their rigorous humorlessness. Peterson appears to laugh genially at Billy's suggestion to write a memoir during the long delay as they wait for their boat to be repaired—"Very funny. I like an associate of mine to have a sense of humor. A good laugh does more for the stomach muscles than five minutes setting-up exercises"—but he then proves that he faked his good humor when he abruptly stops laughing and barks, "And now that we've had our moment of fun, and all the better for it, let's get back to the question." Furthermore, Peterson cannot understand the rather obvious fact that Gwendolen is an inveterate fantasist, solemnly avowing of her and her husband, "These are two very clever and dangerous antagonists." He respectfully assesses his adversaries for their wily acumen—which they do not possess. Steadfastly refusing to see the ridiculousness of their situation, Peterson, O'Hara, Ross, and Ravello play the straight men to Capote's queer comedy, which further highlights the disjunction between the film's camp and caper registers.

Capote's camp humor, which aligns with a queer vision of the world, frequently dismantles normative codes of gender and sexuality. Fabio Cleto notes that "naïve camp works by emphasising or demystifying the artificiality that passes for natural" in a process that he terms "queering straightness." He further affirms that such camp performances necessitate "an external perception that travesties the object of perception and debunks its seriousness."[28] "Queering straightness" subverts assumptions of seamless heterosexuality and its presumed normative status, and Capote codes his four criminals as uninterested in, if not alienated from, codes of normative 1950s masculinity and sexuality. The film's opening and closing shots parade this homosocial syndicate in pairs, linking them as queer couples, and Gwendolen's initial response to them casts the men in a sexually suspicious light, as she assumes that they must be "desperate characters" because "Not one of them looked at my legs." Billy taunts Peterson, O'Hara, and Ravello for their childlike masculinity—"Rub-a-dub-dub, three men in a tub"—when they struggle to close a suitcase, with O'Hara resting his hand on Ravello's shoulder. In Africa the four men pass themselves off as traders in domestic goods—vacuum cleaners and sewing machines. When Peterson attempts to ingratiate them to Ahmed, the African inquisitor, he proclaims gamely, "Surely, your excellency, in our case one look is sufficient to convince you of our innocence." As Ahmed examines them, Peterson smiles with unconvincing joviality, then the camera pans to a grimacing Ross. The shot cuts momentarily to Maria prettying herself with her compact and then returns to Ravello, who smiles broadly if unconvincingly, and ends with O'Hara, who glumly stares and blinks. Ahmed replies, "No, one look is not enough"—a sure sign that their attempt to pass themselves off as innocent merchants has failed, that their performance of normativity does not pass even casual observation.

Still, although Capote wrote a camp script, it was by no means certain that his dialogue would result in a camp film (as it is also never certain that an ostensibly serious script will not derail into a camp classic). He shares a screenplay credit with Huston, and so it is impossible to disentangle who wrote which line during their hurried collaboration. Also, the script's camp qualities need to be realized by the actors playing their various roles; in this regard, and as Susan Sontag notes, Gina Lollobrigida stands as a camp archetype.[29] She sensually incarnates the character of Maria, exuding a seductive and bosomy sexuality, and, no matter the unlikeliness of the setting, is frequently dressed glamorously—in an evening dress while Billy remains in his morning robe, in high heels on the beach after they escape their sinking ship. Lollobrigida delivers her lines flatly yet also, with her winsome Italian accent, liltingly. The incongruity between her words and her voice imbues the film with an errant levity, such as in her description of herself to Harry as temperamentally English: "Emotionally, I am English. I serve tea every afternoon with crumpets, and I always kept up my subscription to *Country Life.*" Purring about her English sympathies, Lollobrigida's Maria undermines the stereotypes of the hot-blooded Italian sex goddess while simultaneously reinforcing them in her determined pursuit of Harry. When he lies ill in bed, she tries to seduce him with tea, singing "Tea for two, and two for tea." Harry, oblivious to her affections, fetishistically fixates on his hot-water bottle. Maria seductively appeals to him, "Only you could make a woman feel like this," but it is always unclear why she finds him so attractive—other than for his artificial status as an English squire.

In a similar vein, Jennifer Jones's performance as Gwendolen is either horribly arch or brilliantly insouciant, depending on whether she understood the effect she was achieving, yet either style connects effectively with the film's campiness. The delivery of her lines often feels strained, as if she

Far from the rarefied emotional heights of her Academy Award–winning role in *The Song of Bernadette* (1943), Jennifer Jones as Gwendolen Chelm either delivers a perfectly pitched comic performance or stumbles through the film without a clear sense of her character's motivations or lines. Through the lens of camp, however, it matters little which option more accurately describes her acting.

were ad-libbing or simply having difficulty remembering them, and she fails to maintain a convincing British accent. Within a camp perspective, such slips merely accentuate that the character is performing this charade to dupe the ne'er-do-wells surrounding her, all the while duping herself. Bogart plays the role of Billy Danreuther with an affable ease, and in many ways he appears more an amiable bystander to the narrative action than its instigator. When his driver demands reparations for the car that has tumbled over a cliff, Billy protests, "Why, you fat bandit, I *gave* you the car in the first place!," to which the driver coolly declares, "How I came into possession of it is beside the point." Bogart's style of careless geniality carries his performance, such as when Ahmed asks Billy to betray Peterson and chides him for resisting the proposed deal—"Your demands are very great, under the circumstances"—to which Billy deadpans: "Why shouldn't they be? Fat Gut's my best friend, and I will not betray him cheaply." In his ode to Oscar Wilde and queer illusion, Neil Bartlett extols the pleasure of forgeries and faked emotions in camp humor, exclaiming, "*Who wants to be consistent?* What kind of integrity is that? We are all fakes, all inventions. We are making this all up as we go along,"[30] and his words capture the pleasure of Bogart's performance. The actor metamorphoses through numerous facades as the picture progresses yet achieves a consistency through his very inconsistency as circumstances change—there is an integrity in his lack of integrity.

In *Beat the Devil,* Capote's camp sensibility elevates an otherwise pedestrian enterprise into a gem of a film, one that crackles with sharp humor, effortless charm, and the pleasures of artifice. Capote called *Beat the Devil* "a marvelous joke,"[31] "a mad camp," and "the camp of all time,"[32] indicating his pleasure in the film's jaunty sensibility and erratic humor. A unique text in Capote's canon, *Beat the Devil* encourages readers to ponder whether his camp stylings are submerged in other works—and how these works appear if one uncovers their camp potential.

Camp Gothic in *Other Voices, Other Rooms*

Upon the publication of *Other Voices, Other Rooms* in 1948, many critics decried its queer excesses, faulting it in particular for its outré style and for its shocking storyline of Joel Harrison Knox's maturation into homosexuality. Writing for the *Boston Herald,* Rudolph Elie Jr. castigated Capote's variable prose and provocative subject matter: "The writing ranges from passages of great brilliance and insight to awkward, sophomoric constructions, to elaborately self-conscious artiness to strongly lavender implications and back again to brilliance."[33] ("Lavender" has faded from the gay lexicon but commonly signified homosexuality in the early to mid-twentieth century.)[34] Richard Boulton agreed with this assessment, titling his review "Lavender Pastiche" and condemning the novel as "lavender eyewash."[35] The critic for the *Boston Daily Globe,* observing Capote's "feminine perception," compared *Other Voices, Other Rooms* to "machine-made filigree lace,"[36] and Charles Rolo, writing for the *Atlantic,* concluded that it is "too formless and too choked with gaudy blossoms."[37] Jesse Cross's succinct evaluation in *Library Journal* urged librarians to safeguard their patrons from its pathologies: "Much lush writing, frequently trailing off into illusory fancies of sick brains, losing its way, yet withal picturesque. Not recommended for libraries."[38] Carlos Baker's review encapsulated the prevailing critical response to Capote's novel as simply *beaucoup trop*: "This interest is something like that of a spectator at a Mardi Gras parade: the wonder is what will be thought of next."[39] What happens, however, if rather than criticizing these critics for their literary homophobia—given the mores of the era, they were hardly alone in their prejudices—readers assent to such charges of queer excess yet defend these stylistic flourishes as evidence of Capote's camp play with the tropes of the southern gothic novel? At what point, that is, does Capote's southern gothic novel become, in Sontag's formulation of camp, a "southern gothic novel"?

Certainly, Capote paints the gothic setting of *Other Voices, Other Rooms* with a broad brush. Decay, horror, and freakishness darkly color the novel, as is readily evident in its opening revelation that Joel's destination is "Skully's Landing," with the image of death foreshadowed in Sam Radclif's truck, in which a "toy skull ornamented the gear shift" (9).[40] The novel contains a strikingly high population of people of short stature, including the "pygmy" Jesus Fever (28), the "little Negro dwarf" who attends to Ed Sansom when he convalesces from a gunshot wound (152), and the "midget" Miss Wisteria (191). Miss Wisteria's stunted physical growth mirrors her stunted sexual development, as evident when she pedophilically attempts to seduce Joel: "She placed her hand on his thigh, and then, as though she had no control over them whatsoever, her fingers crept up inside his legs" (195). Freakish reimaginations of the human form populate Capote's landscape. Joel perceives Amy and Randolph to be "a kind of freak animal, half-man, half-woman" (120), and even Zoo, the novel's most sympathetic character, bears the physical markings of southern gothic grotesquerie: "The length of her neck was something to ponder upon, for she was almost a freak, a human giraffe" (54). And while many additional examples of Capote's gothic touches could be listed, it suffices to conclude with the novel's backstories, including the "tale of Gothic splendor" concerning the town's "freakish old house": "it is said that once three exquisite sisters were raped and murdered here in a gruesome manner by a fiendish Yankee bandit who rode a silver-grey horse and wore a velvet cloak stained scarlet with the blood of Southern womanhood" (17–18). The legend of the Cloud Hotel and the Drownin Pond (98–100), which features a dead child, a dead gambler, and a dead society matron in its cast of characters, likewise permeates *Other Voices, Other Rooms* with a twilit atmosphere of gloom, doom, and darkness.

At the same time, how seriously are readers to take these numerous gothic features, which conglomerate into a hyperbolic landscape of horror? The grotesquerie of this southern landscape also registers in the immoderate facial and body hair that afflicts its women: Miss Roberta "had long ape-like arms that were covered with dark fuzz, and there was a wart on her chin" (22); Joel notices that Miss Amy has "the vague suggestion of a mustache fuzzing her upper lip" (44); and Zoo reports of the family matriarch Angela Lee: "Honey, a mighty peculiar thing happen to that old lady, happen just before she die: she grew a beard" (124). The celebrated allure of southern women's beauty, within Capote's camp gothic imagination, is reconceived as a hirsute masculinity waiting to pierce through a feminine façade. Furthermore, the apelike, bewarted Miss Roberta hangs a certificate on her restaurant's walls that announces, "This is to certify that Roberta Velma Lacey won Grand Prize in Lying at the annual Double Branches Dog Days Frolic" (23), which hints that prevarication and artifice are esteemed values within the novel's imaginary. Capote's gothic touches in his depiction of Noon City's business establishments include the "combination barbershop-beauty parlor that is run by a one-armed man and his wife" (17); he leaves unanswered the question of how a one-armed barber would practice his trade. As Jerry Leath Mills documents in his tongue-in-cheek (yet impressively detailed) study, many esteemed southern novels feature a dead mule, yet Capote exaggerates the contours of this already embellished trope: "John Brown reared back, snorted, pawed the floor; then, as if insane with terror, he came at a gallop, and lunged, splintering the balcony's rail. Joel primed himself for a crash which never came; when he looked again, the mule, hung to a beam by the rope-reins twisted about his neck, was swinging in mid-air" (225–26). Mills sees in Capote's demented and suicidal mule a "notoriously decadent scene"—one impossible to imagine within the mores of realism and even implausible within the mores of gothicism, yet nonetheless amusing in the risible excesses that embroider Capote's nightmare world.[41]

In this respect Baker's comparison of *Other Voices, Other Rooms* to a Mardi Gras parade, in which spectators delight in the unexpected wonders that pass before their eyes, becomes particularly apt, for Capote's moments of gothic excess encourage readers to see the landscape as horrific but with an undercurrent of sly humor. While fear and laughter may appear to be contradictory reactions to gothic literature's terrors, Jane Austen, with her gentle parody of the genre in *Northanger Abbey,* was surely not the first to ponder the possibility of humor emerging from darkness, and Avril Horner and Sue Zlosnik insist on the necessity of recognizing the comic potential evident, if often overlooked, throughout this literary tradition: "We have suggested that it is perhaps best to think of Gothic writing as a spectrum that, at one end, produces horror-writing containing moments of comic hysteria or relief and, at the other, works in which there are clear signals that nothing is to be taken seriously."[42] Gothic literature invites such apparently oppositional responses, and Capote thematizes the necessity of dual perceptions throughout the novel. When Joel sees himself in a mirror at Skully's Landing, his reflection fails to capture the truth of his image: "it was like the comedy mirrors in carnival houses; he swayed shapelessly in its distorted depth" (50). Along with Baker's comparison of *Other Voices, Other Rooms* to a carnivalesque panoply of eye-popping amusements, a funhouse mirror aptly symbolizes the experience of reading the novel for its latent humor. One can enjoy the text as a southern gothic novel, but a new, complementary pleasure arises when it is held up to itself as a carnivalesque reflection.

Such a funhouse effect develops throughout the novel as characters fail to, or simply cannot, recognize Joel as a gay adolescent. Sam Radclif's reaction to Joel, that he "had his notions of what a 'real' boy should look like, and this kid somehow offended them" (4), establishes the theme of Joel's alienation from normative southern masculinity. When Joel asks Zoo if she recognizes the name Alcibiades—the young, attractive Greek who attempts to seduce Socrates in Plato's *Symposium*—she admits she does not and then attempts to explain Joel's ostensible mistake: "You musta heard wrong, honey. The name he most likely said is Alicaster. Alicaster Jones is a Paradise Chapel boy what used to sing in the choir. Looks like a white angel, so pretty he got the preacher and all kinda mens and ladies lovin him up" (160). Although Zoo does not understand Randolph's reference to Alcibiades, she correctly yet naively posits Joel's connection to a modern-day Alcibiades in Alicaster. Incapable of seeing homosexuality in the classical past, apparently overlooking the scandal of homosexuality in her southern present, Zoo broaches the possibility of homoerotic attraction only to dismiss its relevance to Joel, and thus she exemplifies an interpretive process mirrored by many critics, in which they comment superficially on surface presentations without recognizing the very depth of that surface.

Much of the excess for which contemporary reviewers condemned *Other Voices, Other Rooms* circulates around Randolph and his theatrical displays of queer flamboyance. Again, while one might regret the homophobia implicit in these observations, they are nonetheless on the mark: as Capote announced of his character in a 1948 interview, "everything about him is baroque and highly ornamental."[43] Randolph's letter to Joel's Aunt Ellen abounds with rhetorical flourishes ("to again assume my paternal duties, forsaken, lo, these many years" [7]), and the narrator describes Sam Radclif's reaction to this epistle. He sees "a maze of curlicues and dainty i's dotted with daintier o's" and wonders, "What the hell kind of man would write like that?" He later exclaims, "And the cousin . . . yes, by God, the cousin!" (15). When Randolph is "cleaning his nails with a goosequill," Capote stresses that he is "stylized in his attitude" (120–21). Randolph's baroque sensibility paints him not merely as a homosexual but as one epitomizing various stereotypes of the rarefied queen. He quips with Wildean wit—"All children are morbid; it's their one saving grace" (77)—and feigns emotion through his cosmopolitan ennui. When Joel expresses sympathy for Zoo, stating simply, "Poor Zoo," Randolph's world-weary resignation counterbalances the boy's concern: "'Poor everybody,' said Randolph, languidly pouring another sherry" (80). Randolph's dry sense of humor animates his conversations with Joel, such as when, in contrast to Zoo and her terror over the murderous Keg Brown, Randolph casually admires a former lover who schemed to kill him: "for little Kurt, that was his name, turned out to be a perfect horror, and tried twice to murder me . . . exhibiting both times, I must say, admirable ingenuity" (136). Praising his adversary for his cleverness, Randolph models a bemused insouciance that distances him from the normal registers of emotion.

Early critics of *Other Voices, Other Rooms* also attacked Capote's symbolism, as did the *Newsweek* reviewer who bemoaned the book's "deep, murky well of Freudian symbols."[44] Martin Bucco similarly diagnosed the text and its author within a Freudian framework: "Freudianism in Capote's work might rest less on conscious appropriation than on a neurotic condition in Capote himself. The Freudian critic reports the Capotesque world one of infantile repression."[45] The longstanding charge that gay men have failed in their psychosexual development into normative heterosexuality cannot be refuted within the circular reasoning of Freudian thought—gays become gays because they do not become straight—yet Capote cagily engaged with and refuted such analysis of his novel. In one interview he vehemently denied any interest in Freudian symbolism: "All I want to do is tell the story, and sometimes it's best to choose a symbol. I wouldn't know a Freudian symbol as such if you showed it to me."[46] But with a typically Capotean contradiction, he stated of the novel that "Everything in it has double meanings."[47] He also affirmed in a 1968 interview, "the book is a prose poem in which I have taken my own emotional problems and transformed them into psychological symbols. Every one of those characters represented some aspect of myself."[48]

While many great novels feature multilayered symbolism and allusions, Capote's symbols frequently introduce camp humor into *Other Voices, Other Rooms*. Harold Beaver suggests that excessive play with signs and symbols builds queer levity: "Most diverting, because most evasive, of all is the multiplication of signs. [Camp] seems an infinite world wholly devoted to a switching of signs based on shifting of context."[49] In the novel, an early allusion to Sam Radclif's employer, the "Chuberry Turpentine Company" (3), refers to the jazz saxophonist Chu Berry (1908–1941), thereby imbuing a playful, improvisatory air into the ensuing deployment of names and symbols. A longstanding trope of southern manhood—the patriarch's sword—apparently symbolizes Joel's ascent into masculinity when Zoo bestows it on him. She says, "This here was Papadaddy's proudest thing . . . Now don't you bring it no disgrace" (166), but Joel finds himself powerless to use it when confronted with the possibility of his death. While traveling through a swamp, he and Idabel encounter a cottonmouth. Failing to access the sword's power, Joel stands dazed: "How did Mr. Sansom's eyes come to be in a moccasin's head?" (180). It is difficult to conceive that Capote would not have understood the compounded symbolism of a phallic sword confronting a phallic snake, which then leaves his protagonist frozen until a female character proves the false congruency linking symbols to genders as she "pull[s] the sword out of his hand" (180) and kills the animal. A girl wielding phallic weapons need not necessarily introduce a comic sensibility into a novel, yet as Idabel bosses Joel about—"Outa the way, sissy-britches" (108)—she dismantles traditional notions of gender identity. Correspondingly, in lines with muted levity, Capote depicts his protagonist as cowed by the phallic authority symbolized by Idabel's concealed weaponry: "Joel thought of the knife in her pocket, and despite Florabel's pleas, concluded it might be wise to move elsewhere" (108).

A string of overdetermined symbols throughout *Other Voices, Other Rooms* follows Randolph's artistic interest in birds and paints Joel in avian terms, with these images becoming deeply implicated with hyperbolic sexual iconography. Within the avian world roosters (i.e., "cocks") commonly signify the penis, with the word *bird* denoting it as well.[50] After Amy kills a bluebird in Joel's room, Zoo tells Joel that "Mister Randolph likes the dead birds, the kinds with pretty feathers" (63). Capote's avian symbolism assumes a deeper queer meaning when chicken hawks menace Skully's Landing. In queer slang, the synonymous terms *chicken hawk* and *chicken queen* refer to, as Richard Spears attests, "a male homosexual who is particularly attracted to teenage boys."[51] Capote's narrator notes that "A pair of chicken hawks wheeled with stiffened wings above smoke" (109) and soon reiterates, "Like kites being reeled in, the chicken hawks circled lower till their shadows revolved over the slanting shingled roof" (110). Zoo blasts her shotgun to frighten the birds away: "The wings of the hawks raged as they fled over tree tops, their shadows sweeping across the road's broiling sand like islands of dark." She then explains her objective: "Miss Amy, them hawks fixin to steal the place off our hands less we shoo em away" (115). Lest the reader miss the connection between Joel and birds, Idabel tells him, "You look like a plucked chicken . . . So skinny and white" (132). With phalluses symbolically flying around this southern landscape, Randolph's pursuit of Joel is threatening but ineffective, for he also confesses his impotence: "You are quite right: my bird can't fly" (169). Chickens and chicken hawks succeed as symbols in Capote's novels, as Joel and Randolph assume the respective positions of prey and predator, yet such terminology within queer circles often carries with it a humorous undertone, one that cannot be shaken from their deployment in the novel.

Beyond the avian realm, the comic undertones of Capote's symbolism emerge in his suggestive depiction of Joel's anal deflowering. When Joel tussles with Idabel after his misbegotten attempt to kiss her, his buttocks proleptically identify his future sexual pleasures: "The dark glasses fell off, and Joel, falling back, felt them crush beneath and cut his buttocks. 'Stop,' he panted, 'please stop, I'm bleeding'" (135). If any readers doubt Joel's homosexual identity, his anus testifies to his truth. In another scene of exaggerated symbolism that becomes comic in its excess, a phallic symbol slaps Joel in the face: "a Prince Albert poster swept like a bird through the air and struck him in the face: he fought to free himself, but it was as though it were alive, and, struggling with it, it suddenly frightened him more than had the sight of Randolph: he would never rid himself of either" (197). While ostensibly this "Prince Albert" refers to the brand of tobacco named in honor of Victoria's husband, the *Oxford English Dictionary* defines a Prince Albert as "A metal ring inserted into the end of a man's urethra and out through the glans penis (also called *dressing ring*)."[52] Within the language of queer and piercing cultures, the phallic connotations paint this scene as one in which Joel is literally slapped in the face by a penis. This symbolism also compounds with the avian images found throughout the novel, as Capote writes that the Prince Albert poster "swept like a bird" until striking Joel in the face, thus triggering his realization that he will never free himself from close, intimate, and oral encounters with penises.

Along with learning to accept his homosexuality, Joel must come to appreciate camp humor as part of his initiation into the South's queer subculture. To stress this aspect of Joel's development, Capote depicts the adolescent as initially resistant to Randolph's comic sensibility. When

Joel mentions Zoo's fear of the murderous Keg Brown, Randolph laughs, apparently inappropriately:

> "Don't tell me!" cried Randolph, and giggled in the prim, suffocated manner of an old maid. "Already?"
>
> "I didn't think it was so funny," said Joel resentfully. "He did a bad thing to her."
>
> Amy said: "Randolph's only cutting up."
>
> "You malign me, angel."
>
> "It wasn't funny," said Joel.
>
> Squinting one eye, Randolph studied the spokes of amber light whirling out from the sherry as he raised and revolved his glass. "Not funny, dear me, no. But the story has a certain bizarre interest: would you care to hear it?" (77)

While within most conventional interpretive practices the attempted murder of a woman provides scant fodder for humor, Randolph indulges himself in a "caustic lilt of sarcasm" (78), even finding his memories of her terror "exquisitely humorous" (79). For Joel, in contrast, understanding Randolph and his humor is "like trying to decipher some tale being told in a senseless foreign language" (80). Gay men often foster a sense of community through queer and camp humor, as they reveal themselves to one another through their jokes and comic sensibilities. Indeed, Capote underscores the dialogic nature of such communication. At the commencement of their acquaintance, just as Joel does not understand Randolph's humor, Randolph finds Joel's conversation drab: "Randolph had heard him out in the colorless way one listens to a stale joke, for he seemed, in some curious manner, to have advance knowledge of the facts" (82). Still, the mutuality that later defines their relationship is foreshadowed in their early wrangling over humor and its meaning when Joel ponders whether Randolph is mocking him or simply mirroring him: "Joel was used to compliments, imaginary ones originating in his head, but to have some such plainly spoken left him with an uneasy feeling: was he being poked fun at, teased? So he questioned the round innocent eyes, and saw his own boy-face focused as in double camera lenses" (86). At this moment when Joel does not yet understand Randolph's queer sensibility, he nevertheless sees himself in his eyes.

Toward the novel's close, as Joel recuperates from his illness following the carnival, he comes closer to accepting his homosexuality and thus finds himself able to communicate with Randolph: "The mist which for him overhung so much of Randolph's conversation, even that had lifted, at least it was no longer troubling, for it seemed as though he understood him absolutely" (208). Communication, once hindered between the two, now flows. Furthermore, Capote couples Joel's new sense of understanding with the blossoming of his queer sense of humor, as Randolph camps for his companion's amusement: "He was Charlie Chaplin to a T, Mae West too, and his cruel take-off on Amy made Joel double up on the bed, finally absorbed in laughter for its own sake, and Randolph said ha! ha! He would show him something really fun: 'I'll have to fix up, though . . . But if I do . . . you mustn't laugh'" (209). While Randolph's cruel parody of Amy does not register at the same level of savage humor as his jokes about Zoo's attempted murder, this scene stresses the ways in which a queer sensibility often finds levity in pain and insult—and shows that Joel now finds such humor pleasing.

Congruent with their overarching distaste for *Other Voices, Other Room*'s queer gothicism, several early reviewers also pilloried its conclusion. In her review for the *Nation,* Diana Trilling diagnosed the novel as an exploration of queer pathology: "At the end of the book the young Joel turns to the homosexual love offered him by Randolph, and we realize that in his slow piling up of nightmare detail Mr. Capote has been attempting to recreate the emotional background to sexual inversion. What his book is saying is that a boy becomes homosexual when the circumstances of his life deny him the other, more normal gratifications of his need for affection."[53] Leslie Fiedler espied in the image of a gay adolescent the dark roots of Capote's novel: "Once the child has been remade by homosexual sensibility into the image of an ambiguous object of desire, the lust for the child is revealed as a flight from woman, the family, maturity itself! and unless the writer sentimentalizes pederasty on some romantic, English public school model, he finds himself confronting a subject as dark and terrible as Dostoyevsky's evocation of the child rapist."[54] Again, however, such views overlook the potential for lighter modes to complement the tale's surface narrative, in this case the ways in which Capote embeds the structure of a fairy tale to lay the groundwork for a "happily ever after" ending. Joel's Aunt Ellen reads "The Snow Queen" to him as a boy, and he grows up to enjoy the company of his own snowy queen. In his alter-ego as the "the queer lady" with "white hair . . . like the wig of a character from history: a towering pale pompadour of fat dribbling curls" (67), Randolph drags about for his amusement, and another scene similarly showcases his clowning: "Randolph stuck on his head . . . a wreath of pine needles and tiger lilies . . . and galavanted around

. . . the whole evening" (95). At the novel's end, Joel unites with his "Snow Queen": "Gradually the blinding sunset drained from the glass, darkened, and it was as if snow were falling there, flakes shaping snow-eyes, hair: a face trembled like a white beautiful moth, smiled. She beckoned to him, shining and silver, and he knew he must go" (231). The incongruent melding of fairy tale and southern gothicism turns each genre into a carnivalesque reflection of the other; the childish pleasures of fairy tales filter through the horrors of the gothic, and an errant humor emerges in their disjunctive, yet strangely complementary, union.

In sum, a deeper pleasure arises in reading *Other Voices, Other Rooms* not merely as a southern gothic novel but as a "southern gothic novel" with queer and campy comic undertones, even if the humor is sometimes challenging to distill. Randolph proclaims of his life, "do not take seriously, what you see here: it's only a joke played on myself by myself . . . it amuses and horrifies . . . a rather gaudy grave, you might say" (138). If readers perceive *Other Voices, Other Rooms* as Capote's gaudy take on the gothic tradition, with its excesses and extravagant symbolism piquing both horror and amusement, then its accomplishments come into sharper focus, and its unique place in the southern literary tradition shines forth more clearly. "They came upon the Landing from the rear, and entered the garden" (228), Capote writes as Joel and Randolph return from their foray to the Cloud Hotel, with the allegorical garden of sexual pleasure found in the posteriors. It need not be read as a funny line, but in Capote's carnivalesque funhouse of comic and erotic humor, it metamorphoses into a blatant statement of queer desire—only remaining buried under the trappings of gothicism for those who refuse to dig through them.

Answered Prayers and Other People's Wit

While Capote's camp humor pulses in the subterranean realms of *Other Voices, Other Rooms,* it splashes on the surface of *Answered Prayers,* while also proving that Capote's ability to draw on the comic varied. Because *Answered Prayers* remained unfinished at the time of Capote's death, it cannot stand as a certain indictment of his waning talents, but its flagging humor emerges as a likely reason he never completed the project. Still, in publishing three of its chapters—"Unspoiled Monsters," "Kate McCloud," and "La Côte Basque"—Capote allowed his readers insight into the book's progress, and these chapters demonstrate a striking failure of his comic sensibility. Capote promised a masterpiece in *Answered Prayers,* declaring, "Proust and I are both accurate in description. For instance, you could never find anything more sensually exact about La Côte Basque than that chapter,"[55] and Capote's biographer Gerald Clarke cites an editor who, after reading early drafts, called it "brilliant, malicious, very funny, acerbic, bitchy, and unputdownable."[56] Its humor, however, fails to match that of Capote's earlier efforts.

Many of the funniest lines in *Answered Prayers* are not Capote's. In his gossipy accounts of the rich and famous, he quotes other people's humor. For instance, when Cecil Beaton laments, "The most distressing fact of growing older is that I find my private parts are shrinking," Greta Garbo, "after a mournful pause," deadpans in reply, "Ah, if only I could say the same" (14).[57] Dorothy Parker remarks on her repeated suicide attempts, "If I don't stop doing this, someday I'm going to hurt myself" (108). After Parker asks about Montgomery Clift's sexual orientation—"I mean, he is a cocksucker, isn't he?"—Tallulah Bankhead placidly replies, "Well, d-d-darling, I r-r-really wouldn't know. He's never sucked *my* cock" (109). Cole Porter, rejecting a gigolo charging astronomical sums, denies himself the pleasures of oral sex while casting himself as the eponymous protagonist of one of his songs: "Miss Otis regrets she's unable to lunch today. Now get out" (143). One cannot deny the humor of these witticisms, yet they stand in isolation from one another as memorable encounters unmoored from their contexts and unreflective of Capote's uniquely comic sensibility.

Beyond pilfering from his witty circle, Capote recycles old aphorisms, such as the "Old Texas saying" that "Women are like rattlesnakes—the last thing that dies is their tail" (23). He expresses his personal dislike for certain authors and celebrities through his narrator P. B. Jones, such as in Jones's snide assessment of Mary McCarthy's physical appearance: "Creative females are not often presentable. Look at Mary McCarthy!" (15). While the pleasure of many romans à clef lies in decoding which characters represent which celebrities, Capote's chapters are unchallenging in this regard, such as in the portrayal of Tennessee Williams as "Mr. Wallace" (58–64) or of socialite Slim Keith as Ina Coolbirth, "a big breezy peppy broad, born and raised on a ranch in Montana" (140). Some proclamations appear designed to shock, such as P. B. Jones's statement, "I was a kind of Hershey Bar whore—there wasn't much I wouldn't do for a nickel's worth of chocolate" (5). Capote does not camouflage homosexuality in *Answered Prayers* as he did in *Other Voices, Other Rooms* and other earlier works, yet unvarnished candor about sexual desire does not necessarily result in more compelling literature. The strictures of the 1940s and 1950s required Capote to encode multiple layers of text and subtext into his early fiction, whereas his greater openness about human sexuality in *Answered Prayers* renders its comic touches more broad, less challenging.

In sum, *Answered Prayers* fails as camp because the public response to homosexuality had shifted radically after the sexual revolution of the 1960s and 1970s, which also revolutionized sexual humor. As Andrew Britton explains of the nature of camp humor, "'Subversiveness' needs to be assessed not in terms of a quality which is supposedly proper to a phenomenon, but as a relationship between a phenomenon and its context—that is, dynamically. To be Quentin Crisp in the 1930s is a very different matter from being Quentin Crisp in 1978. What was once an affront has now become part of life's rich pageant. The threat has been defused—and defused because it was always superficial."[58] After approximately thirty years in the national limelight, Capote's camp and humor did not achieve the same result that they had earlier in his career, and *Answered Prayers* showcases the ways in which time and cultural context affect readers' responses to humor. Such an observation should be counterbalanced by the recognition that much humor is truly timeless—Aristophanes, Chaucer, and Austen continue to amuse, as does Capote with *Beat the Devil* and *Other Voices, Other Rooms.* In aiming to shock, *Answered Prayers* misses the mark of provoking laughter, rendering this unfinished novel the least satisfying work in Capote's dynamic corpus.

Conclusion

Capote's camp humor in *Beat the Devil, Other Voices, Other Rooms,* and other works allows readers to see more clearly his unique talents and his inimitable contributions to southern literature. Some critics have alleged that Capote was little more than a literary chameleon: Gordon Merrick observes parallels between *Breakfast at Tiffany's* and F. Scott Fitzgerald's *The Great Gatsby,* including their "stylish, detached, and colloquial" prose and their "unabashed use of theatrical device,"[59] and Linda Mizejewski sees in Holly Golightly a tribute to Christopher Isherwood's Sally Bowles in *Goodbye to Berlin.*[60] Tennessee Williams traced the source of Capote's dislike for Gore Vidal to the following exchange, in which the two denigrated each other as literary magpies: "Gore told Truman he got all his plots out of Carson McCullers and Eudora Welty. Truman said: 'Well, maybe you get all of yours from the *Daily News*.'"[61] Capote defended himself against such charges: "Like any artist, such as a singer or a pianist, I change my tone and color range to suit my subject; and as a result, it seems as though there is some extraordinary difference of approach and style, when there is none whatever."[62] Still, it is apparent that these allegations gnawed at him, and in an interview with Andy Warhol, he stated, "For me, every act of art is the act of solving a mystery. They say, 'Why is he so inconsistent, moving from one thing to another?' But the reason is, if I don't, then I'm not doing, in a sense, what it is I want to do. Just to solve a stylistic problem. Just to solve a problem that I create for myself."[63] Additionally, in an acerbic denigration of the proponents of stylistic uniformity, he sniped: "Anyone consistently consistent has a head made of biscuit."[64] Shifting styles among various works, Capote pioneered new forms, new genres, and new modes of southern literary expression, and the comic edge that embellishes some of these works merits them even greater acclaim. In a 1972 self-interview, when asking himself what he finds frightening, Capote replied, "The thought that I might lose my sense of humor."[65] If readers see Capote's humor as merely an amusing part of his public persona rather than as a core aspect of his cinematic and literary achievements, then they lose the wonder of his accomplishments through the stifled silence of laughter denied.

3

FLORENCE KING'S QUEER CONSERVATISM AND THE GENDER POLITICS OF SOUTHERN HUMOR

A longtime columnist for William F. Buckley Jr.'s conservative journal *National Review,* Florence King also penned *Confessions of a Failed Southern Lady,* a memoir detailing her southern upbringing and her bisexual affairs. In this work she outs herself with a pointed wisecrack that demolishes any pretense of southern propriety: "No matter which sex I went to bed with, I never smoked on the street" (2).[1] Through this admission, which threads the needle between transgressive passion and regional decorum, King assures readers that she satisfied her ostensibly errant sexual desires while simultaneously respecting her grandmother's admonitions about southern womanhood. King's ferocious wit links her disparate literary endeavors, in that her voice—caustic, precise, and unmercifully funny—unites them into a unique corpus of queer southern humor. Her comic musings span the 1970s through the early 2000s and include her mock sociological studies *Southern Ladies and Gentleman, WASP, Where Is Thy Sting?* and *He: An Irreverent Look at the American Male;* her novel *When Sisterhood Was in Flower;* and her essay collections *Reflections in a Jaundiced Eye, Lump It or Leave It, With Charity toward None: A Fond Look at Misanthropy, STET, Damnit!,* and *Deja Reviews.* Blossoming from this multiplicity of form, King's writings teem with contradictions: she is a groundbreaking feminist who expresses starkly antifeminist sentiments; she is a bisexual woman evincing little sympathy for gay and lesbian rights; and she proudly trumpets her conservative, southern politics while lambasting leading Republican figures. Her humor provides ample explanation for many of these contradictions—after all, a joke is just a joke—but King entwines her wit with questions concerning the social value accorded to women's humor and to the very meaning of conservatism in southern and queer cultures.

To put it mildly, gay conservatives perplex many of their fellow queers, who often seek to explain away political views diverging from the left while also diagnosing the conditions that would lead otherwise normative homosexuals into the ostensible perversion of conservatism. Kenneth Cimino, in his sociological analysis of gay conservatives, ponders, "why don't LGBT conservatives use sexual identity as the main group identification?"[2] Cimino's corollary assumption appears to be that queer conservatives *should* connect their sexualities seamlessly to their political views and that if they did so, they would liberate themselves from their conservatism. By framing the question of why some gays become conservative, scholars tacitly naturalize liberalism as the de facto, if not proper, political identity for queers, with conservatism serving as an aberration needing correction. Given the prejudices the gay community has endured over the years, such an interpretive formulation is ironic, for it reasserts the type of binary of identity that queer liberation otherwise dismantles.[3] Yet the effort to explain queer conservatism suffers from a similar intrinsic bias, as it pathologizes a political worldview, often with flippant assertions decrying greed as a primary motivation for gay conservatives presumably more concerned about their pocketbooks than the advancement of queer equality.[4] Still, it appears that roughly one-fifth of gays and lesbians identify as conservatives; thus, although they are a minority within the wider minority of queer culture, they are a sizable subpopulation.[5] And so although some readers might desire to view King's queerness and her conservatism as being at odds, in the early 1990s she defended her sexual identity and her conservative political views in the same breath: "I don't mind being regarded as perverted and unnatural, but I would *die* if people thought I was a Democrat" (*LI* 173).

Interpreting King's humor either through a queer feminist or through a conservative antifeminist lens would unnecessarily stifle the rich play of southern gender politics with which she engages and would only reinforce the binary that her caustic comedy subverts. Furthermore, such a binary approach would also overlook surprising points of convergence between queer and conservative theories, namely, in their questioning of identity politics. Following Foucault, many queer theorists decry identity categories, including such basic ones as heterosexual and homosexual, seeking instead a more disruptive sense of queerness unconstrained by prevailing social ideologies and their disciplinary apparatuses. Queer theory resists the state's purchase in taxonomizing its citizens, with Michel Foucault describing the potential freedoms from regimes of identity achievable through bodily pleasures: "It is the agency of sex that we must break away from, if we aim—through a tactical reversal of the various mechanisms of sexuality—to counter the grips of power with the claims of bodies, pleasures, and knowledges, in their multiplicity and their possibility of resistance. The rallying point for the counterattack against the deployment of sexuality ought not to be sex-desire, but bodies and pleasures."[6]

While not phrasing their celebration of the individual in Foucauldian terms of the body's pleasures, many conservatives likewise decry group-identity politics in favor of celebrating the individual as master of his or her own destiny. Milton Friedman, praising the accomplishments of such figures as Isaac Newton, Albert Einstein, William Shakespeare, John Milton, Thomas Alva Edison, and Henry Ford, argues that "[t]heir achievements were the product of individual genius, of strongly held minority views, of a social climate permitting variety and diversity."[7] F. A. Hayek similarly advocates "respect for the individual man *qua* man, that is, the recognition of his own views and tastes as supreme in his own sphere, however narrowly that may be circumscribed, and the belief that it is desirable that men should develop their own individual gifts and bents."[8] A significant strain of conservative theory criticizes the inhibitory force of group identities, those that would hem in the superior individual who must instead transcend them. Writ large, such themes dominate the writings of objectivist novelist and philosopher Ayn Rand, whose *The Fountainhead* and *Atlas Shrugged* feature protagonists who cast off the shackles imposed on them by their societies. Of her allegiance to Rand's philosophy, King wryly recalls: "She liked people to be tall, slim, and beautiful, and I was now slouched, dumpy, and pustular, but I took up Objectivism anyway" (*CF* 99).

King's comment that she "would *die* if people thought I was a Democrat" indicates her steadfast allegiance to conservative politics, but the queer play of identity as she simultaneously resists the tides of social conservatism in her personal sexual practices unsettles her group affiliations with both queers and conservatives. In this light, her writings display a rhetorical and performative disidentification with feminist and antifeminist discourses simultaneously. As José Esteban Muñoz argues of such disidentificatory strategies, "Disidentification is a performative mode of tactical recognition that various minoritarian subjects employ in an effort to resist the oppressive and normalizing discourse of dominant ideology. Disidentification resists the interpellating call of ideology that fixes a subject with the state power apparatus. It is a reformatting of self within the social. It is a third term that resists the binary of identification and counteridentification. Counteridentification often, through the very routinized workings of its denouncement of dominant discourse, reinstates that same discourse."[9] Within Muñoz's matrix, the two prevailing responses to societies' ideological superstructure are identification and counteridentification. Through these perspectives, individuals see themselves in harmony or in conflict with their culture, primarily because of the ways in which their value as citizens is determined. Disidentification opens new possibilities of understanding how an individual sees herself in relation to her culture. As valuable as Muñoz's paradigm has proved in exploring tactical deployments and subversions of prevailing ideologies, it cannot fully capture King's play with identity politics, for she disidentifies with both conservative and queer discourses simultaneously: she is a member of the dominant culture of the U.S. South and proudly asserts her sense of privilege arising from her Wasp background, yet she is also a countercultural figure who bucked the sexual and social mores of the 1950s through her active and queer sex life. In sum, King is doubly disidentificatory in her humor, undermining and fortifying structures of both discourse and counterdiscourse.

Given the overarching cultural misogyny denigrating women and women's humor, disidentification emerges as a valuable strategy for female humorists, particularly for southern female humorists whose society validates a genteel and sophisticated model of womanhood. To interpret King's humor through a disidentificatory lens necessitates an analysis of the genders of women's humor, as well as paying particular attention to the ways in which she presents herself in relation to feminist and queer cultures. Foremost, it requires understanding wit—King's preferred comic mode—as a rhetorical weapon, which, as she argues, is inherently anti-egalitarian: "It's no accident that *wit* is practically an archaic word in American English. Wit has never played well in America, for reasons not hard to discern. . . . Wit is not a democratic form; the two adjectives most often used to modify it are those weapons of Renaissance aristocrats, *rapier* and *stiletto*" (*RJ* 140). Amid the cultural striving of America, she hypothesizes, "wit was drowned out in the clamor of democracy and the rise of the middle class" (*RJ* 141). As a female wit pillorying feminism, as a bisexual woman celebrating homoerotic passion while denouncing queer social agendas, King straddles multiple rhetorical, cultural, and political worlds, delimiting the necessity of multiple disidentifications for her wit to cohere. As Stephen A. Smith trenchantly observes, "[King] peddles full-frontal satire, wielding her weapon sometimes as a scalpel but more often as a machete."[10] She did not care much who or what she hacked through in clearing the underbrush of gender and sexuality in southern society, simultaneously identifying and disidentifying with discourses of both queer and conservative cultures.

Feminist Humor, Conservatism, and King's Double Disidentifications

Many theorists of women's humor expect it to advance a feminist agenda by reflecting ironically on women's unique perspectives on society. In their 1988 anthology of women's humor *Redressing the Balance*—a collection that does not include King—Nancy Walker and Zita Dresner outline the resistant strategies of female comedy: "By exposing the discrepancies between the realities of women's lives and the images of women promoted by culture, between the inequities to which women have been subjected and the egalitarian ideals upon which the nation was founded, American women humorists have targeted the patriarchal social system."[11] Regina Barreca similarly sees women's humor as a zingy curative to patriarchy: "Women's comedy is 'dangerous' because it refuses to accept the givens and because it refuses to stop at the point where comedy loses its integrative function. This comedy by women is about de-centering, dis-locating, and destabilizing the world."[12] Bisexual comedian Margaret Cho, in an exaggerated declaration with little humor but much power, states, "Feminism is nonnegotiable. If you are not a feminist, you do not deserve to live."[13] From these perspectives, women's humor dismantles patriarchy through its cagey rhetoric, with female comics fighting to liberate women from the constraints of patriarchal sexism.

But what about women like King who do not align themselves with mainstream feminism and evince little interest in advancing its collective goals? Claims that women's comedy shares a guiding ethos of empowerment acknowledge the role of humor in the struggle for gender equality, yet they also carry undertones of essentialism, constructing some women's humor as that of all women.[14] All stereotypes about women, even positive ones, carry with them the potential to limit women's lives, and clichés about female humor as resisting patriarchy, while true in many regards, circumscribe its proper realm as the politically emancipatory. Such a perspective threatens the foundations of humor, for a comic with a moral message faces the perpetual threat of losing her joke to didacticism. Even when critics argue that women's humor should not be marked as distinct from men's, the presumption that female comics speak to an essentialized sense of women's experience perseveres, such as in Sean Zwagerman's admonition that "[it] is more useful to understand women's humor not as formally distinct or ideologically homogenous, but as the use of humor by women in response to situations that impact (and often inhibit) women's opportunities to speak and be heard."[15] Acknowledging the problems with describing women's humor as somehow different from men's, Zwagerman nonetheless defines female humor as a fundamental need to speak against discourses inhospitable to women's experiences.

This brief theoretical overview of women's humor points to the difficulties of analyzing Florence King's wit and placing it in the context of a women's comic tradition for the simple fact that she blatantly rejects the feminist premises behind that tradition. A more ecumenical view of women's humor acknowledges the situational nature of humor and women's deployment of it, no matter their positions on the political spectrum. Distinguishing between women's and men's humor, as well as discerning an essentialized and satiric subversion of patriarchy in women's humor, obscures the shared objective of all talented wags: the laugh. This is not to conclude that the comic theories of Walker, Dresner, Barreca, and Zwagerman have no merit; on the contrary, they offer rich and powerful analyses of the ways in which women's humor has historically served to undermine sexist discourses and ideologies. In *A Very Serious Thing: Women's Humor and American Culture,* Nancy Walker outlines a more labile model, proposing that "women's humor is an index to women's roles and values, and particularly to their relationship with American cultural realities. Being a female humorist in America has been problematic in a number of ways that are tied closely to other issues in women's history: the tension between intellect and femininity, male and female 'separate spheres,' women's status as a minority group, and the transforming power of a feminist vision."[16] One cannot shoehorn King's wit into prevailing conceptions of women's comedy as a feminist endeavor; her disidentificatory rhetoric precludes such a categorization. Nonetheless, as Walker suggests, readers can use King's humor as an index for gauging her assessments of gender and sexuality in the South, examining the disconnections between satire and sensibility that illuminate her queer conservatism. As King notes of women's humor, "The witty woman is a tragic figure in American life. Wit destroys eroticism and eroticism destroys wit, so women must choose between taking lovers and taking no prisoners" (*RJ* 147, cf. *SD* 5). As is apparent from her humor and in her frank depictions of her sex life, which she ultimately rejected in favor of a proud spinsterhood, King took no prisoners.

When second-wave feminism began sweeping the United States in the early 1960s, King was a recent college graduate who had experienced sexism on the job market. For many women of this period, undergoing sexual discrimination served as a clarion call to feminist politics, but it was not so for King: "When I graduated from college in 1957 and found no employment doors open to me but the one to the secretarial pool, I blamed college and wallowed in guilt for having gone. A bigotry-wise ethnic would have blamed the unfairness of the system—in this case, the anti-feminism then rife in the business world—but being a Wasp, it never occurred to me that I could be undesirable simply because I was what I was" (*WW* 122). This passage is notable for its contradictions: refusing to blame the businesses that would not hire her, King instead censures her college for the education that she could not parlay into a career. She also ridicules any "bigotry-wise ethnic" who might denounce the unfairness of such prejudicial practices, yet it is unclear why one should not expose this discrimination. Her proclaimed naiveté—"it never occurred to me that I could be undesirable simply because I was what I was"—builds the passage's humor, as she assumes the persona of the conservative individualist confident in her inherent superiority. In this role she denies the relevance of her sex to the discrimination she faced, as she also acknowledges the "anti-feminism then rife in the business world" that overlooks her Wasp pedigree, which should assert her cultural position over that of any "bigotry-wise ethnic." These tortuous rhetorical ploys acknowledge yet refuse to blame misogyny as King's problem.

Because of King's experiences with discrimination, one might expect that she would appreciate the efforts of second-wave feminists to advance women's rights, but she pillories their work. As a whole, she sympathizes with men targeted by feminist critiques—"In the last ten years or so, men have been beset by some of the bluntest women in history—Galileos with tits, so to speak" (*H* 196)—as she also snipes at various leaders of the movement. She dismisses Germaine Greer—"There were feminist books before *The Female Eunuch* but they were not written by matey Australians" (*H* 196, cf. *DR* 335)—and ridicules Shere Hite: "Today's woman is tripping the Hite fantastic and men know it. Her Poor Peter Pecker books are strewn all over the office" (*H* 197). Of Betty Friedan, she mocks, "Our era produced Betty Friedan, an unhappy Smith graduate who polled other unhappy Smith graduates and concluded that the housewives of America were clamoring to leave their 'comfortable concentration camps' for careers" (*SD* 17). She denigrates Gloria Steinem as "the divine afflatus of feminism who has made a career of leading the herd to trendy saltlicks" (*DR* 23) and states in mock-awe, "She conquered male-dominated publishing like a Marxist Scarlett O'Hara" (*DR* 118). Citing Mark Twain's caustic assessments of his contemporaries, she writes that he "could not abide . . . mediocrities, the Eleanor Smeals and Gloria Steinems of his day" (*DR* 51). Through these various barbs, King rejects allegiance to mainstream feminism and ridicules the movement's leading intellectual figures as lightweights.

Beyond such attacks on prominent feminists, King revels in misogynist humor, aligning herself with voices ridiculing women's causes. Prizing female beauty and denigrating unattractive women, she attributes her esteem for beauty to her southern upbringing, such as in her response to *Ms.* magazine—"There is a little bit of the Southern misogynist in every Southern woman—including myself. Occasionally, when I look at the coverperson on *Ms.* Magazine, I catch myself thinking, 'Oh, the poor thing, I bet no man ever looked at her'" (*SL* 157). In a similar vein, she signals her distaste for feminism's shibboleths: "In anticipation of the distress that my consistent use of *Miss* will cause, I should like to explain that I am sick of *Ms.* I agree with Archie Bunker; it sounds like a bug" (*H* ix). The foremost reactionary conservative of 1970s television, Archie Bunker of Norman Lear's *All in the Family* caustically resisted the changing mores of American culture, and so by siding with him, King disidentifies with feminism to the point of identifying with the defining pop-culture symbol of angry patriarchy. Also like Bunker, King revels in the opprobrium that feminists have bestowed upon her, delighting in "the feminist editor who called me 'Fascist Flossie'" (*LI* 132), crowing that "liberals don't call me Ku Klux King for nothing" (*LI* 74), and applauding "the feminist group on the Internet who called me an elite psychopath" (*DR* 164). Conjuring an image of feminism's purported excesses, King concludes that "the All-Purpose Feminist Goal is an abortion performed by a gay black doctor under an endangered tree on an Indian reservation" (*H* 203–4, cf. *SF* 98), a skewering of politically correct sensibilities that takes a concern for the marginalized to an extreme—and thus ridiculous—incarnation.

Given her pointed attacks on Gloria Steinem and *Ms.* magazine, it might appear incongruous that King published in its pages during its heyday in the 1970s and continuing through to its maturation in the 1980s, yet such a contrast further illuminates her double disidentifications with feminism and conservatism.[17] Despite the strong antifeminist streaks in her writing that expose her sharp disconnections with the movement, King's humor is expressly feminist in many of its sentiments, as she dismantles the prerogatives accruing to masculinity and the stereotypes constricting femininity. In several instances, she brushes away the fictions of gender, dividing humanity not between male and female but between workers and lovers: "Sexual differentiation exists only between the legs. Otherwise, there are people with work temperaments who need to be left alone, and those with love temperaments who need 'meaningful relationships' to occupy them" (*H* 71). Sneering at those seeking "meaningful relationships," King implies that an individual's temperament, not monolithic constructions of sex and gender, is the key distinguishing factor among all people. King rejects sex as an organizing principle of society, defining genitalia as biological markers of women and men but not of any corresponding characteristics associated with them. In another passage building upon her belief in "people with work temperaments," with its latent feminist argument that many women pursue professional careers, she skewers men apparently ignorant of working women: "The misogynist always believes that any lone woman in a hotel is either a prostitute or an easy make; it never occurs to him that she might be in New York on business just as he is" (*H* 78). Both of these ripostes focus on women's business endeavors, sketching out the necessity for men and women to use the lens of labor to see gender as an outdated archetype. King's exasperation with sexism echoes many feminist arguments about the importance of women's work; similarly, her dismissal of gender difference allows only for a biological distinction between the sexes rather than any distinction based on cognition or emotion.

Deriding feminists yet embracing central tenets of feminism, King's disidentificatory strategies emerge further as she subverts southern femininity by satirically pinpointing the roots of female promiscuity in misogyny, as she further demonstrates that promiscuity hardly merits paternalistic handwringing. For King, sexual promiscuity is caused by sexism: "much female sexuality is a substitution for success, money and fame, a way to become a VIP without endangering one's femininity. The Southern woman is more susceptible to this psychological transference; she frequently throws herself into a virtual debauch simply because she has a human need to excel" (*SL* 43). King's writings weave in and out of the autobiographical, yet it seems safe to assume that she counts herself as one of the southern women who, because of her stifled ambitions, "thr[ew] herself into a virtual debauch" during her years in college and graduate school. King dispels such canards as the "fallen woman" trope and tosses aside countless other stereotypes of southern femininity, foremost among them the propriety expected of female sexuality: "*All* I wanted was sex. I did not want the coffee shop flirtations, sock hops, frat parties, sorority sweetheart songs, hayrides, and proms, but it was the fifties, so I had to endure them because they were vital preliminaries in that mad ballet known as 'making out'" (*H* 14). In this passage King reveals the ways in which she enacted the cultural expectations accorded to her gender, thereby attesting to the utility of Judith Butler's theories of gender performativity some forty years before Butler penned them. King knew she must play the role of the southern sweetheart, with its endless rituals, so that she could then subvert her own performances of gender and enjoy the carnal pleasures denied her by southern cultural mores.[18] Complementary to this ploy and its rebuttal of a masculinist vision of female sexuality, King also dismisses ideological constructions of southern women's asexuality, which contrast with the widespread cultural perception of men's physical needs: "I had heard all the whispers about those male problems known as 'blue balls' or 'lover's nuts,' but there was no name for the comparable pain that women feel because officially, women were not supposed to feel it" (*H* 20). Both proving and debunking the fictions of gender and of biology, King interprets her body in defiance of southern patriarchal codes that deny the possibility of a woman's body experiencing the fire of libido and its subsequent pleasures.

Few women—or men, for that matter—find sexual violence a laughing matter, yet King includes several comic anecdotes about rape in her writings, a rhetorical ploy that further alienates her from standard feminist discourses. Foremost, she rejects the vision of the caring male lover and concomitantly mocks women who prize such masculinity: "Feminists get incensed when anyone says that a woman wants a man to treat her roughly, but whenever Michael gave me his tender smile and murmured his 'Shall we make love?' I started to think longingly of the Earl of Bothwell, Marcus Agrippus, Hotspur, and Alaric the Goth" (*H* 103). Fantasizing of Goths rather than Romeos, King dismisses gentle masculinity in favor of a more rough-and-tumble vision of sexuality. On another occasion, she nonchalantly recounts a violent encounter with a suitor at Ole Miss: "I refused to go out with him, so he decided to rape me." She foils his attack with a kick to the groin, and her attacker apologizes the next day, at which point she reveals her ambivalence over the encounter: "Suddenly I felt terribly, horribly sorry for him. For a moment, I wanted to go to bed with him; I contemplated it, then decided not to do it. I imagine he would have been impotent with me anyhow, after an attempted rape followed by flowers from Shucks Ma'am's florists, but every once in a while I still wish I had" (*SL* 90). King offers little insight into her sympathy for this potential rapist, but in her telling of the tale she transmutes the horrors of rape into a failed comedy of manners, recasting the rapist, holding a limp bouquet symbolizing his flagging masculinity, as an impotent swain in need of feminine forgiveness. Elsewhere, King sardonically outlines the utility of rape as a plot device for her historical romance *The Barbarian Princess* (1978), written under the pseudonym Laura Buchanan: "In keeping with the typical sweet savage, mine was a sadomasochistic daisy chain of incidents based on the popular wisdom of the hour: 'When in doubt, rape'" (*RJ* 161).[19] She also chuckles over the sexual depravities inflicted upon her protagonist: "Just to keep her virginity perking along, I made [her husband] a sodomist who forces her to submit to beastly practices that leave her hymen intact" (*RJ* 163).

In maintaining rape as a trope in her arsenal of humor and narrative, King disavows any confederacy with feminists, and in an incendiary dismissal of them, she imagines a particularly brutal rape as their appropriate punishment: "I had nothing to say to a feminist readership. I hoped they *all* got raped by a battalion of Turkish cavalry. Not by the Turks—by the horses" (*SF* 13–14). While this line appears in *When Sisterhood Was in Flower,* her comic novel published in 1982, little daylight distinguishes the narrator's voice from King's, particularly in this narrator's identity as a conservative writer. The savagely exaggerated image of equine rape establishes the narrator's strident character by voicing a satiric style flouting the dictates of feminist discourse. King also theorizes that rapists are motivated to attack women because of the sexual liberalism brought about by feminism: "Female chastity (or at least the pretense of it) keeps us civilized, but *Cosmo* had aroused in men the ancient dread of the insatiable female. I decided rapists were saying, in effect: 'Here's some sex you *won't* enjoy'" (*SD* 51). Blaming the victim of sexual violence—a particularly odious rhetorical ploy designed to punish violated women and to exonerate their perpetrators—King justifies rape as men's rational response to the perceived threats of feminism. Indeed, she uses rape in an almost wistful moment of self-deprecating humor: "Nothing described at the Palm Beach rape trial [of William Kennedy Smith in 1991] could possibly happen to me now unless we're invaded by some Slavic republic whose soldiers aren't fussy" (*SD* 15).

With these rape jokes, King aims her fire at feminists in the 1970s and

1980s who viewed rape—and sometimes even female sexuality—as an ideological tool for suppressing women. During the so-called Feminist Sex Wars (also known as the Lesbian Sex Wars), women debated such issues as pornography, prostitution, and sadomasochism, disagreeing passionately about the role of sexuality and desire in a patriarchal world. While feminists uniformly sought to dismantle patriarchy through their political activism, many did not agree on how women's sexuality, in a postpatriarchal culture, should be articulated and enacted.[20] Andrea Dworkin, for instance, believed female desire to be simply a coerced response to men's sex drives: "Every woman—no matter what her sexual orientation, personal sexual likes or dislikes, personal history, political ideology—lives inside this system of forced sex. . . . Every woman is surrounded by this system of forced sex and is encapsulated by it. It acts on her, shapes her, defines her boundaries and her possibilities, tames her, domesticates her."[21] Robin Morgan linked pornography and rape in a telling formulation: "*Pornography is the theory, and rape the practice.*"[22] In contrast, other women articulated their right to assert their own sense of sexual independence, even in terms of ostensibly masculine sex acts, such as in Pat Califia's defense of pornography and the male phallus and in Joan Nestle's ode to her mother's active sex life. On pornography and the phallus, Califia stated, "A lot of feminist antiporn ideology puts out the idea that cocks are ugly weapons that do nothing but defile or murder women. This symbolic system is very harmful. If cocks really have an inherent power to pollute and damage women, the only solution is to forcibly excise them from the male body. Instead I'd like to see women become more phallic (i.e., more powerful)."[23] In her essay "My Mother Liked to Fuck," Joan Nestle rebutted Dworkin's arguments by celebrating her mother's sex life: "As Andrea Dworkin's litany against the penis rang out that afternoon, I saw my mother's small figure with her inkstained callused hands, never without a cigarette, held out toward me, and I saw her face with a slight smile," as she then ponders how her mother had "*sensed the sexual order of life*" and "felt its pull."[24] Participating in this debate, King's rape jokes, while starkly antifeminist in tone, concomitantly envision a woman's sense of the erotic—and more importantly, of the humorous—valences of rape, as they further distance her from the feminist movement.

Targeting both feminists and herself with rape jokes, King expands the borders of women's humor to a realm where readers of both sexes experience difficulty following her, but through such disidentifications with feminism, she requires any feminists among her readers to confront the longstanding stereotype of their humorlessness. Certainly, King endorses this stereotype, describing one of her liberal characters in *When Sisterhood Was in Flower* as earnestly seeking enlightenment regarding humor: "She even went so far as to *buy* a paperback called *How to Develop a Sense of Humor,* with worksheets in the back" (*SF* 117). Moreover, in commenting on women's humor, she dismisses feminist efforts to reimagine the comic: "The women-and-wit conundrum came to a head in a 1976 book called *The Curse: A Cultural History of Menstruation* by Jane Delaney, Mary Jane Lupton, and Emily Toth. In a chapter on menstruation jokes, this earnest trio came up with one of the finest oxymorons of all time: 'We would like to think that feminism will help women develop a different sense of humor, one that is warm, loving, egalitarian, compassionate.'" To this gentle vision of humor, King cracks wise, "That's like telling people to have calm orgasms" (*RJ* 148). Through her rape jokes, King implies that if feminists cannot laugh with her about sexual violence and other controversial matters, then the stereotypes of femininity that she breaks are the ones that still control them. Rather than disidentifying with feminism by herself, she compels her audience to experience the fracturing of identity inherent in disidentification, for to read her writings and to refuse their pleasures is to privilege one's political beliefs—no matter how deeply, indeed, rightly held—over the humor of her texts.

From these examples, it is clear that King's humor echoes misogynist discourses, yet here too she finds rhetorical power, as her writing enacts the suppleness of gender. Along with her breezy depictions of her lesbian relationships (which are discussed in the following section), King details numerous heterosexual affairs in her writings, yet in a particularly biting passage, she summarizes her college suitors' inability to think for themselves as a key reason for her disenchantment with them: "They refused to read *Daniel Deronda* because they considered it a waste of their time, so they borrowed my notes. Thus when I necked with them, I was, in a sense, necking with myself" (*H* 24). Dismantling patriarchal southern views of women, King rebuilds men by constructing her suitors in her own image. Ultimately a disappointing endeavor, her narcissistic make-out sessions expose the pliability of southern masculinity and the indomitable power of this southern woman to rewrite the cultural narratives that would control her.

Furthermore, as much as King takes advantage of the suppleness of ostensibly rigid gender roles, she condemns men for ceding their cultural prerogatives: "A woman can easily come to hate a nice man because his kindness, patience, and passivity are the very qualities that the world demands of her. His niceness reminds us of the nice roles we are forced to play. Nice men, in short, are us. We are really kicking ourselves" (*H* 96). Seeking the power, both sexual and cultural, of men, King reverses the gendered trope of the "fallen woman" canard and dreams of treating men as her sexual playthings: "I fantasized about a room where I could go with a fallen boy. It would contain a couch where we would do the things I wanted to do, and when I was finished, I would turn his picture to the wall and forget about him until the next time. Being easily shamed like all fallen boys, he would permit himself to be forgotten" (*CF* 118). These fantasies speak to King's desire to act like a man and to enjoy male social and sexual prerogatives, and in her litany of gendered speech stereotypes, she demonstrates her ability not merely to think like a man but to effect this metamorphosis: "Women talk. Homosexuals chatter. Therefore a real man must say as little as possible. To be laconic is to be masculine. Bite it off. Like this paragraph" (*H* 115). By abruptly concluding her paragraph, she negates stereotypes of the garrulous female author, as she also displays the utter ease with which a woman may assume a man's voice. Moreover, King sees in masculinity a hierarchical power denied to most women yet accessible to her in her vocation as a writer: "Second, no one wants to write 'like men.' Many women regard authority in any form as a male trait to be avoided at all costs. . . . But an author is, after all, an authoritarian" (*RJ* 190). Identifying in the writer's profession her desire to disidentify with feminism and its communal ethos, King adopts an authoritarian style reflective of her sense that an artist must create in response to her vision. Assuming the prerogatives of masculinity facilitates this goal.

As King disidentifies with feminism and ridicules its leading figures, as she jokes of rape and adopts a masculine voice when rhetorically expedient, she may appear simply to express archconservative views in her humor. Indeed, she candidly admits, "I'm slightly to the right of Baby Doc" (*RJ* 2). By pillorying Republican luminaries as well, she refuses to grant conservative readers the comfort of aligning themselves with her political sympathies and forces them to experience similar moments of disidentification. In some of her more memorable lines, she describes George H. W. Bush as "doing his impersonation of a grasshopper trying to be a regular guy" and dismisses Barbara Bush as a simpleton who is "all wifed out and breathing on cue." She comments that Gerald Ford "look[s] happy as only the seriously dumb can" and rebukes "simpering Nancy Reagan" for her efforts in "securing her husband's Place in History with the vacuity of a teenager wrapping thread around her boyfriend's oversized class ring" (*SD* 187–88). She admits that she "once adored" Pat Buchanan (*SD* 256) but later decides that he "has a real feel for the jawbone of an ass" (*SD* 329) and derides his sister Bay for her "torturous efforts to imitate her brother" (*SD* 262). Of Elizabeth Dole, she snipes, "E. Doli is the woman who keeps cropping up in my life as a vacuous nemesis" (*SD* 311). She excoriates George W. Bush for his weak work ethic—"He's lazy and diffident without having the excuse of being a reader" (*SD* 381)—and later concludes resignedly, "I can't stand the sight or the sound of him. It's visceral, not political" (*SD* 476). She even despairs of the conservative vox populi, Rush Limbaugh: "I can't listen to Rush anymore. Those hokey populist conservatives drive me up the wall" (*SD* 484). In a lament over the intellectual state of the Republican party, she regrets, "we produce Duh Republicans—they prefer 'populists'—who are forever reaching out to 'the real people' with the boastful assurance that it pays to be ignorant" (*SD* 401). A feminist in lifestyle if not in her politics, a conservative in politics if not in her sympathies, King's double disidentifications erase categorical certainties through a mordant wit that dismisses the possibility of a stable gendered identity yet finds authoritarian power over her own life through these rhetorical ploys. King may not have smoked on the street in deference to her grandmother's southern social codes, but it appears that she got away with virtually anything else she desired.

Homosexuality and King's Southern Humor

King's discursive disidentifications with feminism and conservatism deny readers a firm hermeneutic perspective, confronting them with the possibility of their own disidentifications if they are to enjoy her humor, and such a strategy is also apparent in her treatment of homosexuality in the U.S. South. As a whole, King's depictions of lesbian sexuality are bracingly and welcomingly forthright. She pens joyful odes to sapphic pleasures, such as in her ribald jingle presenting lesbianism as an expedient means for satisfying women's sexual desires: *"Candles melt / Carrots are tough / Bottles can hurt you / You might as well muff"* (*CF* 225). Congruent with her dismantling of gender roles, she depicts lesbianism in the South as a natural, if unintended, consequence of the landscape's rigid construction of gender: "In a region drenched in sexual tension, where flirting is literally an ingrained habit in women who are so sexually competitive that they study every inch of each other's persons, intrasexual awareness is unavoidable. Add to this southern woman's proneness to physical affection . . . and there is bound to be a sensual component in many female friendships" (*SL* 161). As Jaime Harker argues, King's candid account of her bisexuality in *Confessions of a Failed Southern Lady* upends southern codes for portraying homosexuality—"King's portrait of 'transgressive' sexuality in the South is surprising not only for its candor but for its absolute absence of angst"—particularly because readers are virtually conditioned to expect treatments of same-sex desire in southern fiction to be muted, if not distressing, in tone.[25] In much southern lesbian literature, including Lillian Hellman's *The Children's Hour,* Alice Walker's *The Color Purple,* and Fannie Flagg's *Fried Green Tomatoes at the Whistle Stop Café,* as well as in such queer male literature as Tennessee Williams's *Cat on a Hot Tin Roof* and Truman Capote's *In Cold Blood,* homosexuality is secretive or otherwise occluded, such that same-sex desire is treated as traumatic rather than triumphant. In contrast to such tropes, King's writings are refreshingly direct and devoid of shame. For example, she denies that she and Bres, her first female lover, experienced any hesitations in acknowledging their sexualities: "I suffered no coming-out trauma; Bres, who had come out at sixteen, said she hadn't either. . . . Southern women tend to go completely to pieces after a homosexual experience and have to be 'put away,' or else we take it eerily in stride" (*CF* 222). In a confidently tautological syllogism, she proclaims of Bres, "She was a Lesbian because she was a Lesbian. *Finis*" (*CF* 223). Refusing to narrate a woman's long journey from self-discovery to rejection and then to self-acceptance, King rewrites the coming-out genre of queer literature with a few short sentences, modeling for readers an image of sexual confidence virtually unparalleled in twentieth-century southern literature.

King balances such candid statements of lesbian desire by acknowledging, with a coolly detached humor, both the poisonous homophobia of 1950s Mississippi and its ironic blindness to homosexuality. As she explains of her bisexual exploits, in part adopting a virulent voice of white, male privilege, "According to the tenets of Mississippi logic, what we had done automatically made us 'niggah-lovin' Jew Communists" (*CF* 221, cf. 226). This passage underscores the invisibility of homosexuality in the South: she transgresses against its sexual mores, yet these transgressions can only be registered by association with other ostensible offenses involving African American civil rights, religious ecumenism, and enforced economic egalitarianism. Indeed, while recognizing the potential violence she faced because of her sexuality, King pays an unexpected paean to southern hospitality: "It would have been no more surprising to look up from Bres's twat and see a shotgun coming through the window than to see a smiling face saying, 'Hey, how y'all doin'?'" (*CF* 232). Such are the contradictions of southern culture, in that King envisions a shotgun blast and a friendly greeting as equally plausible reactions to the discovery of her lesbian affair. She nonetheless frames this hypothetical encounter in a comic mode, visualizing herself unexpectedly discovered in the middle of cunnilingual pleasures.

King's celebration of homosexuality also emerges in her treatment of lesbianism as a joyfully open possibility for satisfying wide-ranging sexual urges. In sketching her libidinous character Royal in *Southern Ladies and Gentlemen,* King explains the appropriateness but also the limitations of the word *lesbian:* "Strictly speaking, it would not have been libelous because rumor had it that she was not all that fussy about her sex partners. She did not have proclivities, she had a vulva" (*SL* 123). Both debasing and elevating (and humorous in the intersection of these divergent poles), King's vision of Royal's sexuality synecdochically constructs the woman as her genitalia, yet it also liberates Royal from southern gender constructions that degrade women by seeing them only as their genitalia but not on their own terms. King continues her ode to Royal by celebrating her sexual style: "There was a difference between Royal and the so-called swingers of today. There are plenty of sluts, tramps, and whores around now, but how many hoyden minxes? . . . She did everything that is physically possible to do with one or more partners of both sexes, yet she did it so well, with a style and dash that are sadly missing today" (*SL* 126). King opens *Southern Ladies and Gentleman* with the standard disclaimer that "all the names used in this book were invented by me" (*SL* 6), but it appears likely that Royal serves as an appropriately regal alias for King herself. Ten years before she outed herself in *Confessions of a Failed Southern Lady,* King foreshadowed her own sexual freedoms through her libidinous heroine untethered by southern sexual mores.

Much of King's humor based on same-sex desire ridicules the homophobia of the South by exposing the ubiquitous potential for homophobes to enact the gender transgressions they self-righteously deplore. In detailing the fears of Wasp mothers that their children might be gay, King satirizes how these women inadvertently foster their sons' homosocial, and potentially homoerotic, activities: "Above all, she does not want him to be a homosexual, so to ward off that fate, she encourages him to spend as much time as possible squeezed into a car with ten other horny adolescent males" (*WW* 60). Fostering homosociality to ward off homosexuality—an ineffective tactic in such settings as boarding schools, navies, and prisons—these mothers assume they are successful in their quest because, as King explains, "The important thing is, Johnny is not in the library turning queer" (*WW* 61). Ironically, in King's scenario of such mother-henning, the mother's biological sex metamorphoses so that she exceeds the physical masculinity of her offspring: "Thanks to all the nonsense in Waspdom about masculinity, the Babe believes that *everybody* should be a real man, herself included, so she smothers her son by competing with him in the arena. She does not castrate him, she simply grows a bigger pair of her own" (*WW* 67). With this polymorphous image of the mother modeling the gender transgression forbidden to her son, King's Wasp mother enacts the suppleness both of gender and of the sexed body, metaphorically transfiguring maternal femininity into a hermaphroditic hybrid marked by enlarged testicles.

King depicts male homosexuality as always latent in southern culture, as perpetually on the verge of piercing through the façade of masculine heteronormativity. Straight men's interest in football, in her hands, simmers with repressed homoerotic tension: "The sexual identity that Southern men drew from football boggled [one's] mind. They could talk and think of nothing else but The Game, and although they were all planning bacchanal weekends with women, they got very anal with each other. There was a great deal of butt-slapping and goosing. It was all accompanied by detailed descriptions of their potency with women, of course. . . . Other American men weren't like this . . . were they?" (*SL* 17). As southern men define themselves through their passion for sports in general and for football in particular, the homosocial world of athletics brims with an erotic frisson of misdirected sexual energy. These men transpose into their living rooms the homosocial butt slapping they view on their televisions, where they escalate the submerged eroticism of a game waged by players who take such positions as "tight end" and "wide receiver," in which the ultimate objective is to reach the "end zone." Giddily goosing one another in King's depiction of southern homosociality, these men enact the homoeroticism banished from their culture, proving that its sexual specter haunts their fellowship.

King also connects latent southern homoeroticism to the Civil War, claiming that the white southern man, humiliated by his forefathers' defeat, now fetishizes black men, "perhaps because he wants to be sodomized by the black man, whom he looks upon as the archetype of maleness, since blacks were the only southern men who won the Civil War. He sees the black penis as Excalibur, whence all male power and excellence spring" (*SL* 99). King limns masculinity as a free-floating signifier, ostensibly attached to white southern men but labile and mobile, one that resurfaces in a submerged desire for interracial sodomy. Even heterosexual intercourse can generate queer panic in southern men, as when King outlines the mating rituals of a Good Ole Boy who finds himself sexually interested in a woman: "She does think like a man—i.e., her thoughts interest him. Now he is openly threatened; suddenly, she *is* a man—yet he is sleeping with her as well as talking with her. He enters into a distraught state of psychic pseudo homosexuality in which he projects all of his rage onto the woman, and the lovers begin to clash" (*SL* 105). The Good Ole Boy seeks a reflection of himself in the opposite sex but then finds himself distraught by the latent homoeroticism of his narcissism. Through her pop-psychology diagnoses, King construes southern men who denounce homosexuality as pathologically conflicted over the potential for homosexual desire to flourish even during their heterosexual acts.

As the South refuses to see homosexuality and thus unintentionally embraces gender and sexual transgressions, southerners' quests for their roots likewise reveal the region's queer underbelly. King satirically describes the genealogy fetish of southern women determined to trace their lineage to English royalty: "They would have loved being descended from Mary Stuart or Bonnie Prince Charlie, but this is hard to manage because the Queen of Scots had only one child and the Young Pretender was a little funny" (*SL* 28). "A little funny" is King's recurring phrase for denoting homosexuality, such as in her chapter title from *Southern Ladies and Gentlemen,* "'He's a little funny, but he's nice,' or, The Gay Confederation" (*SL* 141). The phrase's queer undertones are likewise evident when she writes, "She expects the worst from men, and if she doesn't get it, she wonders if they are 'a little funny'" (*H* 158).[26] In seeking to link themselves to Bonnie Prince Charlie, these southern women questing for their lost roots in royalty, would only, if successful, create a queer lineage from a royal usurper characterized by his indeterminate sexuality and his transvestism. (He assumed the appearance of the maid Betty Burke during his flight to safety in France.[27]) As much as the South prides itself on its sense of history, this historical impulse can lead its citizens back to their queer roots despite the region's overarching homophobia in its present.

Indeed, not only homosexuality but all sexualities become unrecognizable when people are so frightened by or ignorant of desire that any sex act represents homosexuality to them. In a particularly biting account of the ignorance of the repressed, King recounts a heterosexual liaison with a fellow boarder at a rooming house. When their landlady catches them in *flagrante delicto*—"I was sprawled across the bed with her best Sears spring-flowers sofa bolster under my stomach, there was an opened jar of cold cream on the table, and Claude was hunched over me on all fours"—this horrified woman screams in shock, "Homosexuals!" (*H* 162).[28] If heterosexual intercourse can be frantically perceived as homosexuality, sexual acts lose their ability to signify their actors as straight or gay. Sexuality ceases to function as a marker of identity in this scene, other than as a blanket transgression of cultural mores inhospitable to erotic expression in any form.

But as homosexuality finds some degree of power in the South because its citizens either refuse to or simply cannot recognize it, an additional irony arises in King's own inability to locate her fellow queers. In some incidents, her alienation from lesbian culture structures the anecdote's humor: "Merely by walking in and sitting down, I once emptied what I took to be a nice Schrafft's like cocktail lounge that catered to women. As the bartender explained afterward, it was a Lesbian bar, and everybody thought I was a cop" (*WW* 174). The scene is painted so sparsely that numerous questions arise: How did King unintentionally stumble across a lesbian bar? Why did the patrons mistake her for a policewoman? Toward the close of *Confessions of a Failed Southern Lady,* King recalls how she stopped searching for lesbian companionship: "If I let myself look for pinkie rings, I would end up looking for Lesbian lunch boxes, Lesbian Thermos jars, and women who went around whispering, 'Hot Ralston for your breakfast'" (*CF* 268). As much as the South's inability to see homosexuality results in humorous gender paradoxes, King's inability to find Washington, D.C.'s lesbian subculture testifies to the efficacy of gender policing. She wryly realizes that her grandmother, always eager to join social organizations, would have been a willing, if ignorant, ally in this pursuit: "The Daughters of Bilitis had been launched in San Francisco but I didn't know about it, and even if I had, the name would have been an insurmountable stumbling block in my case. However, if they had had a Washington chapter, I don't need to tell you who would have joined it proudly as a matter of course without even knowing what it was. That would have solved all my problems because every dyke in Washington would have been up at the house" (*CF* 269).[29] A seamless synthesis of her sexual desires and her grandmother's sexual ignorance, King's vision of her grandmother naively hosting luncheons for lesbians, and thus providing her granddaughter with potential sexual encounters, captures the ways in which the South facilitates what it refuses to see.

Despite her bisexual experiences and her satiric depictions of southern homophobia, which appear to align her as an advocate for gay rights, King opposes basic measures of equality, and in these moments her disidentifications with queer culture come to the forefront. Indeed, some readers have criticized her treatment of homosexuality, such as Margo Jefferson's observation, in a 1975 review of *Southern Ladies and Gentlemen,* that "At times her sallies are poorly and tastelessly aimed—as when she turns them on Southern homosexuals."[30] Over two decades later, in a 1997 essay, King argues against same-sex marriage—"to paraphrase the Vietnam general, 'We had to destroy marriage to save it for homosexuals'" (*SD* 216)—and curiously dismisses the significance of lesbian sexuality to society: "The lesbian sex drive has no effect on society. . . . A woman may be exclusively attracted to women and repelled by men, but she can still reproduce the species. All she has to do to conceive is be present, but if a man feels no desire for the female, conception won't occur and the race will die out" (*SD* 216). Repeating one of the most offensive slanders against gay men, she confuses male homosexuality with pedophilia: "First, Lesbians do not lust after little girls as some homosexual men lust after little boys" (*RJ* 96). Again merging pedophilia with homosexuality, she notes, "A 'Man-Boy Love Association' to promote the acceptance of sex between men and boys has already been formed" (*LI* 154). Given these opinions, it is difficult to see King as endorsing a progressive queer agenda, despite the presumption of many critics and readers that queer writers should join efforts to dismantle homophobia. Much like the scholars of women's humor who argue that it speaks against patriarchy, Mab Segrest, in analyzing the works of Angelina Weld Grimké, Carson McCullers, Lillian Smith, Rita Mae Brown, and Dorothy Allison, endorses a vision of "Southern lesbian literature that explores the connections between *seeing* the world differently and *making* it different."[31] King's writings, through her double disidentifications, endorse and condemn, embrace and reject homosexuality, and so once again she eludes the type of binary categorization that many critics employ and rejects any presumption of queer liberation as the unstated telos of lesbian authorship.

In fracturing identity categories, King dismantles the gendered fantasies of the South: this land of chivalric men and elegant ladies is merely a façade that her humor mercilessly derides. But more than exposing the artificiality of gender and sexuality as social and ideological constructions, she exposes the artificiality of the South, a land that's "a little funny," a little queer, no matter the efforts of its citizenry to present the region as defiantly normative. And while there is much of King's humor for feminist and queer readers to enjoy, her complementary antifeminist and homophobic sentiments render many of her jokes unsettling. Through her double disidentifications with feminist, queer, and conservative cultures, King forbids her readers from ever settling too comfortably into a sense of security with her wit, and she thereby foists disidentifications upon them as well, for she continually troubles the possibility that one can laugh through her rhetorical strategies that leave no binary identity possible. Gay/straight, male/female, southerner/northerner, feminist/conservative—King demolishes them all with a wit as deadly and precise as a rapier yet as thorough as a bulldozer. As she observes, "America's either-or sexual steamroller is still at work. Today a man is either straight or gay" (*H* 193), and her humor crushes this binary and proves its ultimate uselessness. And as much as King cannot be conscripted seamlessly into a pro-gay-rights camp, she models a queerness of identity that refuses all attempts to pin her down while celebrating her protean humor: "The most important reason why wit fails in America is sexual insecurity. Wit is aggressive and therefore masculine; at the same time, it's waspish and therefore feminine. Therefore, witty people are queer" (*RJ* 147). Through her wit that she labels queer, King proves the potency of humor to embrace and to offend, to affirm and to subvert, and any sense of self-satisfaction in her readers will fall to the thrusts of her wit that respect no boundaries.

In the end, King will always have the last laugh over her readers and exegetes, as she has popped the bubble of critical interpretation in favor of the perpetual play of her humor. Mentioning that some of her essays have been anthologized and assigned in college classes, she derides any effort to turn them into objects of study: "One of [the anthologies] asks: 'Why did the author wait until the end of the article before revealing her own tastes in music?' implying there was a deep intellectual reason for my choice of sequence. The correct answer is: 'Because she forgot to mention it earlier and she didn't feel like retyping'" (*H* 152). Despite her many learned allusions to Western culture, including a particular fondness for the oft-overlooked War of Jenkin's Ear, she mocks the idea of studying her humor: "Too many snap courses like this, and too many papers on—God help us all—'Symbolic Undercurrents in Florence King' are why we are increasingly becoming a nation of ignoramuses" (*LI* 69). Having undertaken just the sort of analysis King would decry as a symbol of fallen academic standards, I do not doubt that she would dismiss this chapter as a similar exercise in distilling unintentional meaning from her body of humorous writing. Nonetheless, in the disjunctures of gender, sexuality, and desire recorded in King's corpus, her strain of queer conservatism reveals its affinities and double disidentifications with both queerness and conservatism, creating a unique body of southern humor disruptive of the ensconced opinions of both left and right. "The only person I have libeled is myself" (*H* ix), King affirms, as her wit upholds a queer vision of homosexuality and of the South, a land where she pursued taboo pleasures and then told all, serving her wit before allegiances to gender, sexuality, and conservatism, and proving the ample humor possible through double disidentifications.

4

RITA MAE BROWN'S QUEER FEMINISM AND THE GENDER POLITICS OF SOUTHERN HUMOR

With the breakout success of *Rubyfruit Jungle* in 1973, Rita Mae Brown smashed encrusted stereotypes of the humorless lesbian. Depicting her puckish protagonist Molly Bolt on a journey of self-discovery throughout the South and into New York City, Brown celebrates the pleasures possible for women who refuse to allow social stigma to condemn them to lives of loneliness and misery. Since this breakthrough, Brown has published many more lesbian comic novels, including *In Her Day, Southern Discomfort, Sudden Death, Venus Envy, Riding Shotgun,* and *Alma Mater,* and in the series of novels featuring sisters Julia and Louise Hunsenmeir—*Six of One, Bingo, Loose Lips,* and *The Sand Castle*—Brown's protagonists share the stage with the town's lesbian leading lady Celeste Chalfonte and Julia's bisexual daughter Nickel.[1] Expanding her literary interests beyond the realm of lesbian comedies, Brown has proved herself prolific in numerous genres, including poetry, mystery, historical fiction, memoir, political tracts, and screenplays.[2] In this chapter, I focus primarily on Brown's lesbian comic novels, but to illuminate her sense of the comic and the literary tradition, I also employ commentary from her autobiography *Rita Will,* her political tract *A Plain Brown Rapper,* and her writer's manual *Starting from Scratch.* Throughout these works, Brown raises issues pertinent to southern women's gendered and sexual identities, as she also undermines easy conceptions of the meaning of southern lesbian literature.

Classifying literature into genres inevitably elicits a range of vexing questions, and one could well argue that all of Brown's corpus fits within the rubric of lesbian literature simply because she identifies herself as a lesbian—although, as shall soon become apparent, not without some qualifications to this label. Even this simplistic classification raises interpretive issues. For instance, should a corollary characteristic of lesbian literature be that gay characters play leading roles in their plots? If so, then several of Brown's novels would not be considered lesbian fiction: her mystery novels, for example, are noticeably less invested in issues of homosexuality than her lesbian comic novels. Gay characters and subplots occasionally enter these stories, but their protagonists, Mary Minor "Harry" Haristeen and "Sister" Jane Arnold, are sufficiently identified with heterosexuality to be a divorcée and a widow. Despite the gimmick of having sentient animals comment on the unfolding crimes, Brown's mystery novels do not evince a particularly fetching comic sensibility, and her historical novels likewise engage less directly with issues of humor and homosexuality. In *Dolley: A Novel of Dolley Madison in Love and War,* Brown recounts and fictionalizes the former first lady's life, paying particular attention to events during the War of 1812, and in *High Hearts,* the heterosexual heroine dons male garb to fight in the Civil War. In so doing she subverts gender norms, but she then falls in love with her (male) commanding officer. Of course, one could counterargue that this polymorphous gender play of *High Hearts* sufficiently intervenes in constructions of sexual normativity to warrant its inclusion under the heading of lesbian literature. Rather than miring this chapter with such taxonomical quandaries, it is sufficient to reiterate that this book addresses intersections of homosexuality and humor in southern narratives, and these themes unite *Rubyfruit Jungle, In Her Day, Six of One, Southern Discomfort, Sudden Death, Bingo, Venus Envy, Riding Shotgun, Loose Lips, Alma Mater,* and *The Sand Castle* as a coherent subset of Brown's fiction.

Although Brown's lesbian comic novels advance feminist themes by exposing the biases of patriarchy, many feminist and gay readers have sharply criticized her depictions of queer communities. These tensions between Brown's progressive political views and gendered critiques of her work are paralleled by her contrasting depictions of the U.S. South. While she mocks the region with savage humor in some novels, she also extols the virtues of southern living and chivalric honor. In many ways the South serves metonymically as a conservative counterbalance to her feminist message, and thus her defense of the South appears to temper the revolutionary lesbian vision that her audience expects in her fiction. Brown's comic sensibility, vacillating between a progressively feminist and a conservatively southern ethos, upends conventional assumptions about gender and humor, as she also describes her literary mission as expanding the comic tradition from its male roots in the literary canon.

Brown's comic voice and fiction are uniquely her own, and while her narratives should not be mistaken for romans à clef, nor should the parallels between her life and her storylines be overlooked. Certainly, Brown admonishes her readers not to see her life reflected in her narratives: "As a reader it's tempting to assume that a novel is a complete reflection of the author. It isn't. It may reflect part of an author's personality, pursuing themes that hold the author, but the creator of a work is separate from the work" (*HD* xi). Implicitly opposing this argument while reminiscing over the limits of her literary education, she also derides any critical approach that would ignore the author who wrote a given work: "In my day the fashion was New Criticism. This is an idea so patently foolish I can't believe anyone paid attention to it. The idea, simply put, is that you must approach any text without reference to the time it was written or the life of the person writing it" (*RW* 222). As many readers have noted, and as Brown herself readily admits, numerous plotlines from her novels—Molly Bolt's expulsion from the University of Florida in *Rubyfruit Jungle,* Harriet's clandestine romance with a professional tennis player in *Sudden Death,* Nickel's precarious birth and adoption in the Hunsenmeier novels—mirror moments from her life.[3] Within these novels that fictionalize her life story and embellish it with additional fictional layers, Brown's endorsements and critiques of feminism illuminate the ways in which her identity as a southern lesbian complicated her relationship to progressive women's social networks.

For certainly, as Brown recalls, discrimination against southerners and lesbians occurred frequently among otherwise progressive women committed to second-wave feminism. Such bias influenced Brown's experiences with the feminist movement in the late 1960s and early 1970s, ultimately resulting in her expulsion from the National Organization for Women. When asked whether she resigned from the group, she tartly responded, "Hell no. They threw me out. Here I am, a southern country girl, so I was easy to write off as a stupid kid. I still had my accent. . . . I raised the issue of class differences between women and racial differences. At this point this was really quite an important band of women in America, but not necessarily representative of all women's concerns. Then, of course, I raised the issue of gay women. That was all it took. [Betty Friedan] got rid of me in a hurry."[4] In her telling of these events, Brown was expelled from N.O.W. because of her lesbianism, which rendered her participation in the United States' leading feminist organization unwelcome, and was also discriminated against because of her southern roots. As a southerner, she was dismissed as unintelligent, and as a lesbian, she was feared as too controversial for the cause—an unseemly distraction from the organization's goal to advance equality for (straight, white, middle- and upper-class) women. Yet history has proved Brown's viewpoints remarkably prescient; her call to consider the varying experiences of women predated the concerns of third-wave feminism in the 1990s through to the present. Given Brown's sharp-sighted analysis of the limits of second-wave feminism, it is thus more surprising that she has fallen into critical disfavor with many feminist and queer readers. The confluence of humor, feminism, and the South illuminates her work, as it also points to reasons behind her fall.

Brown's Comic Tradition

Does a lesbian humorist owe greater allegiance to her sexuality or to her comic voice? Such a question institutes a false binary, for numerous lesbians and bisexual women—Rosie O'Donnell, Jane Lynch, Kate Clinton, Wanda Sykes, Margaret Cho, and Alison Bechdel, to name a few—have proved themselves capable of voicing queer humor while delighting straight audiences as well. The issue of lesbian self-representation through humor is nonetheless fraught with questions of how an individual woman represents her wider queer community. While Western culture is progressing toward equality for gay people, lesbian stereotypes remain entrenched in patriarchal traditions and were, of course, much stronger in the 1970s and 1980s when Brown was establishing her literary reputation. Martha Gever and Nathalie Magnan declare of lesbian identity that "An enormous rift exists between how we are portrayed and portray ourselves as deviant women in patriarchal, heterosexist societies and how we function and represent ourselves within our own subculture."[5] To this end, humor provides a key means of rewriting cultural scripts about lesbian identity. As Janet Bing and Dana Heller explain, much lesbian humor refutes biases that denigrate same-sex desire as perverse: "lesbian humor and joke-telling challenge the categorical oppositions that would define the lesbian body as unnatural or abnormal by subverting the very terms of sexual nature and social normality."[6] For women employing humor to build camaraderie and to resist derogatory social views, jokes revise prevailing social categories of the normative and the abnormal. Dorothy Painter concludes persuasively, if tautologically, that humor enhances queer women's sense of belonging: "through laughter and reinforcing comments in response to breaching stories, . . . the lesbian speech community continues to be constituted *as a lesbian speech community*."[7] Gary Alan Fine describes such humor as functioning in an *idioculture,* which constitutes "a system of knowledge, beliefs, and customs which are particular to a group, to which members can refer and employ as the basis of further interaction."[8] Within these paradigms, lesbian humor builds lesbian subcultures and strengthens ties among women socially marginalized because of their sexuality.

In complementary contrast to women employing humor to strengthen queer camaraderie, Brown sees comedy as a means of integrating society as a whole, of sharing lesbian perspectives on life with the wider culture. Thus, whereas concepts of lesbian humor as described by Bing, Heller, and Painter, as well as Fine's theory of idiocultural humor, focus on how comedy builds subcultural networks, other humor theorists demonstrate the role of laughter in integrating and assimilating people from diverse communities. John Morreall sees a comic sensibility as congruent with ecumenical outlooks, arguing that "Humour is correlated with open-mindedness . . . and the willingness to see things in new ways makes us more understanding of other people, what they think, and how they act."[9] In a similar vein, Matthew Hurley, Daniel Dennett, and Reginald Adams propose, "In telling a joke, we show that we appreciate a particular instance of humor—and think our listeners will, too. . . . Humor evolves into a medium for the display of intelligence and mutual knowledge and opinion."[10] Such formations of mutual knowledge can occur within subcultures or across entire cultures, and Brown stresses that her humor is directed toward the latter goal. To this end, she compares herself to African American humorists advancing racial integration during and after the civil rights movements of the 1960s: "And I'm funny. . . . Funny people are dangerous. They knock down barriers. It's hard to hate people when they're funny. I try to be like Flip Wilson, who helped a lot of white people understand blacks through humor. One way or another, I'll make 'em laugh, too."[11]

Thus, as much as Brown's novels detail lesbian experiences, her aim is to reach beyond a primarily queer readership, a strategy that she outlined early in her career: "I see my political writing going to the feminist press while in time my fiction will go to establishment presses."[12] For Brown, the promulgation of feminist politics entailed her strategic deployment of the power of the establishment press to reach a mainstream audience through comedy. Brown's rambunctious Molly Bolt expresses a similar sentiment regarding humor's power in her plan to integrate her high school's community (rather than in forming or finding a lesbian subculture): "I decided to become the funniest person in the whole school. If someone makes you laugh you have to like her. I even made my teachers laugh. It worked" (*RJ* 62). Appealing to her peers and authority figures with her quick humor, Bolt succeeds in winning allies throughout her travels, even as her lesbianism frequently invites suspicion and more overt forms of discrimination, such as her alienation from her family and her marginalization from her film-school classmates.

Brown's sense of humor speaks to her unique sensibilities as a southern lesbian attuned to women's marginalized status in American culture, yet she forthrightly professes her admiration for male authors of the Western comic tradition and aligns herself with this heritage. Foremost, she praises the South's great humorist Mark Twain as a comic role model, lionizing him as equivalent to his classical forebears: "Those writers who have most influenced me are Aristophanes, Euripides, and Mark Twain."[13] Twain's influence shines through much of Brown's fiction, for Molly Bolt in many ways appears to be a lesbian counterpart of Huck Finn, and Brown models her time-travel romance *Riding Shotgun* on *A Connecticut Yankee in King Arthur's Court.* (This structural allusion becomes evident when the narrator affirms of protagonist Cig Blackwood: "She remembered Mark Twain's *A Connecticut Yankee in King Arthur's Court.* Not much of a fiction reader, she loved Twain" [*RS* 185].)

In tracing Brown's comic influences beyond Twain, one finds many references to the Western literary tradition. She admires Chaucer, declaring that he "understood the peculiar affinity of our language/people for comedy/comic relief" (*SS* 216), and she often echoes the inspired lunacy that Cervantes portrays in his masterpiece *Don Quixote,* such as when, in *In Her Day,* Carole recounts to Ilse her comic misadventures with Adele and states, "We've been off tilting windmills" (140). Lillian Faderman sees Henry Fielding's influence on Brown and describes Molly Bolt as a "female Tom Jones."[14] Brown affirms her affection for the masterful comedies of manners of the eighteenth century when Cig Blackwood, having time-traveled to the 1690s, marvels at the amazing minds and literary talents who will populate the approaching century: "Franklin, Jefferson, Madison, and Monroe would walk the earth, as would Sheridan, Goldsmith, Congreve, and Gibbon" (*RS* 250). In particular, she states of William Congreve's *The Way of the World,* "You can't get much better than this" (*SS* 226). Also, she follows the lead of Richard Brinsley Sheridan and the amusing verbal slips of his most famous character, Mrs. Malaprop of *The Rivals,* through her characterization of Louise in the Hunsenmeir novels. Of Louise's many malapropisms, some of the more amusing include her observation, "People walk their dogs on other people's property and in the parks so the animal can illuminate," to which Fannie Creighton deadpans, "I'd like to see that" (*SO* 192). Louise pronounces grandly, "Our economic situation is garrulous" (*SO* 196), and pontificates on the "anals of history," to which Nicole smirks in reply, "*Annals* of history" (*B* 121). Further extending her expansive view of the comic tradition, Brown's appreciation and admiration for the humor of gay men is evident when, in *Sudden Death,* Carmen exclaims: "How many accomplished people can you name who have told the truth about themselves? Americans are such cowards they import Quentin Crisp to do the dirty work for them!" (143). Crisp's coolly queer humor plays on his refusal to accept any cultural shame for his homosexuality, recording the incidents of his life with ironic detachment, yet also with an openness that cannot be constrained by the closet.

From this literary pedigree reaching to the roots of Western culture, Brown's comic ethos emerges. Discussing her belief that humor should integrate society, she cites her debts to classical Greek playwrights to underscore her dedication to a vision of communitarianism achieved through comic means: "I feel that my responsibility is very similar to the responsibility of an Aristophanes or a Euripides or even old Aeschylus, in that I have a responsibility to the community, even though that community is so gigantic that I don't have face-to-face recognition with most of the people in it."[15] She further proves her commitment to an ecumenical audience in outlining her ideal readership of *Rubyfruit Jungle:* "I wanted my novel to be so witty that even Republicans would be forced to enjoy it" (*SS* 13). With this statement she invites all readers to enjoy her lesbian fiction, regardless of their gender identities or political affiliations. Republicans (and Democrats as well) in the 1970s and 1980s often held explicitly homophobic views, but for Brown, lesbian humor could build bridges to readers beyond queer subcultures.

Through her literary debts to Aristophanes, Twain, Chaucer, and others, Brown uses the comic to build community and further deploys her humor to reimagine women's place in traditionally patriarchal literature and society. Thus, as much as she sees herself as part of a longstanding comic tradition, one defined primarily by male authors, she also excoriates this tradition's bias. In her political writings she passionately decries the consequences of patriarchy and calls for women to resist prevailing cultural forms of art and literature and thereby to reimagine their possibilities: "As women artists we are in deep revolt against this rotting art just as we are in revolt against the syphilitic political structures that damage us and endanger world peace. . . . Our task is to achieve a synthesis of poetry and politics, theater and experience, love and society" (*BR* 164). Such is the paradox of Brown's place in the history of laughter: widely acknowledged as the author of the first lesbian comic novel, a woman deeply invested in rethinking the scope, method, and aims of art, she primarily aligns herself with male humorists from the Western tradition to create this new voice of humor.

Brown's affinity for the masculine heritage of Western humor has limits, and a consistent thread in her fiction expresses dissatisfaction with an over-intellectualized form of humor that she sees as gendered male. Molly Bolt ponders her distaste for such humor while watching a production of Tom Stoppard's absurdist tragicomedy *Rosencrantz and Guildenstern Are Dead:* "The play made no impression on me at all, but I clapped wildly at the end to let off all that trapped energy" (*RF* 210). Outside her fiction, Brown also registered her dislike: "Philip Roth, that other stuff, I don't know what that's all about. It's so self-indulgent I just can't bear, that whole white male trip."[16] An accusation of self-indulgence is difficult for any author to disprove, for surely the very act of writing a novel indulges one's unique sense of aesthetics and narrative, but it nonetheless appears that Brown sees these men as advocating comic forms distinct from hers and the other male humorists she admires.

Brown's critique of Stoppard's and Roth's comic sensibilities as excessively erudite and archly satirical, however, should not be taken as blanket condemnations of their preferred forms of humor, for she employs wit and satire at key moments in many of her texts.[17] Despite this potential overlap with sensibilities she otherwise condemns, it is apparent that she distills a new form of southern women's humor in her novels, and a key element of this comic style involves rejecting excessively intellectual humor. Carole, the protagonist of *In Her Day,* finds herself fatigued by wit and states a concomitant desire for a new comic form: "I've lost my sense of play. When I laugh it's over words. Wit. Intellect" (34). To further register this character's disappointment with intellectuals and their overweening humor, Brown mocks the academic pretensions of several minor characters. In *Rubyfruit Jungle* Polina Bellantoni is "completing her Ph.D. in Babylonian underpants for Columbia University" (189), and her husband's work is equally ridiculous and obscure: "His original thesis was cataloging cows in nineteenth century French paintings and he had expanded this original interest to a thorough knowledge of cows in Western art" (190). Polina's lover Paul Digita specializes in poetry and punctuation and delivers a "lecture on Yeats' use of the semicolon" (196–97, cf. *SS* 47); later he is described as "work[ing] himself into a lather over the horrible idea that poetry was ditching punctuation" (205). In *Six of One* Julia laments, "It's hell having a daughter that went to college" (3), and Hortensia describes schools as "Slaughterhouses of the imagination" in *Southern Discomfort* (133). Counterbalancing such dismissals of academic erudition and excessive intellectualism, several characters endorse the necessity of an education: "Put your money in your head. No one can ever take it from you then" (*SO* 335, cf. *SoD* 71, *SC* 33). By phrasing this advice as homespun wisdom, Brown acknowledges the importance of learning while mocking the intellectualism that would privilege the wit of Stoppard and Roth over the humor of Aristophanes and Twain—and of her own comic voice as well.

As these barbs against intellectuals and intellectual humor demonstrate, Brown does not shy away from satirizing targets in need of comic deflation, yet as a whole, her humor is less invested in wit and satire than in zaniness and a playful sense of the comic. As Louise Kawada argues of women writers' resistance to heterosexism and the power of the comic to rewrite prevailing cultural scripts, "Women writers, and in particular, Lesbian writers, already marginalized and in possession of different truths, have begun to reshape the template of comedic form. . . . Often the vehicle for this exploration has been a revised expression of comedic form that has privileged the spontaneous and the zany, the marginalized and the disempowered."[18] Along these lines Brown pronounces her literary ambitions: "I am aspiring to be silly. If you ever read Aristophanes you know there are moments of such sublime silliness in his plays that you shout at the sheer pleasure of being so assaulted. That's what I want to do" (*SS* 18). Again the paradox of her humor should be noted; she voices a feminist woman's comic form as part of a Western literary tradition heavily rooted in the classics, yet she does so by creating fictional worlds where women impart the wisdom of humor through farcical shenanigans.[19] Furthermore, while the lion's share of Brown's comic role models are celebrated male authors, she also cites the humor and comic play of such cinematic and television comedians as Mabel Normand, Marie Dressler, Lucille Ball, and Eve Arden as informing her comic sensibility (*RW* 210, 104–5).

To this end Brown's novels exalt silliness and dismantle seriousness, as is evident in their comic themes. In *Venus Envy* Frazier's Aunt Ruru teaches her that “Seriousness is the refuge of the shallow” (103, cf. *SS* 13, for Brown’s reiteration of this axiom as her key comic precept). Likewise, Frazier’s friend Mandy cites Chaucer’s Wife of Bath before intoning, “We’re not here for a long time but we’re here for a good time” (210). In the Hunsenmeir novels, the narrator repeatedly describes the characters celebrating ridiculousness and joyful folly. During a country jaunt scouting for antiques, a woman sees through Celeste Chalfonte’s disguise, with amusement following for all: “Ramelle, in the front seat, couldn’t stop laughing. The entire affair was absurd, but you have to be absurd sometimes. Nothing is more deadly than routine rationality” (*SO* 57). *Bingo* closes with Nicole’s letter to her deceased father, to which she adds the postscript, “*Life is too important to be serious*” (351). Another comic theme recurring throughout Brown’s fiction is, “Sex makes monkeys out of all of us” (*AM* epigraph), and the inevitable follies of desire strip her characters of their social pretensions.

Brown further endorses thematic silliness with numerous scenes of scatological humor. From a Rabelaisian perspective, the lower elements of the body enable a regenerative mode of humor, one in which laughter erupts from the embarrassments of corporeality. As Mikhail Bakhtin observes, “To degrade also means to concern oneself with the lower stratum of the body, the life of the belly and the reproductive organs; it therefore relates to acts of defecation and copulation, conception, pregnancy, and birth. Degradation digs a bodily grave for a new birth; it has not only a destructive, negative aspect but also a regenerating one.”[20] Few forms of humor are as far removed from the intellectual realms of wit than the crude laughs of scatology, and with a gleeful reveling in the lower bodily elements, Brown creates comedy from the body rather than through the mind. In *Rubyfruit Jungle* Molly Bolt devises a coprophagic revenge against a childhood enemy, as she explains: “I scooped up a handful of tiny, perfectly round rabbit turds and put them in the Sunmaid raisin box” (14). After her plot succeeds, she pronounces triumphantly to her cousin, “Come on, Leroy, let’s leave him here full of shit” (16). Later in the novel she hides an “agreeable specimen of dogshit” (183) in an enemy’s desk, which culminates in the discovery of her plot and the victim’s cry: “Shit! Shit! My desk is full of shit. Every drawer has turds and crap and yuk in it” (186). *In Her Day* features the parrot Lester screeching vulgarities—“Piss, shit, corruption, snot. Twenty-four dupers tied in a knot. Apeshit, batshit, fuckaroo. All you girls lay down and screw!” (127–28). A comic scene unfolds in *Six of One* as Fanny Thatcher, driven to desperation, must defecate outdoors. Her fastidious manners prohibit her from leaving Nature befouled, but her friend Fannie Creighton upbraids her for the socially inappropriate repercussions of her modesty: "My God, if you're going to have a bowel movement in your purse, you could at least leave it there instead of making us suffer" (58). Later, Julia exacts revenge against her sister Louise by urinating on her rug (346), and in another of her schemes, she plans to startle Louise with fake vomit during mass, which culminates as "Nickel gave it a weak pitch and it splattered in front of Mary Miles Mundis. The sight of it made her sick as a dog" (*LL* 361). In *Southern Discomfort* a judge dies in a brothel, and, to protect his reputation, his fellow debauchees wrap his body in a filthy rug to surreptitiously return it to his chambers. His secret remains hidden, but as the narrator notes, "no one could explain the mouse turds in his hair" (65). *Sudden Death* depicts a practical joke at a tennis tournament where, after the singing of the national anthem and the unfurling of the flag, "a cascade of brassieres and jockstraps delicately floated to the earth below," leading one character to label the protagonist Harriet a "Lesbian flag desecrator" (12). Brown also mocks the ridiculousness of commercialism in sports through an imagined endorsement contract for the women's tennis circuit, in which she conflates vaginal cleansers and urine: "Wags had it the ladies even flushed out with Tomahawk's super douche, Tee Pee" (13).

In many such moments as these, Brown invigorates her fiction with a sense of play lacking in more intellectual forms of humor, which she perceives as reflecting a masculine sensibility. Focusing on the human body as a source of equalizing comedy, Brown confronts her readers with, and asks them to laugh at, the sheer joy of folly, the necessities of excretion, the potential embarrassments of sex, and the vulnerability of the naked body. For Brown, seriousness is the refuge of the shallow, and silliness is the playground of women's comedy. Through her humorous plotlines, Brown advocates social acceptance of lesbians and other sexual nonconformists. That she has nonetheless received sharp criticism from many queer readers points to disjunctions among her comic sensibility, her portrayal of queer life, and her treatment of the South—as well as her readers' expectations for how these themes should be treated.

Laughing at or with Feminism in Brown's Queer South

In bringing to readers, regardless of their gender or sexuality, a communitarian vision of lesbian humor, Brown's comic novels forthrightly advocate women's and gay people's equality and stress their cultural contributions. She has nonetheless received withering criticism for her characterizations of lesbians, particularly for portraying them as individual protagonists rather than as members of a queer community enjoying the benefits of sisterhood. As Leslie Fishbein writes of *Rubyfruit Jungle,* "It is an utterly individualistic tale that has no social consciousness or sense of commitment to a lesbian community. When lesbians are portrayed in groups, they are viewed as butches and femmes, as sexual predators. . . . The novel never evokes lesbian support networks or genuine gay friendships."[21] W. C. Harris criticizes the novel in similar terms: "Still, what does it mean when one of the most popular lesbian novels of the last fifty years continually eschews alliances, acknowledges no sense of community with lesbians or women . . . ?"[22] James Mandrell, in a reading of the roots of *Rubyfruit Jungle* in the picaresque tradition, concludes, "By offering this 'good and true account,' Molly/Brown changes nothing, shows no possibility of change, but, rather *acquiesces* to and *confirms* the marginality experienced by those who are not straight, white middle-class males."[23] Jonathan Dollimore bemoans Bolt's construction of other lesbians, in that, as Bolt seeks to find her authentic self, "the charge of inauthenticity extends to one's own kind, or rather precisely distinguishes associated others as not properly of one's kind."[24] Despite its status as a beloved, instant classic of lesbian fiction, *Rubyfruit Jungle* has increasingly been derided for its perceived transgressions against the queer community and its superficial questioning of heterosexual privilege.

Brown's later novels have been castigated in similar terms for their purported disloyalty to feminist ideals. Martha Chew notes "the disappearance from the novels of the lesbian feminist political vision that is set forth with revolutionary fervor in the early writings."[25] Jan Clausen, ruing how many poets "have lapsed from feminist fashion, or met with feminist wrath," singles out Brown as a case study of a writer losing her way because of the pleasures of financial success: "it is a sobering experience . . . to read early 'underground' heroine Rita Mae Brown's musings on the joys of owning a Rolls Royce."[26] This line of criticism casts Brown as a former firebrand who lost the fervor of her youth and settled into a life of comfort and complacency that, as reflected in her fiction, repudiates her political and literary commitments to feminism. Much of this commentary is political rather than aesthetic, and it also raises the question of whether authors should be required to depict their protagonists participating fully within their social networks. (One does not often hear criticism of *Hamlet* based on Shakespeare's failure to depict the young prince's lack of "social consciousness or sense of commitment to" the Danish community while individualistically pursuing revenge for his father's untimely death.)

Even critics sympathetic to Brown are challenged in their efforts to recuperate her legacy. Assessing Brown's output, Sharon Boyle concedes in a 1994 essay, "Despite the impressive amount of writing Brown has produced, critical attention paid to her work remains scarce," but she predicts that "[a]s Brown continues to grow and change as a writer, critical attention paid to her work will increase as critics and scholars come to appreciate her contribution to writing and to the reading public."[27] Boyle's optimism about Brown's critical reception appears as yet to be unfounded. Indeed, in an essay addressing Brown's ethics and advocacy of feminist nonviolence, Kathleen Martindale opens with a disclaimer about the literary merits of Brown's fiction: "Though the novels are successful as entertainments, I make no case for them as literary works of art."[28] In her history of twentieth-century lesbian life in the United States, Lillian Faderman summarizes Brown's fortunes, observing that the author "had been a great hero in the lesbian-feminist community before her popular success, but became the target of strong criticism after."[29] Barbara Grier, the publisher of Naiad Press, agrees that "as an icon she slipped a little from grace and glory because her career seemed to go off in other directions."[30] *Rubyfruit Jungle* brought Brown a meteoric rise, which, with her subsequent lesbian comic fiction, precipitated a long descent into critical disfavor.

Such rejections of Brown's writing due to her perceived feminist failings are surprising, given her sustained attention to and endorsement of feminist goals. In the prefatory pages of *In Her Day,* she begins with a "Note to the Feminist Reader" that advocates accepting individuals despite their imperfections as a key step in advancing feminist objectives: "In art as in politics we must deal with people as they are not as we wish them to be. Only by working with the real can you get closer to the ideal." On the facing page, counterbalancing this gentle admonition, she includes a quick barb in her "Note to the Nonfeminist Reader": "What's wrong with you?" With these dual statements, Brown envisions a readership individually unique yet uniform in their feminism. The barb bracingly asks readers how they could refrain from supporting women's equality, while the admonition reminds readers who already identify as feminists that all people—including feminists such as the author of the book in their hands—will not conform to a single vision of political or personal identity.

Developing these perspectives, Brown's lesbian comic novels endorse strong feminist sentiments. In *Six of One,* which ranges temporally over much of the twentieth century, the indomitable Celeste Chalfonte criticizes American democracy for its failure to allow women to exercise their franchise: "What kind of great country is this when half the population can't vote!" (105). In an argument with her sister Carlotta, who piously proclaims, "God made man first. Adam and Eve," Celeste inverts the patriarchal bias encoded in her sister's beliefs: "Man was the experiment. Woman is the final product" (*SO* 106). Much feminist literature, ranging from Aemilia Lanyer's *Salve Deus Rex Judaeorum* in the seventeenth century to Virginia Woolf's *Orlando* in the twentieth, and before and beyond them as well, decries the ways in which gender is constructed through biology, and Brown's novels emphasize that women are capable of asserting the prerogatives of masculinity as necessary. In an argument between Hortensia and Carywn in *Southern Discomfort,* Carwyn insults his wife—"You should have been born a man, my dear"—and she archly replies, "Apparently that's a misfortune we both share" (49). Their exchange highlights how constructions of gender are based on the assumption of a congruency between bodies and identities, to which the women and men who inhabit and engender these bodies often refuse to conform. Physical bodies do not limit sexual expression in Brown's novels. Consider the magical realist ménage a trois that Frazier enjoys with Roman gods in *Venus Envy,* in which Venus advises, "Never let gender stand in the way of pleasure," as her body metamorphoses ("Venus, now sporting a cock") so that she can penetrate Mercury (353). Likewise, in a moment of erotic one-upmanship in *Alma Mater,* Victoria's boyfriend Charly pants, "You know I can't even think of you without my dick standing straight up"; Victoria deadpans in reply, "Charly, if I had a dick, it would be stiff, too" (209). Such episodes in Brown's corpus prefigure (and postdate) the theories of Judith Butler and other feminist theorists concerning social and performative constructions of gender.[31] These themes carry into Brown's plots, particularly in the baseline assumptions that all people, irrespective of gender or biological sex, should accept one another as they are, with the implicit corollary that doing so will promote feminist goals.

Further advancing her feminist perspectives, Brown rewrites the meaning of gender in the South. While in the American cultural imaginary the region promotes itself as a land of eternal chivalry, thereby whitewashing its history, Brown deploys this trope of southern identity but reimagines it as a woman's virtue.[32] When the villainous Brutus Rife derides Celeste Chalfonte for her moral compass, he sneers at her southern sensibilities: "you live in another world, a world of cavaliers, courtliness and romance. You don't understand how the world really works, nor do you want to understand" (*SO* 127). She then kills him to prove her commitment to cavalier values. When Celeste and her friends learn that Fairy Thatcher has died a political prisoner in a World War II concentration camp, they grieve but celebrate her passing as an epitome of honor: "She found something she believed in, and right or wrong, the cause gave her dignity. And her Southern upbringing made her understand honor. Fairy Thatcher died with honor" (*SO* 310). In *Venus Envy* a transplanted northerner learns "that the myth of the Southern Belle was just that. These women were polished, achingly polite, and heroically poised, but damn, they were tough as nails and they were straight shooters" (37). Rewriting the cavalier legend for women, Brown's female characters resist the stereotypes of frail southern femininity and choose instead the ostensibly male characteristics of chivalry, courtliness, and honor.

Comic authors respect few subjects as sacrosanct, and as much as Brown endorses feminist politics and dismantles regional conceptions of gender, she concomitantly lampoons feminism as a movement for its lack of humor. In *In Her Day,* the narrator condemns Carole's love interest Ilse for her overzealous commitment to feminism, which has robbed her of her ability to laugh: "Ilse spent the last two years of her life 'in struggle' and while she learned a lot she lost more: her sense of humor" (14). The narrator also records that Ilse's unblinking feminism has blanched her comic sensibility: "Gaining a feminist viewpoint taught her that art was nothing but an extended commercial for the rich. They celebrated their values or lack of them, their petty morality or latest conquest. And so she threw the baby out with the bathwater. She forgot about Mark Twain" (94). For Brown, a woman's loss of Mark Twain represents an unnecessary sacrifice of humor to politics, and while she endorses feminism as an essential intervention into patriarchal social structures, she gently mocks the movement for refusing to acknowledge any immoderation in pursuing its worthwhile goals. In *Six of One* Nickel criticizes her mother Julia for wearing nail polish, seeing in her grooming rituals a concession to male constructions of female attractiveness. Her mother's response is sharp: "Well! Julia Ellen twitched like a broody hen and told her in no uncertain terms that a political movement that worries about fingernails ain't worth two shits" (184). Indeed, Nickel soon admits that her friends in the women's movement have succumbed to its excesses: "Well, a friend of mine got so carried away with the birth movement she made a stew out of her placenta" (350). In *Sudden Death* a male character, Ricky, disparages "the women's movement [as] a home for aging Campfire Girls" (103). A feminist jibing at feminism, Brown employs the women's movement in her fiction for humorous effect, with such jokes contributing to a new sense of what feminism might mean, as she calls for a movement as deeply invested in humor as it is in politics.

As the critical reception of Brown's literature suggests, some queer readers have rejected her fiction for its political implications and its depictions of gay characters, and she, in turn, has registered her alienation—albeit often with tongue in cheek—from the gay community. In numerous public statements she self-deprecatingly jokes about her identity as a lesbian, such as in a 1978 interview when she flatly rejected the label of "lesbian writer": "Next time anybody calls me a lesbian writer I'm going to knock their teeth in." In rebuttal Brown asserted that sexual labels constrict individuals' identities, and thus people's sexual orientation can be turned into a weapon against them: "Sexuality is the key of our oppression. . . . We are continually seen in sexual terms."[33] In an ironic statement of sexual identity—apropos of her rejection of sexual labels—Brown affirms her lesbianism while also suggesting its irrelevance to her sense of identity: "I'm a lesbian in name only. I'm much too busy to practice what I preach."[34] (Nickel echoes this sentiment in *Six of One:* "Sex is my only vice, and I don't have much time for that. I'm bisexual in name only. I'm too busy to practice what I preach" [257]). To see such statements as repudiations of lesbianism misses their acerbic humor, as well as their deeper communitarian import of freeing all of society from constructions of compartmentalized identities based on sexuality.

These themes in her novels illuminate Brown's sense both of the limitations of identifying oneself too strongly with a group and of embracing the freedoms of a queer sense of one's sexual desires. In her early essays Brown undermines the very concepts of heterosexuality and homosexuality: "To define yourself by your genitals or by a sexual act (heterosexuality, homosexuality) is to fall into the trap our sexist society has set for you" (*BR* 30). As she further explains, "Our culture is so sexist, so narrow-minded, so frightened that it can only function in terms of roles. These roles are simplified: Male = power and dominance; female = nurture and passivity. There is no such thing as human" (*BR* 33). Molly Bolt similarly deconstructs social categories based on gender and sexual orientation, delighting in herself through such resistance: "Why does everyone have to put you in a box and nail the lid on it? I don't know what I am—polymorphous and perverse. Shit. I don't even know if I'm white. I'm me. That's all I am and all I want to be" (*RJ* 107). In many ways Brown's humor throughout her corpus prefigures the move from gay and lesbian studies to queer theory: as gay and lesbian studies concentrated on the role of homosexuality in culture, fighting back against centuries of discrimination opposing same-sex eroticism, queer theories have pursued the ways in which all sexualities—even heterosexualities—are socially constructed and thus potentially inhibitory.[35] From this perspective, Brown's lesbian comedies appear, not as dismissive of gay and lesbian identity, but as proleptically and insistently queer.

Bolt's simple plea to be herself, while couched within the humor of her jaunty adventures, argues thematically for the possibility of a society embracing the polymorphous and the perverse among its members and thereby forming an honest community, rather than one forged in the hypocrisies of sexual secrets. Although Brown focuses on the wider community rather than on sexual subcultures in much of her humor, she ultimately does so with the intention of liberating all people from any type of sexual discrimination, as Nickel explains: "If you accept my theory, then coming out is not an issue of individual liberty; it is a matter of communal responsibility. Communities must have truth and trust. Not understanding that sexual information is crucial to our building communities is going to weaken the community as well as harm the individual. So it's actually in everyone's self-interest to make coming out easy for gay people" (*B* 209–10). And so while *Bingo* does not depict Nickel's fellowship with other lesbians, as Brown's critics correctly note, a message of queer liberation nonetheless stands at the thematic heart of her novels. Refusing to be tied down to the terms *heterosexual* and *homosexual,* Brown endorsed a queer version of sexuality in her 1970s and 1980s novels that advanced an ecumenical understanding of desire unconstrained by labels and bodies.

Although Brown queries the limits of the label *lesbian,* instead claiming the pleasures of a polymorphous perversity, she embraces her identity as a southerner—"I'm a writer and I'm a woman and I'm from the South and I'm alive, and that is that"[36]—which further complicates her humor and her fiction. A defining feature of her sense of self, Brown's southern roots are key to her fiction's comic sensibility, with numerous motifs coloring her depiction of the landscape. One of her lighter touches celebrates the region's virtual addiction to Coca-Cola, which she repeatedly refers to as "Southern champagne" (*HD* 7, cf. *SO* 9, passim). This motif reaches its acme during Frazier's orgy with gods of classical mythology in *Venus Envy,* when

Eros summons her favorite beverage: "Yes . . . but I've also brought a Coca-Cola, since I know you are from the American South. As I recall, you all swim in Coke" (334). Indeed, in *Loose Lips* the narrator reports, "Juts put Coca-Cola in her baby bottle and Nickel gurgled with glee" (248), a dietary practice likely to horrify nutritionists yet that rings true of southern child-rearing. With a more serious tone, and echoing Margaret Mitchell's paean to southern soil in *Gone with the Wind,* Carole's friend Adele in *In Her Day* proclaims, "If there ever was a Southern philosophy, that's it. The land." (174). Of most relevance to her comic sensibility, Brown appreciates the ways in which the South, despite its social conservatism, allows unique individuals a place in society: "Actually I think [*Six of One*] is rather southern. The South allows eccentrics, and, of course, if you're going to be a writer it's fabulous to grow up with that."[37] Moreover, she believes her southern roots encourage her to express her emotions: "I pretty much dislike Yankees. . . . They're no fun. They don't have a wild streak in 'em. They're too rational. Art is intensively emotive, and at least in the South you are allowed your emotions. . . . In the South, you can do anything you want as long as you have impeccable manners."[38] Such a perspective colors various characters in her comic novels, most notably the Hunsenmeier sisters, but extends to a range of minor characters in other works as well, each of whom refuses to take calls for southern decorum seriously.

In several instances Brown's jibes at northerners combine with her critique of feminism. It is her sense that northern feminists, during the critical years of second-wave feminism in the 1960s and 1970s, dismissed the South—and the women of the South—as intellectually and socially retrograde. In discussing the Equal Rights Amendment, which in 1982 failed to pass sufficient state legislatures for ratification, Brown identifies northern stereotypes about the South as a key factor in the amendment's failure, as well as a source of her dissatisfaction with aspects of the feminist movement: "The South was the key to passage of the amendment. Too many feminists held the attitude that southerners are backward, so why bother with them? Then, too, coming from me the argument was seen as special pleading for my region" (*RW* 260). In this analysis of the Equal Rights Amendment's failure, one can hear echoes of Brown's critiques of identity politics. From her perspective, northern feminists constructed southerners as unsympathetic to feminism, and this assumption bore real repercussions for women's equality. It is yet another case of a stereotype perpetuating, rather than questioning, the image it upholds. Brown's condemnation of northern feminists parallels her critiques of lesbian gender roles, particularly in *In Her Day* when Carole complains of New York City's lesbian community: "I can't stand that lady-butch crap. Second, and worse, far the worse, she said I had a Southern accent and I'd be far more attractive if I lost it" (51). Carole soon returns to this theme: "You try living in the North with a Southern accent and see how far you get. People make incredible assumptions about you" (80). With scenes such as these, Brown exposes how some northern feminists constructed communities as reflective of their sense not only of gender and sexuality but also of geography, from which southern lesbians were marginalized.

A feminist who criticizes feminism while defending the South against feminist aspersions, Brown is also a southerner who criticizes the South. Proudly proclaiming her southern identity in some texts, elsewhere Brown does not hesitate to excoriate the region and its hidebound mores. With a particularly memorable metaphor, Molly Bolt opines that "Gainesville, Florida, is the bedpan of the South" (*RJ* 111). In *Sudden Death,* the narrator wryly remarks, "There are worse places to be than Jacksonville, but when there, one can't think of them" (150); Brown also describes this region's aroma as similar to a "moist paper-mill fart" (*RW* 108). With a more serious tone, the narrator of *Southern Discomfort* records a minor character's thoughts while contemplating the disconnection between the South's image of itself and its actuality: "The New South seemed anything but new—old wine in new bottles was more like it. All the blather about honor, ideals and sentiment. Sentiment was the soft outside of cruelty" (65). This narrator also pays close attention to the racial injustice and sexual hypocrisy of the South, noting the prevalence of "what Southerners used to call 'our special problem'" (*SoD* 192)—mixed race children born from clandestine relationships and unprosecuted rapes. In *Loose Lips,* the narrator reports Julia's disdain for southerners' unreasoned pride in their ancestry: "Illustrious ancestors had never put a penny in Julia Ellen's pocket, so she abstained from the great Southern vice of ancestor worship" (33), a sentiment that Nickel later echoes: "Mother hated the Southern snottiness over genealogy" (*SC* 29). Brown also condemns the South for refusing to acknowledge homosexuality—"In Virginia the word *lesbian* doesn't even exist in a polite person's vocabulary" (*VE* 88).

While criticizing the South for its hypocrisies and homophobia, Brown also depicts her impatience with southern homosexuals' perpetuation of prejudice through their acquiescence to heterosexism and its call for silence:

“That was the great Charlottesville way: straight in Charlottesville, gay when you left it” (*VE* 187). Some readers may discern latent homophobia in Brown’s statement, in that she partially blames the victims of discrimination for their complicity in their marginalization. Reinforcing her call for sexual honesty within communities, a recurrent theme of her novels proposes that gay people would gain greater acceptance if they would simply come out of the closet. In *Sudden Death* Harriet fantasizes of a world in which queerness cannot be hidden: “I wish every gay person and bisexual person in America had a blue dot in the middle of her forehead so she couldn’t devour herself with deceit, anxiety, and fear, that’s what I wish!” (210). Likewise, in *Bingo* Nicole registers her impatience with closeted lifestyles: “If on a given day every single person who has ever had homosexual sex woke up with a blue dot on his or her forehead, either three quarters of adult America would stay in bed or they’d be brazen and hit the streets, and finally all this huffing and puffing over who sleeps with whom would be *over*” (56). Ironically, Nicole’s vision has already come true in the narrative during Julia and Louise’s dab-a-dot war, in which they attacked each other with bingo markers (*B* 23–24), thereby publicly marking themselves, if not as homosexuals, then as eccentrics within their community.

Along these lines, it is easy to condemn the conclusion of *Bingo* as in some measure homophobic when Nickel and Pierre, despite their queer sexualities, marry to raise Nickel’s as yet unborn child and seem to become straighter in their appearances. Nicole reports that Pierre “used to fight back with his ‘fairy act,’ as we called it between ourselves, but now he dropped it. He remained the best-dressed man in town but his style changed” (349). Nicole likewise undergoes a fashion makeover: “And, as he promised, Pierre transformed my wardrobe. He finds me comfortable clothes that enhance whatever attractiveness I’ve got. He drags me into stores and fusses over me and I let him do it because he knows more than I do. I even like the way I look” (349). While it is certainly possible, if not likely, to read such scenes as advocating conformity with heteronormativity, Brown paints Nickel as willing to sacrifice her own preferences to ensure her unborn child’s place in the community. Rather than retreating into a queer subculture or an urban refuge such as New York City, Nickel and Pierre commit themselves to a community not entirely hospitable to their desires, thereby widening its parameters, if only gradually. A queer sense of anti-urbanism imbues these passages showing Nickel’s preference for life in the small town of Runnymede rather than a gay-friendly metropolis. Scott Herring criticizes New York City's outsized role in U.S. queer culture: "That this city is framed—naturalized—as the epicenter of contemporary queer life 'around the world' smarts as much as the implicit assumption that the metropolis is the final destination point for queer kids of any gender, class, race, or region."[39] Much like the end of *Rubyfruit Jungle,* in which Molly Bolt does not succeed in her filmmaking dreams but promises to pursue them in the future, the dénouement of *Bingo* does not celebrate queer liberation from discrimination as much as point to the sacrifices required of southern queers. Yet there is optimism in this ending, for in their refusal to cede their home entirely to heterosexuals, Nickle and Pierre imbue their southern community with queerness, thereby widening its cultural boundaries. As many other southern lesbians and gay men have realized, living in their homes may require sacrifices, but the courage of such decisions reflects a desire to change the parameters of the South itself. As a communitarian lesbian humorist, Brown ends *Bingo* with hope leavening her recognition of homophobia, with the South both celebrated and criticized but nonetheless standing as the home—loved despite its limitations—of her queer characters.

But Is She Funny?

She who builds her literary reputation through humor must in the end be judged for this humor, and as much as Brown is capable in her novels of building some uproariously comic crescendos, many other moments fall flat. Numerous critics have derided puns as the lowest form of humor, and Brown, during her studies of the English literary tradition, would have done well to heed Joseph Addison's diatribe against them: "There is no kind of false wit which has been so recommended by the practice of all ages as that which consists in a jingle of words and is comprehended under the general name of punning." He ruefully laments, "It is indeed impossible to kill a weed which the soil has a natural disposition to produce."[40] While her fondness for puns is most evident in her Mrs. Murphy mysteries (*Purrfect Murder, Puss 'n Cahoots*), they often appear elsewhere in her work. The title *Southern Discomfort* echoes creakily off the famous liquor Southern Comfort. In *Sudden Death* Harriet and Carmen pun endlessly and tiresomely on words beginning with *cat:* catalogue, category (50), caterpillar (65), catnip (86), catalyst (126), catapult, catatonic (157), and catastrophe (204). In an uninspired bit of repartee in *Alma Mater,* Mignon's Aunt Bunny criticizes her outfit—"You look like a fifteen-year-old tart"—as the observing characters enter the fray:

> "Fig," Vic said, playing off "tart."
> "Newton," Jinx added.
> "Bar," Chris jumped in. (*AM* 59–60)

Brown's characters become less interesting, less engaging when such banal banter unfolds.

Brown also undercuts her unique comic sensibility by relying on time-worn groaners, many of which she acknowledges as such. In *Sudden Death* Jane asks Beanie, "what's the definition of a macho woman?" The answer: "One who kickstarts her vibrator" (62). Carmen groans and dismisses this exchange as an "old joke" (62). Such chestnuts pop up with dismaying frequency throughout Brown's novels. In a moment of exasperation, Cig Blackwood in *Riding Shotgun* envisions her life along the lines of an old joke about the woes depicted in country music: "I'll write the reverse country song . . . I'll make a goddamned fortune and be out of this mess. The lyrics will be: 'Got back my car. Got back my dog. Got back my house. Got back my wife.' She laughed" (307). Cig may laugh, but if readers do, it is not because the joke is original. Brown also pilfers clichés of the T-shirt variety ("This cat is on a seafood diet. Everything she sees" [*B* 212]). Indeed, in *Sudden Death,* the narrator describes Carmen's appreciation for a T-shirt witticism: "'The one that says Smith College, A Century of Women on Top.' Carmen coveted that T-shirt" (*SuD* 21). Other tired one-liners, including "Aside from that, Mrs. Lincoln, how did you like the show?" (*B* 147) and "Men are like streetcars, there's always another one coming around the corner" (*LL* 215), hamper Brown's development of her characters, who, given such clichéd lines, degrade into clichés themselves.

As no clown should copy another's face, no comic should steal another's jokes, but Brown pilfers freely. In the opening of *Venus Envy,* Frazier, believing her death is imminent, contemplates the aesthetics of her surroundings: "every time she glanced at the saccharine wallpaper, a dusty rose with tiny little bouquets, she thought, 'One of us has to go'" (*VE* 1). Oscar Wilde famously expressed this mordant sentiment prior to his death.[41] In one of the comic climaxes of *Loose Lips,* Nickel tosses Baby Ruth candy bars into a swimming pool, which the guests mistake for excrement; a similar escapade unfolds in Bill Murray's comedy classic *Caddyshack* (dir. Harold Ramis, 1980). While Brown's characters respond amusingly to the situation, with Louise proclaiming, "I did not defecate in Mary Miles's pool!" (347), the scene loses any sense of comic vitality because of its lack of originality. Brown also borrows from herself, using the same jokes in different narratives. A comic debate in *Six of One* over irregular verb forms and a slang term for female genitalia—"Is [twit] the present tense of twat?" (271)—is trotted out again in *Bingo* (122). A tired joke appears in *Riding Shotgun* when a suitor queries, "Again, mademoiselle, I ask for your hand," and receives the reply, "Would you like my foot, too?" (173). This exchange is repeated between the Hunsenmeier sisters: "He's going to ask for her hand," Louise proclaims, to which Julia wisecracks, "Better than her foot" (*LL* 420).

Such rehashed moments as these invariably disappoint, for so often, Brown's humor is fresh, brash, and uniquely feminist, queer, and southern. As Carole and Ilse's relationship winds down in *In Her Day,* Carole feels a pang of regret when she sees a reminder of their passion and then ponders: "Christ, how can anyone get sentimental over a pubic hair?" (148). In *Venus Envy,* Frazier mulls over the possibility of a relationship with a gay male friend and wistfully upbraids herself: "Hard to be star-crossed with a man who enjoys snorting cocaine off erect black penises but still, what if things had been different?" (3). When Jinx and George discuss a local scandal in *Alma Mater,* their understanding of sexual desire conflicts with their understanding of southern decorum. Jinx asks, "Is it statutory rape if a woman engages in oral sex with a minor?," to which George replies, "I don't know, but it's certainly bad manners" (130). Here Jinx and George enact southerners' reliance on etiquette to resolve all social questions, even the most ludicrous imaginable. When Brown writes fresh material, her novels sparkle with a humor that respects few boundaries of southern and sexual propriety—which makes her failure to adhere to this standard in other moments all the more regrettable.

Brown has repeatedly pronounced her commitment to humor, and she sees it as the foundational aspect of her self: "Descartes said, '*Cogito ergo sum.*' I think, therefore I *am.* I say, '*Rideo, ergo sum.*' I laugh, therefore I am" (*HD* xii). A comic and communitarian philosophy guides Brown's life and her protagonists throughout their journeys in the South, infusing *Rubyfruit Jungle* and Brown's best writing with a liberating sense of freedom and fun. Despite the misgivings of some, *Rubyfruit Jungle* will likely remain a widely read and widely enjoyed novel. Alongside such classic lesbian works of the twentieth century as Radclyffe Hall's *The Well of Loneliness,* Djuna Barnes's *Nightwood,* Ann Bannon's *Beebo Brinker* series, Audre Lord's

Zami: A New Spelling of My Name, and Jeanette Winterson's *Written on the Body,* among others, *Rubyfruit Jungle* signaled the refusal of lesbians to stifle their tongues and pens any longer. Among these other great works of twentieth-century lesbian literature, Brown's fiction stands out as uniquely humorous, uniquely feminist, and uniquely southern. With moments of riotous sexual humor piercing cultural constructions of docile femininity and southern mores, Brown has reimagined the meaning of women's humor, lesbian identity, and southern gender roles. Her mixed legacy points both to her own failures to develop her comedic talents to a sustained pitch and to the difficulties of asserting a humorous critique of feminism and urban homosexuality without alienating core segments of her audience.

5

DOROTHY ALLISON'S BRAVADO AND THE COMIC LIMITS OF TRAUMA

Poverty, pedophilia, and neglect: Dorothy Allison's literature treats these topics with raw grace and fierce power, candidly exploring the dignity as well as the daily tribulations of lives constrained by external forces, whether merely ambivalent or callously cruel.[1] Allison also recounts the prejudices aimed at lesbians in the South and throughout the United States, detailing the pervasive fog of bigotry and its effects on her sense of her sexuality. In light of these themes, the lion's share of critical interest in Allison's corpus contemplates her treatment of trauma and its repercussions, particularly in her account of child sexual abuse in *Bastard Out of Carolina.* Cathy Caruth theorizes that "the history of a trauma, in its inherent belatedness, can only take place through the listening of another"—an apt formulation for describing the power of Allison's testimony of abuse and its effects on readers.[2] Critical readings informed by trauma theory have plumbed the profound depths of her poetry, essays, and narratives, in which she grapples with the harsh realities of life for families whom others disparage as "white trash." As Kelly L. Thomas explains, "Allison's trashiness operates as a means of opposing class prejudices, heteronormative notions of sexuality, and naturalized constructions of whiteness."[3] Notwithstanding the emotionally somber register of these recurring themes, Allison's literature features many richly comic moments, and so to focus primarily on its traumatic aspects overlooks the ways in which she braids humor into her overarching consideration of her characters' struggles for survival. Allison deploys humor frequently while recognizing its ambiguity for contemplating traumatic topics, yet when coupled with a sense of women's bravado, this comic sensibility illuminates with hope the horrors of homophobia and pedophilia depicted in her work.

Allison and Humor's Ambiguity

Certainly, my intention is not to topple interpretations probing the traumatic themes of Allison's fiction, for these studies illuminate the cathartic, indeed, therapeutic, force of her work. Allison has repeatedly recognized writing's purgative effects, stating that the writing process "became the way out of an enormous amount of guilt. It became the way I figured things out." She adds, "Writing became the way that I could say things that otherwise I had no other way to talk about."[4] In "Deciding to Live," the preface to her short-story collection *Trash,* she explains that facing her childhood traumas allowed her to transcend these experiences and thus to find her path to forgiveness and love: "Writing it all down was purging. Putting those stories on paper took them out of the nightmare realm and made me almost love myself for being able to finally face them. More subtly, it gave me a way to love the people I wrote about" (*T* 3). By writing about painful subject matter, Allison liberated herself from the suffering of her past, casting off the shackles of trauma and thereby inviting readers to experience a similar catharsis.

As much as Allison foregrounds these themes of trauma and testimony in her works, and as much as she acknowledges the therapeutic power of literature, she cautions that a singular focus on these aspects in her fictions diminishes their artistic scope and complexity: "You know, the problem is, if you reduce art to psychology, it is a reduction. And talking about trauma and testimony is a reduction. It takes away from the complexity of what you try to accomplish as a writer, what I try to accomplish as a writer. But, damn, trauma is plot. Something has to happen."[5] With this perceptive observation, Allison reveals the foundational role of trauma for her fiction: it is an essential catalyst and provides obstacles for her protagonists to confront and overcome. Focusing exclusively on trauma's role in her work, therefore, risks overstressing plot devices at the expense of her wider authorial agenda, which not only speaks to the struggle to overcome adversity in the forms of poverty, abuse, and prejudice but also celebrates the power of individuals to form their own lives. As Ann Cvetkovich opines, "Allison's work circulates within lesbian public cultures that create a collective audience for trauma rather than consigning its representation to therapeutic contexts."[6] Creating this "collective audience for trauma" necessitates a wide array of literary strategies, and Allison repeatedly employs a strong, earthy humor to counterbalance the traumas her characters confront. Within a world that often attempts to ignore the possibility that child sexual abuse occurs, thereby consigning suffering to the individual and the personal rather than confronting it communally, Allison's corpus speaks publicly and openly, professing a commonality of experience that would deny any attempt to cordon off trauma to the margins of society. Moreover, she accomplishes this objective without sacrificing the possibility of humor to imbue deeper meaning to her characters' lives and to create deeper pleasure for her readers.

The difficulty of discussing Allison's humor in conjunction with the traumatic aspects of her fiction arises in the apparent gulf between the two. She herself has noted the limits of the comic and how, if exploited or otherwise used injudiciously, it would distend her narratives' force. In an appraisal of her early writings, she criticized her humorous efforts for bleaching her writing of its power: "the funny stories I was telling people were better, were the work of someone who was going to be a 'real' writer. It was three years before I pulled out those old yellow sheets and read them, and saw how thin and self-serving my funny stories had become" (*T* 5). In many ways, these early efforts at humor whitewashed the truth of her authorial agenda, and she realized that they would never effect the cathartic response that her mature works deliver: "The stories I told about my family, about South Carolina, about being poor itself, were all lies, carefully edited to seem droll or funny. I knew damn well that no one would want to hear the truth about poverty, the hopelessness and fear, the feeling that nothing I did would ever make any difference and the raging resentment that burned beneath my jokes" (*S* 22). With a curt yet insightful analysis of humor's limitations, Allison observed that her comic sensibility prevented her from telling the truth of her life: "Every attempt stalled on my fear. Easier to be funny than honest" (*S* 88). Allison also registers her suspicions of humor as a tool that permitted her family to ignore the dysfunction surrounding them. Laughter sugarcoated the pains they refused to acknowledge: "The tragedy of the men in my family was silence, a silence veiled by boasting and jokes" (*TT* 28). Yet another reason for Allison's reticence about humor arises in its frequent antifeminism. Humor can be used to devalue and degrade human lives, particularly within traditions of southern misogyny. In *Two or Three Things I Know for Sure,* Allison's Aunt Dot voices her frustration with men's jokes: "Men and boys, they all the same. Talk about us like we dogs, bitches, sprung full-grown on the world, like we were never girls, never little babies in our daddy's arms. Turn us into jokes 'cause we get worn down and ugly" (*TT* 35–36). Comedy's variability and adaptability allows it to serve endless narrative possibilities, but, as these passages imply, Allison frequently rejects humor for its superficiality, for allowing her to dodge the deeper meanings and contexts she sees as integral to her developing voice and to the truth of her family's experiences.

Still, despite these hesitations, Allison describes how humor functions as a coping mechanism, allowing one to develop new perspectives on past events: "You get older, you get skills for dealing with it, you develop a sense of humor, you get Jesus."[7] For Allison, humor and laughter truly offer life-saving force, such as when she recollects, in the essay "Never Expected to Live Forever," how she survived an armed robbery by laughing, and her gun-wielding mugger ended their encounter with a strained yet pleasant "Have a nice day" (*S* 42). Moreover, Allison describes herself as part of a southern literary heritage, which she paints as "a lyrical tradition. Language. Iconoclastic, outrageous as hell, leveled with humor."[8] In assessing her place in southern fiction, Allison cites Flannery O'Connor, the region's preeminent voice of dark comedy, as an aspirational figure: "If one cannot be James Baldwin or Flannery O'Connor, I decided long ago, it wouldn't be a bad thing to wind up a little like Morton Thompson, to write the kind of book a young girl hides like a talisman to protect and burnish, brightening the memory and lighting up an otherwise dark and secret history" (*S* 81).[9] Allison endorses humor in several interviews, yet she also points to its limits in her fiction. In particular, she laments, "There's a lot of Southern humor that's just so caricature-driven." She also admits the challenges of resisting its allure: "So yeah, I can make those comic portraits, and I always feel that pull towards making it more comic, going for the easier way. Now that is a genre of Southern literature that I find really unpleasant and painful" (667). Limning the benefits of comedy while recognizing its limitations in the southern literary tradition, Allison, in effect, creates a new kind of comic voice for southern women, one arising from her past yet filtered through her literary treatment of them.

In this regard, Allison underscores repeatedly that, although many of her works are fictional, she bases them on her experiences, for she uses her past to create fictions that speak deeper truths: "The fiction I make comes out of my life and my beliefs, but it is not autobiography, not even the biomythography that Audre Lorde championed. What I have taught myself to do is to craft truth out of storytelling" (*S* 55). Of the distance between her life and her literature, she also states, "I haven't written a biography,"[10] and places much of her work in a borderland between fact and fiction: "It was not biography and yet not lies" (*T* 7). Allison's rejection of autobiography highlights her decision not to write an account of her life but to create art from her past through a process of reimagining, reconceiving, and reshaping events, whether real or imagined, into an amalgam of fact and fiction: "even the fiction I write . . . is never wholly fictive. I change things. I lie. I embroider, make over, and reuse the truth of my life, my family, lovers, and friends. Acknowledging this, I make no apologies, knowing that what I create is as crafted and deliberate as the work of any other poet, novelist, or short story writer" (*S* 180). Part of Allison's crafting includes the judicious deployment of the comic, for this bridging of trauma with grace notes of humor illustrates the simple fact that even lives overshadowed by pain and hurt are not devoid of life's simple pleasures.

In sum, Allison tells her stories to reimagine the lives of poor southern families such as her own. To a culture that diagnoses and demonizes the poor—and Allison self-identifies as a woman "born poor into a world that despises the poor" (*S* 14)—she insists on their full humanity and their counternarratives, in which they laugh.

> The stories other people would tell about my life, my mother's life, my sisters', uncles', cousins', and lost girlfriends'—those are the stories that could destroy me, erase me, mock and deny me. I tell my stories louder all the time: mean and ugly stories; funny, almost bitter stories; passionate, desperate stories—all of them have to be told in order not to tell the one the world wants, the story of us broken, the story of us never laughing out loud, never learning to enjoy sex, never being able to love or trust love again, the story in which all that survives is the flesh. That is not my story. (*TT* 72)

Much of society chooses to see poor southern families as broken, bitter, and lonely, as husks of corporeality rather than as fully lived lives. Both in *The Women Who Hate Me* and *Skin: Talking about Sex, Class, and Literature,* her poetry and essay collections detailing her experiences with the women's movement of the 1970s and 1980s, and in her masterpiece *Bastard Out of Carolina,* Allison leavens trauma with laughter, incorporating the pleasure of humor in accounts of alienation and tremendous suffering. Her primary strategy for this humor arises in a fierce, funny sense of women's bravado that rewrites the scripts of trauma and its repercussions, delineating a southern landscape hostile to women's homoerotic desire and indifferent to a young girl's sexual abuse, yet refusing to paint it as uniformly bleak as others desire to see it.

The Women Who Hate Me and *Skin*

As with much of her fiction that imaginatively re-creates her past, Allison's poems in *The Women Who Hate Me* and her essays in *Skin: Talking about Sex, Class, and Literature* reflect her often problematic experiences with the women's movement in the 1970s and 1980s. Building off Allison's statement in *Two or Three Things I Know for Sure* that "I will not wear that coat, not even if it is recut to a feminist pattern, a postmodern analysis" and "*Two or three things I know for sure, and one is that I would rather go naked than wear the coat the world has made for me*" (*TT* 71), Connie Griffin avers of Allison's relationship to feminism that "Allison refuses any paradigm, even a feminist one, that would 'recut' her history and identity in a more simplified form."[11] Allison's conflicts with feminists, despite their shared commitment to women's equality and resistance to patriarchal norms, arose out of her insistence on having her own views of sexual pleasure and its fulfillments. While many of her works express feelings of anger, betrayal, and disappointment, a significant subtheme engages with these tribulations humorously.

Allison frequently links her comic sensibility with a sense of defiant bravado, as evident in *The Women Who Hate Me,* which was originally published in 1983, only one year after the 1982 Barnard Conference on Sexuality that many identify as the beginning of the Feminist Sex Wars.[12] Allison's title can be read as an elegiac statement of loss, loneliness, and exile—of the singular voice cowed into submission by the collective force of a larger group—yet it can also be read nonchalantly, as the speaker shrugging off a disapproving chorus as she cheerfully proceeds along her own path. Indeed, the collection's title page sets these hating women and the lyric speaker in opposition through upper- and lowercase lettering—"the women who hate . . . ME."—that establishes the speaker's sense of her worth despite the antagonism she faces.[13] The poems inside, while addressing numerous themes and expressing various tones, ultimately through a comic sensibility deny these women any power over the speaker's life. Indeed, several of the titles—"dumpling child," "tomato song," "when i drink i become the joy of faggots," "all those imaginary ladies," and "whoring around in my imagination"—point to humor's role in claiming a defiant voice.

The collection's eponymous poem, "the women who hate me," reveals its speaker as traumatized yet ultimately triumphant. Plaintively observing "the women who, not knowing me, hate me / mark my life, rise in my dreams and shake their loose hair" (*WW* 21), Allison's lyric speaker soon defends herself in a spunky statement of defiance and regret:

Say goddamn and kick somebody's ass
that I am not even half what I should be,
full of terrified angry bravado.

BRAVADO.
The women who hate me
don't know
can't imagine
life-saving, precious bravado. (*WW* 22)

In this first canto of the poem, Allison's speaker sees herself as diminished—"not even half what I should be"—with her bravado limned as "terrified, angry." The poem then shifts the characterization of bravado into "life-saving, precious," and it remains beyond the ken of these women who hate her. As the poem continues into its seventh and final canto, the speaker's voice brims with an optimistic spark that carries a comic sensibility as well:

Fact is, for all I tell my sisters
I turned out terrific at it myself:
sucking cunt, stroking ego, provoking,
manipulating, comforting, keeping. (*WW* 29)

The endearing narcissism of the speaker's voice, as she prides herself on her cunnilingual prowess and then celebrates her ability to abide ("comforting, keeping"), bespeaks a comic vision of triumph over trauma. In this poem Allison offers a lyrical and ultimately buoyant account of adversity and conflict, as the speaker achieves confidence in herself; she also hints that she will remain a thorn in the sides of the women who hate her ("provoking") while pursuing her personal sense of pleasure.

Such a voice of bravado—of self-confidence tinged with a humorous but not self-deprecating flair—allows Allison to reimagine the tenor of various aspects of her past. The speaker of the collection's opening poem, "dumpling child," celebrates her identity through food and regional folkways, features of southern culture often denigrated by the larger society.[14] She is "A southern dumpling child / biscuit eater, tea sipper / okra slicer, gravy dipper." The poem then merges its celebration of southern identity with lesbianism when it shifts into its second and concluding stanza: "And ride my lover high up / On the butterfat shine of her thighs" (*WW* 9). In this homage to southern food and lesbian desire, the poem's speaker delights in the buttery excess of her appetites, both gustatory and homoerotic, a stance that requires bravado to recast denigrated desires as unapologetically enjoyed. A recurring motif in Allison's literature, food reveals one's individuality as well as one's group affiliations, often with a comic sensibility emerging as the speaker establishes her unique perspectives on desire and its fulfillment. In the poem appropriately named "appetite," the speaker dismisses the cosmopolitan Epicureanism of the wealthy and instead luxuriates in homespun culinary pleasures:

> it must sound better than it is
> the women who go to France for the summer
> a spiced croissant smeared with yellow butter
> cream in the coffee. I grow fat
> in Brooklyn. (*WW* 51)

The speaker languidly celebrates her body, delighting as it grows beyond the culturally defined norms of corporeal femininity in contemporary Western culture. In contrast to jetsetters journeying across the ocean to enjoy comforts similar to those she finds in her neighborhood, Allison's speaker defends her fatness and thus claims her authority over her taste buds and her body.

Further commingling her comic sensibility with her interest in foodways, Allison's bravado shines throughout "tomato song," in which the speaker proclaims her liberation from her past, as rooted in her name:

> I'm gonna give up my last name
> and maybe my first
> call myself Nite's daughter or Pusskicka
> Or something really crude
> Full of fucks and thrusting gestures. (*WW* 36)

Cruder than Pusskicka? her bemused reader might wonder. The speaker then imagines herself as a giant tomato, one that will "tell low-down jokes / proposition old ladies" (*WW* 36). This lyric speaker refuses to recognize any sense of decorum, whether of humor or of sexuality, and with this brimming bravado Allison counters claims upon women to act with propriety, favoring instead the pleasures of individual appetites.

Much of Allison's alienation from the women's movement arose out of disagreements about female sexuality. She found herself criticized for her unapologetic appreciation of sexual pleasure—specifically, her embrace of dildos. As she explains, "In 1979, the idea of using dildos was still anathema to most feminist lesbians. *Male-identified* was a bigger insult than ever" (*S* 132). Declaring her right to sexual practices that some feminists deemed antipathetic to women's independence from patriarchal traditions, Allison rejected what she perceived as the era's call for sexual conformity among lesbians: "I have been expected to abandon my desires, to become the marginalized woman who flirts with fetishization, who plays with gender roles and treats the historical categories of deviant desire with humor or gentle contempt but never takes any of it so seriously as to claim a sexual identity based on these categories. It was hard enough for me to shake off demands when they were made by straight society. It was appalling when I found the same demands made by other lesbians" (*S* 24). Here readers see the inhibitory influence of group politics, which demands unique individuals to conform to prevailing views. While by no means equivalent to the scenes of child rape in *Bastard Out of Carolina,* Allison's musings over this type of sexual policing point to the difficulties for girls and women to assert their sexual autonomy, whether in the patriarchal South or in feminist communities. In recalling her sexual experiences with a feminist lover, Allison outlines how sex acts perceived as masculine were denigrated, despite their appeal to her. The exasperated tone of her words captures her frustration with stifled desires: "No one admitted using dildos, wanting to be tied up, wanting to be penetrated, or talking dirty—all that male stuff. Sex was important, serious, a battleground. My lover wanted us to perform tribadism, stare into each other's eyes, and orgasm simultaneously. Egalitarian, female, feminist, revolutionary. Were those euphemisms? Euphemisms for *I can't come like that*" (*S* 87). This forthright call for the pleasures of orgasm, denied through the mutuality of egalitarian sexual practices, disrupts the hierarchies of desire established within these feminist circles. The wry ending of this passage—a comic climax of frustration ironically detailing her inability to climax during these past encounters—strips bare the pretensions of sexual identity necessary for group membership that come at the cost of one's most intimate sense of self.

In contrast to these disappointing sexual relationships celebrating mutuality and equivalence, the gender roles of butch and femme, derided by some feminists as antiquated artifacts of heterosexual culture irrelevant to women's experience of mutual pleasure, strongly attracted Allison. In describing her ideal partner, she revels in the stereotypes she was called to deny: "My sexual ideal is butch, exhibitionistic, physically aggressive, smarter than she wants you to know, and proud of being called a pervert. Most often she is working class, with an aura of danger and an ironic sense of humor" (*S* 24). A woman proud in her "perversions" yet simultaneously able to chuckle about them, Allison's vision of her perfect lover bespeaks a comic response to the feminist ideology she otherwise supports. Refusing to apologize for her pleasures in penetration, Allison records, in an essay provocatively entitled "The Theory and Practice of the Strap-on Dildo," her disappointment over a breakup because it entailed the loss of the phallus: "At the time, my greatest regret was that I was losing one of the best sexual partners I had ever found. My second regret was that she retained custody of her dick" (*S* 130). This vision of a lesbian deprived of her lover's dildo wryly portrays Allison's sexual disappointment, yet these pleasures through penetration do not concomitantly undermine her commitment to women's politics.

Both at the Barnard Conference on Sexuality and in the Women Against Pornography movement led by Andrea Dworkin and Robin Morgan, the role of pornography in women's sexuality was hotly debated throughout the 1980s. On this issue as well Allison found herself defending her desires with an insouciant comic flair. In the essay "A Personal History of Lesbian Porn," she recalls a housesitting experience during which she discovered her hosts' pornography collection in a closet and indulged herself in its pleasures. Allison cites Joanna Russ as a key influence in formulating her personal relationship with pornography, with Russ recognizing the ways in which pornography represents some women's desires graphically yet elliptically: "What I'm sure of is that we do not have nearly enough knowledge about female sexuality. For example, 'masochistic' rape fantasies have bedeviled the women's movement for a decade *as if they were a literal representation of what women want,* when they are quite obviously nothing of the kind."[15] Russ's defense of rape fantasies acknowledges simply that a woman's imagination need not reflect her desires in real life. Allison details her growing sexual excitement while reading these friends' pornography—"I found myself examining vegetables with new interest and clotheslines with profound nervous excitement" (*S* 189)—and concludes her essay by refusing to closet herself as a porn-embracing woman: "From now on, no hiding, no confusion. Anyone who comes to my house can see my porn" (*S* 193). The comic bravado circulating in her many poems surfaces in this essay, claiming a woman's right both to her sexual desires and not to be shamed by them. In a similar vein, after explaining her erotic engagement with science-fiction novels, Allison forthrightly admits how genre (rather than literary) fiction enhances her sexual pleasures: "The honest-to-god truth is that I spent most of my adolescence—and I'll admit it, even my twenties—jacking off to science fiction books, marvelous, impossible stories full of struggle and angst" (*S* 93). Indeed, these books, with their decadent eroticism, structure her sense of self: "I am as much a creature of those books as I am of my family, my region, my sexual desire. I am the wages of pulp" (*S* 94).

In pondering the aftermath of the Feminist Sex Wars, Allison wryly wonders if any victor emerged: "The Sex Wars are over, I've been told, and it always makes me want to ask who won. But my sense of humor may be a little obscure to women who have never felt threatened by the way most lesbians use and mean the words *pervert* and *queer*" (*S* 23). Allison's humor, then, permits her the freedom to consider the pleasures of her queerness and her proclaimed perversity, thereby also allowing her to explore and enjoy her sexuality as an expression of her desires, whether with or without dildos, porn, and sci-fi. Throughout her poems and essays, Allison assesses humor's power to combat trauma and alienation, to not allow these "women who hate [her]" to triumph in imposing their viewpoints upon her. This victory of her comic voice testifies to the power of bravado, but a vast gulf stands between an adult lesbian defending her transgressive pleasures and a young girl raped by her stepfather in *Bastard Out of Carolina.* Within the same pages that recount the brash bravado of her lyric speakers in *The Women Who Hate Me,* Allison includes "to the bone," a poem that captures the torment the speaker has endured and her longing for death to ease her suffering.

> That summer I talked to death
> like an old friend, a husky voice
> whispering up from my cunt, echoing
> around my knees, laughing.
> That summer I did not go crazy
> but I wore
>   very close
> very close
>   to the bone. (*WW* 33)

No bravado accents these lines with a lilting humor, and the speaker clearly links laughter to insanity. By no means a panacea for the various traumas that Allison's protagonists endure, the comic provides a necessary, if insufficient, tonic for endurance, as Bone's narrative journey illustrates in *Bastard Out of Carolina.*

Bastard Out of Carolina

"What's a South Carolina virgin? 'At's a ten-year-old can run fast" (*BC* 124, cf. *T* 12). In *Bastard Out of Carolina,* when Aunt Ruth asks Bone if her stepfather Glen has molested her, Bone denies the truth, thus protecting him, and then contemplates the relevance of this cruel joke to her life. It is a scene of searing pain to witness, for readers realize that Bone is so trapped within interlocking circles of abuse, poverty, and denial that she cannot reach out for assistance. Several commentators have noted that Allison's novel thematizes the connections between suffering and transcending trauma, for survivors of trauma often reclaim their lives and their identities through speech and narrative. Along these lines, Leigh Gilmore proposes that narrative serves a curative purpose: "Telling the story of one's life suggests a conversion of trauma's morbid contents into speech, and thereby, the prospect of working through trauma's hold on the subject."[16] For Bone, speaking her story allows her and her readers to better comprehend the ways in which the trauma of sexual molestation influences her understanding of her life and her family. Soyoung Park argues that "fiction-writing not only allows Allison to bear witness to her trauma but becomes a venue whereby she explores and articulates her complex desire,"[17] and Tamara Lea Spira considers the novel an "embodiment of memory as labor," in which Bone faces "the task of coming to terms with forms of violence whose resolution has yet to be achieved."[18] Suzette Henke sees *Bastard Out of Carolina* as an example of "scriptotherapy," in which writing mimics the effects of Freud's talking cure, and thus the pathologies of the past are recovered and analyzed for their effects on the present.[19]

Yet despite the traumas depicted throughout *Bastard Out of Carolina,* the novel ultimately tells a story of survival and salvation. Bone is physically beaten and sexually molested but never defeated, and hope emerges in her ability to endure. The novel's comic elements, then, take on a deeper thematic resonance: they are not side notes to the horror of Bone's life but central to the effort of making meaning from trauma. Conrad Hyers posits that a comic sensibility evinces one's "stubborn refusal to give tragedy . . . the final say. . . . As long as humor exists, the will to live and the determination to continue the struggle, even against insuperable odds, has not been finally destroyed."[20] That is to say, despite the anticomic edge of trauma in events and suffering that no rational person could find remotely funny, humor cannot be wholly evacuated from the realm of human responses to suffering, particularly in relation to lives that continue past the traumatic event. Child rape, the Holocaust, 9/11—such catastrophes will never be funny in themselves, but to cordon off even the possibility of humor to coexist with trauma further elevates the traumatic event into the defining experience of one's life and one's culture. On the one hand, how could it not be? But on the other hand, how can one cede such determinative power to an event that one never sought, never imagined, before it became a life-shattering reality?

I cannot argue, for instance, that everyone would find funny Roseanne Barr's description of her mother living in the shadow of the Holocaust—"Her hobbies were being a credit to her race and hiding in the basement"[21]—yet her mutation of the ultimate nightmare of the twentieth century into a comic ode to her mother testifies to the power of humor to refuse the blanket horror of representing atrocities. In another passage, Barr details how her grandmother's mordant humor inspired her at a young age: "Once when I was out walking with her, and we happened upon a cemetery, which she insisted we cut through, I repeated a learned Jewish law, 'We are not allowed to go into cemeteries!' Fanny replied, 'Hey, it's not the dead ones we have to worry about.' That sentence remains the funniest one I can recall from my entire childhood, and also the most freeing."[22] For survivors of trauma the question of when and how to laugh becomes a fraught issue, one enfolded with the issue of survivor's guilt. Yet even when laughter feels like a betrayal of the ordeal, humor can provide the necessary balm that allows a person to continue. Barr's evolution into a leading comic voice of the late twentieth century was, to some degree, born out of her grandmother's acerbic yet comic response to the defining trauma of her life. She is, of course, not laughing *at* but *despite* the Holocaust. Similarly, neither Allison nor Bone encourage readers to laugh at child abuse but to see the ways in which humor graces lives immersed in suffering.

Bastard Out of Carolina begins with an account of Bone's birth and the state bureaucracy's pronouncement that she is a bastard. Carolyn Kraus notes the novel's deployment of "bastard logic," with this archaic reasoning "caus[ing] Bone to experience herself as fundamentally deficient and, thus, as disenfranchised from normal human rights and expectations."[23]

Bone's family attempts to preserve her from this indignity, yet their efforts fail because of a comedy of errors in which they name competing men as her father: "So Granny gave one [name] and Ruth gave another, the clerk got mad, and there I was—certified a bastard by the state of South Carolina" (*BC* 3). For the most part this episode highlights the variability of laughter, particularly in the community's perverse pleasure in refusing Bone's mother Annie the opportunity to save her daughter from aspersion. When Annie attempts to erase the designation *bastard* from Bone's birth certificate, the clerk "[gives] her a grin that had no humor in it at all," as he declares, "By now, they look forward to you coming in" (*BC* 9). Although the clerk presents himself as sympathetic to her cause, Annie realizes that he enjoys the indignities she suffers: "'Small minded people,' he told her, but that grin never left his face" (*BC* 10). This opening vignette ends happily for Bone and her family when the courthouse, with all of its records inside, catches fire. Annie gloats, "I can't get into any trouble just 'cause I'm glad the goddam courthouse burned down," and Bone further recounts, "She blew at the sparks again, whistling into the phone, and then laughed out loud. Halfway across town, Aunt Ruth balanced the phone against her neck, squeezed Granny's shoulder, and laughed with her. . . . It was almost as if everyone could hear each other, all over Greenville, laughing as the courthouse burned to the ground" (*BC* 16). This incident encodes many of Allison's key comic themes in her otherwise traumatic novel, including the communal derision directed toward the Boatwright family, their realization (sometimes resistant, sometimes resigned) of their marginalized status, and the possibility, even if unrecognized, of humorous endings to degrading circumstances.

Certainly, the Boatwrights appreciate humor as one of their defining family features. They amuse one another with a game of gross-out jokes based on culinary innovations—"Raylene won the prize with her recipe for sugar-glazed turtle meat with poison greens and hot piss dressing" (*BC* 73)—and Bone fondly recalls childhood memories of laughing with her mother as they played this game: "'Peanut butter and Jell-O. Mashed bug meat with pickles.' Mama made us laugh with her imitations of her brothers and sisters fighting over the most disgusting meals they could dream up" (*BC* 73). Family members good-naturedly rib one another over their various failings, such as when Annie teases Earle about his hair: "She looked over at her brother with a crooked smile. 'What you think, Earle, was it school or sin that made your hair so black?'" to which he coolly replies, "Oh, school, little sister. That's why I had to quit, you know. I had to stop the process before it went too far" (*BC* 90). The Boatwrights frequently dispatch sharp one-liners, and Uncle Earle's sarcastic tongue delivers many of the novel's funniest lines, such as his assessment of Glen's milking operations—"Man don't run cows, he just leases the rights to their titties" (*BC* 99)—or his homespun defense of the merits of drinking: "Beau's got worse stuff than beer in his life. Beer's nothing. Keeps you regular, beer and pinto beans. If Beau was to stop drinking his beer, he'd probably swell up and explode" (*BC* 128). His casual diagnosis of his family's dysfunctions—"I swear this family's got shit for brains" (*BC* 150)—speaks to his recognition of their limitations as well as to his resignation to their condition.

In a similar manner Bone's cousin Butch educates her about southern family life through his acerbic humor. Introducing this character, Earle comments that he "Don't seem to have a temper in him at all. And he's got a right strange sense of humor. Don't know what's serious" (*BC* 53). Bone recalls that, although she often found Butch's humor puzzling, she would eventually decipher his meaning: "Sometimes his answers would sound strange if plausible, and it wasn't till much later that I'd figure the joke in what he'd said" (*BC* 53). With a bitingly sarcastic assessment of their clan, Butch explains: "Boatwright women got caustic pussy. Kills off or messes up everything goes in or out their legs, except purebred Boatwright babies and rock-hard Boatwright men" (*BC* 54). Surprised by this vulgar homage to the women of their family and their enduring strength, Bone realizes that she is "pretty sure he was shitting me" yet describes herself as "taken with it all anyway" (*BC* 54). Far removed from the realms of politically correct humor, Butch's riff on the Boatwright women's "caustic pussy" speaks a truth of the family condition—they are survivors who must struggle from birth—with a savage sarcasm that Bone finds appealing. Butch's joke carries a distinct whiff of misogyny, yet the Boatwright women are equally capable of laughing over men, particularly in regard to their sexual appetites:

> Wade's woeful complaint was a joke to all the aunts. "A man has needs," they'd laugh each time they got together. "So what you suppose a woman has?"
>
> "Men!" one of them would always answer in a giggling roar. Then they would all laugh till the tears started running down. (*BC* 91)

Aunt Ruth's exasperated dismissal of men as "just little boys climbing up on titty whenever they can" (*BC* 123) mocks and infantilizes the men of her family, proving the necessity of the comic to cope with the sexism prevalent in the South's discourses of gender.

As Allison's poems in *The Women Who Hate Me* highlight her sense of bravado to an ultimately comic effect, so too do her depictions of Annie Boatwright center around this character's humorous sensibilities carrying her through life's ordeals. Certainly, Bone describes her mother's humor as a defense mechanism that Annie uses as circumstances dictate: "Mama learned to laugh with them, before they could laugh at her, and to do it so well no one could be sure what she really thought or felt. She got a reputation for an easy smile and a sharp tongue, and using one to balance the other, she seemed friendly but distant" (*BC* 10). While for the most part readers do not see Annie as a strong figure because she fails to rescue Bone from Daddy Glen's abuse, choosing instead to remain with him, her moments of bravado make this ending all the more difficult to comprehend. In a scene in the novel's opening, Annie's moxie shines through when, as Bone reports, she declares to the local reverend: "I got no shame . . . and I don't need no man to tell me jackshit about my child." Aunt Ruth revels in her sister's sass: "*Jackshit* . . . She said 'jackshit' to the preacher" (*BC* 14). For Allison, then, the tragedy of Annie's life can be read through her loss of bravado, through the failure of a strength mediated through humor; by the novel's conclusion, she cannot act for herself or for her child.

Raylene, Bone's aunt and the adult character who most fully incarnates Allison's model of female bravado, defies gender norms in virtually all respects, thereby demonstrating the freedoms of voice and lifestyle for women who refuse southern codes of femininity. "Raylene had always been different from her sisters" (*BC* 178), Bone says, as she then details Raylene's history: "Butch told me that Raylene had worked for the carnival like a man, cutting off her hair and dressing in overalls. She'd called herself Ray, and with her short, stocky build, big shoulders, and small breasts, I could easily see how no one had questioned her" (*BC* 179). Ray/Raylene's prior occupation at the carnival identifies her with a liminal world of play and transgression, and she wryly reveals her comic response to life's depredations: "Couldn't stand being that poor anymore, specially since my creditors couldn't hardly stand what I wasn't paying them" (*BC* 188). In her role as foil to her siblings, Raylene models an alternate paradigm of life for southern women. In one of their conversations, she tells Bone, "Girl, you are seriously confused about love. Seriously," which angers Bone: "'Oh?' I drawled at her sarcastically, and rocked to my feet. 'And whose fault is that? Huh? How am I supposed to know anything about love, anyway? How am I supposed to know anything at all? I'm just another ignorant Boatwright, you know.

Another piece of trash barely knows enough to wipe her ass or spit away from the wind'" (*BC* 258). Bone deploys sarcasm as a rhetorical weapon in this encounter, but Raylene responds calmly and, in doing so, demonstrates her restrained bravado: "You think about it, and you'll see that the biggest part of why I live the way I do is that out here I can do just about anything I damn well please" (*BC* 259). Raylene's pithy advice to Bone—"Make people nervous and make your old aunt glad" (*BC* 182)—highlights her belief in the power of bravado, as she also speaks to the necessity of sheer bravery in a community that labels an infant a bastard and does not protect a young girl from her molester. For the traumas that Bone must endure, bravado and bravery provide the necessary strength of character, with Raylene modeling their union in a life of independence and ironic distance.

As much as Allison portrays the Boatwrights' humor as a glue bonding the family together, the absence of laughter in Bone's home contributes immeasurably to her sense of isolation. Allison complements the novel's pedophilic horror by giving the home a pervasively austere atmosphere, and Bone contrasts her circumstances with visions of laughter elsewhere: "It was alive over at the aunts' houses, warm, always humming with voices and laughter and children running around. The quiet in our own house was cold, no matter that we had a better furnace and didn't leave our doors open for the wind to blow through" (*BC* 80). Bone's hunger for humor even carries into her prayers, including her longing for success in the performing arts—"If only He'd let me be a singer! I knew I'd probably turn to whiskey and rock 'n' roll like they all did, but not for years, I promised. Not for years, Lord" (*BC* 140–41).[24] A substantial portion of the humor Bone finds in her life must come from herself and her candid reactions to the people around her, such as when her family visits Daddy Glen's relations, the Waddells:

> One Sunday it was a double, a birthday for James and one of his kids. "One of the children," Daddy Glen's sister-in-law Madeline corrected me. "Kids are billygoats."
>
> Goddam right, I thought, staring over at my puffy cousin in creased pants, an eight-year-old copy of his fat ugly father. (*BC* 101)

Bone stifles her rejoinder to her starchy aunt, yet her defiantly sarcastic musings alert readers to the power of humor for her self-definition. In this scene, she is in many ways her mother's daughter, as Annie voices a similar opinion: "Those little brats need their asses slapped" (*BC* 101). Annie's and Bone's voices converge at key points in the novel, then diverge as the erasure of Annie's bravado leads to the novel's dark resolution.

When reading *Bastard Out of Carolina* for its comic themes, it becomes apparent that Bone's narrative quest is to complement her bravado with bravery. In an attempt to envision her inner strength, she muses, "I am night's own daughter, my great-grandfather's warrior child" (*BC* 207). Then, contemplating Glen's cruelty, she concludes, "I was no warrior. I was nobody special. I was just a girl, scared and angry" (*BC* 209). Following this realization, Bone achieves in play what she cannot achieve in life. Rebelling against the boys' games in which they enjoy the plum parts, Bone invents a new pastime—"Mean Sisters"—to the delight and consternation of her family: "Wade reached out and slapped my fanny. 'Girl, you got a mind that scares me.' He swatted me again, but lightly, and he kept grinning. 'Broderick Crawford's mean sister'" (*BC* 213). Enjoying the freedoms of this play, in which she reconceives the meaning of gender for herself and her family relations, Bone revels in her new identity: "I didn't care. I played mean sisters for all I was worth" (*BC* 213). Such childhood games allow Bone the freedom to express and explore her bravado, and while moments of play afford her no lasting escape from Glen's abuse, through them she rescripts the paradigms of southern femininity and southern families, to the wonder and amusement of her male kin.

As Allison poignantly writes in *Two or Three Things I Know for Sure*, "*Two or three things I know for sure, but none of them is why a man would rape a child, why a man would beat a child*" (43), and *Bastard Out of Carolina* confronts readers with this unanswerable question. Much of the novel's power emerges from Bone's refusal to adhere to the script of a victim, and while her comic voice and her sexuality represent separate spheres of her depicted consciousness, they similarly allow her agency in her life—despite the limitations of this agency in effecting meaningful change in her circumstances because of her youth. In acknowledging her nascent sense of sexuality and confronting the ways in which her desires become implicated with her abuse, Bone masochistically fantasizes and masturbates, creating a vision of ostensible degradation in which she nonetheless finds pleasure: "I'd stare back at him with my teeth set, making no sound at all, no shameful scream, no begging. Those who watched admired me and hated him. I pictured it that away and put my hands between my legs. It was scary, but it was thrilling too. Those who watched me, loved me. It was as if I was being beaten for them. I was wonderful in their eyes" (*BC* 112). Bone repeatedly describes these masturbatory scenes as shameful, declaring, "I put my hands between my legs, more ashamed for masturbating to the fantasy of being beaten than for being beaten in the first place. I lived in a world of shame" (*BC* 113). Similarly, she states, "I couldn't stop my stepfather from beating me, but *I* was the one who masturbated" (*BC* 113). Bone's sexual desire, like her comic voice, refuses to be squelched, for they are key to her affirmation of the self among an environment hostile to her sexuality and her comic bravado. Mary Wiles reads the accounts of Bone's masturbatory pleasures and proposes that "In these fantasies, Bone becomes not only the masochistic heroine but the active agent who is sadistically imposing her scripted scenarios on others rather than a passive object-body."[25] Both Bone's masturbation and her sarcastic, comic rejoinders depict her refusal to acquiesce to southern culture's raping of southern girls and silencing of their voices.

The humorous moments of *Bastard Out of Carolina,* which frequently correlate with its treatment of women's bravado, do not overshadow its consideration of child sexual abuse and the ruts of poverty that trap generations of families. "I always intended for the ending to make the reader angry" (*BC* 319), Allison declared, for the novel's dismal conclusion, in which Annie abandons rather than rescues Bone, denies readers the comfort of a deus-ex-machina resolution that delivers her protagonist into safety and love. Still, as Barbara Bennett urges, the novel's dark conclusion allows for a ray of optimism: "although this novel hardly ends with unqualified happiness and at times is heart-wrenching, it does conclude with a sense of affirmation and hope for Bone's future."[26] In the closing paragraph Bone contemplates her life: "I wasn't old. I would be thirteen in a few weeks. . . . I was who I was going to be, someone like her, like Mama, a Boatwright woman. I wrapped my fingers in Raylene's and watched the night close in around us" (*BC* 309). Raylene—the aunt who encouraged her niece to "Make people nervous and make your old aunt glad" (*BC* 182)—stands by her side, and so this character who best represents responding to life's challenges through a comic sense of bravado remains as her guardian and protector after her mother has failed. Allison has said, "Language can carry us past the horror to the sense of purpose in a life that refuses to surrender to that darkness" (*BC* 318), and part of her language, throughout her poems, essays, and fiction, entails the ability to laugh, not *at* the pains of the past but *amid* the pleasures of a queer life that refuses to be constrained by a past that would otherwise control it. Anthony Dyer Hoefer concludes his rich reading of the novel's apocalyptic themes by declaring that "*Bastard Out of Carolina* evokes the textures of place with neither romanticism nor irony but instead with fury, frustration, longing, and love," and he claims that the novel's sense of place is ultimately emancipatory.[27] Along with fury, frustration, longing, and love, Allison's southern landscape comes alive through her humor. Readers cannot deny the Boatwrights, no matter their manifold troubles, the power of their comic sensibility as they confront a world hostile to them and their aspirations.

Parables, Lies, and Allison's Humor

Allison's refusal to provide a soothing moral to *Bastard Out of Carolina* and her other works unexpectedly imbues them with a comic theme. In the poem with which this study began, "the women who hate me," Allison queries her readers:

> Must I rewrite my life
> edit it down to a parable where everything
> turns out for the best? (*WW* 27)

She similarly rejects the allure of parables in *Two or Three Things I Know for Sure,* denying her audience the moral clarity of a pat resolution: "My stories are no parables, no *Reader's Digest* Unforgettable Characters, no women's movement polemics, no Queer Nation broadsides" (*TT* 51). Parables, a pedagogical genre, teach important lessons of spiritual and emotional truth, but they are not a particularly comic form. As has long been noted within the Christian tradition, Jesus wept in the Gospels (John 11:35) but never laughed. In refusing to translate her narratives, whether inspired by her life or by her imagination, into parables, Allison questions the moral order of the universe, a theme she returns to at several points in her oeuvre. In the short story "River of Names," the narrator's Aunt Cora loses her loved ones in a bridge accident and blames God: "'An Act of God,' my aunt said. 'God's got one damn sick sense of humor'" (*T* 19). Allison returns to this theme in *Cavedweller* when Amanda wonders, "You think maybe God's got a sense of humor?" (*C* 375), and Cissy proclaims toward the novel's end, after surviving a harrowing ordeal while spelunking, "It's ironic . . . It's like God's joke" (*C* 422). Whether in moments resulting in life or in death, God's sense of humor imbues the universe with mystery, if not understanding. In this light, Allison often celebrates the unknowability of life, which further aligns her with a comic sensibility: "Aunt Dot was the one who said it. She said, 'Lord, girl, there's only two or three things I know for sure.' She put her head back, grinned, and made a small impatient noise. Her eyes glittered as bright as sun reflecting off the scales of a cottonmouth's back. She spat once and shrugged. 'Only two or three things. That's right,' she said. 'Of course it's never the same things, and I'm never as sure as I'd like to be'" (*TT* 5). The comfort of knowledge is frequently a false promise, and Allison's literature, as a whole, celebrates the potential for new truths to emerge throughout one's life. Thus, while it is certainly not the case that Bone's abuse is funny, to label it as primarily tragic or traumatic would define her life by the actions of others: to align it with a comic vision of hope and rebirth does not forget its horrors but allows the possibility of a woman's bravado to overcome the haunting troubles of her past.

Allison celebrates both truth and lies for speaking deeper truths of life, with their simultaneous implication bespeaking a comic realization of knowledge's limitations. She praises her grandmother's blunt tongue—"Only my grandmother was shameless. Mattie Lee Gibson would tell people anything. Sometimes she even told the truth" (*TT* 25). In complementary contrast, during the conclusion of "River of Names," Allison's narrator discusses with her lover her penchant for storytelling:

> Jessie puts her hands behind my neck, smiles and says, "You tell the funniest stories."
>
> I put my hands behind her back, feeling the ridges of my knuckles pulsing. "Yeah," I tell her. "But I lie." (*T* 21)

To argue that the traumas depicted in Allison's narratives are the truths and the comic moments the lies would too neatly sever her fiction into easily digestible segments; the truth emerges in the necessity of the comic to counterbalance the tragic, for lives not to become unhinged by the darknesses they did not create.

For Allison, then, humor plays a unique, essential role in establishing her voice in the southern literary canon and in speaking back to those who would hate her, whether feminists who deride her sexual desires, homophobes who vilify her lesbianism, or others who refuse to acknowledge her core humanity. In the essay "Talking to Straight People," she narrates an encounter with a homophobe who sees herself as sympathetic to the purported tragedy of Allison's lesbianism:

> "I know," she said, "you must be a fine young woman, and you think you can't help yourself." Her face was very patient, very Christian. "But my dear," she concluded, "I will always think your life is a tragedy."

> I couldn't help myself. I leaned forward and deliberately touched her, taking her hand. "I understand," I said. "And it's sad. That's just what I could say to you." (*S* 150)

With this ironic rebuff, Allison recodes the cultural meanings of lesbianism and Christianity. In a similar crosscutting of vision, her readers risk fixating on the traumatic aspects of her corpus and thus overlooking her substantial contributions as a southern humorist. To only see trauma where rich comic themes flower denies Allison the complexity of her identity as an artist and denies the complexity of life in the South and elsewhere, where comedy can neither efface trauma nor be squelched. "We become what we did not intend, and still the one thing I know for sure is that only my sense of humor will sustain me" (*T* viii), Allison declares in "Stubborn Girls and Mean Stories." In the end, a southern lesbian, like all people, will suffer in her life, perhaps horribly, yet a comic kick of bravado will sustain her to fight—and to laugh—another day.

6

DAVID SEDARIS'S HUMOR OF THE POSTSOUTHERN SOUTH

Place, Race, and Queer Desire

"When I was seven years old, my family moved to North Carolina," David Sedaris informs his readers (*MT* 194), and so if geography alone determines an author's regional identity, then one must consider him a southern humorist, for he spent the majority of his childhood years in the South.[1] Yet as a transplant from the North, Sedaris brings an antagonistically satirical eye to his new environs, one that positions him as a stranger in a strange land who finds himself perplexed by the mores of this new and unfamiliar geography. In many ways Sedaris embodies the contradictory conditions of the postsouthern South—an oxymoronic coinage that recognizes how southern culture has shifted (and continues to shift) in the late twentieth and early twenty-first centuries while still resisting full assimilation into the wider United States. In treating various topics, including southern traditions, homosexuality, race relations, and his own sense of geographically inflected identity, Sedaris blurs the borders of regionalism. He demarcates the universality of such concerns while also presenting the South as a land undone by its history. Thus, as much as Sedaris endorses a vision of the postsouthern South as integrated into the fabric of the United States, he also marginalizes it as a twilit landscape clinging to antiquated traditions. Reading Sedaris as a queer postsouthern humorist illuminates the ways in which the South of yesteryear haunts the South of the present through their comic disjunction; his comic voice dismantles the meaning of gendered, racial, and sexual normativity as mediated through geography. Regionalism creates conditions ripe for Sedaris's humor, as do the social construction of race and homosexuality (despite their historically denigrated status in the South), yet in the end, he manages to reaffirm this postsouthern South as a place to call home.

Regionalism and Sedaris's Postsouthern South

The South is dead; long live the South! Eulogists of the South have long bemoaned the passing of the region's unique sensibilities. Indeed, Robert Penn Warren and Albert Erskine predicted the demise of southern literature in 1957: "Perhaps twenty years forward from now there will be no place for a collection of Southern writers: the category may by then have outlived its usefulness. Just as regional differences generally in this country are being broken down by the growing influence of mass communication techniques (movies, radio, television), by the increasing ease and speed of travel and by deliberate educational policies, so probably will differences among American writers become less and less regional in nature."[2] The trends noted by Wallace and Erskine have accelerated in recent years, as the Internet and other technological innovations have facilitated national and international communication and travel. With the United States lurching toward cultural homogeneity, with virtually identical shopping malls in virtually identical suburbs linked by virtually identical highways, many southerners regret the loss of geography's idiosyncrasies. Yet to note changes in the southern condition does not necessarily correlate with the South's loss of its regional identity, and, indeed, an enduring theme of its mythmaking weeps over its evanescence, painting it as a historically haunted region, not merely in the "Lost Cause" that views the Civil War as a noble yet failed ambition but in the gradual displacement of the area's peculiarities in the present. Part of the southern condition, it appears, entails lamenting the loss of the southern condition due to the region's sputtering transition into postsouthern modernity.

Of the comic voices examined in this book, Florence King most vocally decries the rise of the postsouthern South, regretting the region's inescapable progress into American conformity and lambasting migrating northerners for diluting the landscape's special flavor: "The latest New South . . . is coping with another trauma. This time it's the invasion of Damnyuppies whose lust for 'relocating' (they never say 'move') is turning our gothic paradise into a homogenized Sunbelt."[3] She also bemoans the population's loss of its most cherished traditions, such as hysterical women: "We know about going to pieces, but what about those poor children growing up now who'll never be able to brag about female relatives who went to pieces? I mean, what's the South without going to pieces?"[4] This postsouthern condition also becomes evident in the emigration of native southerners from their childhood homes to other parts of the United States, where they may or may not maintain southern manners and traditions. Lesbian comedian Ellen Degeneres exemplifies this split between her southern roots and her national appeal, such as when she affirms her love for dancing, which she intones in a southern cadence: "If you know me personally, or watch my television program, then you know I love to dance. I really do, y'all. (Y'all is a New Orleans expression that I felt obliged to include at least once in this book to show that I haven't 'Gone Hollywood.' There, I've used it. Now no highfalutin' critic can say that I've forgotten where I came from)."[5] With tongue in cheek Degeneres models her postsouthern identity in this passage, adopting a southern dialect—rarely heard in her writings and comic performances—to dismiss those who would accuse her of forgetting her past.

Sedaris's relationship to the South is characterized by similar comic contradictions: like King, he rues the loss of the South's regionalist flavor, yet like Degeneres, he performs his southern identity in a humorous manner, both to acknowledge his childhood roots and to distance himself from this past. Still, his affinity for the South is strongly linked to his endorsement of regionalism, which he finds to be a virtue increasingly lost throughout the American landscape. Sedaris's test case for regionalism involves inquiring about states' gun laws. From these conversations he learned, to his wonder, that Texas and Michigan allow the blind to hunt: "I ask about guns not because I want one but because the answers vary so widely from state to state. In a country that's becoming increasingly homogenous, I'm reassured by these last charming touches of regionalism" (*DF* 158). In an acerbic yet poignant elegy to his mother Sharon, who, in his depictions of her, despised the South and its traditions, Sedaris cannot envision her in a syrupy vision of heaven. Nor can he see her in his vision of hell, which he characterizes with the blandness of a sterile American suburbia: "Neither did she deserve to roam the fiery tar pits of hell, surrounded for all eternity by the same shitheads who brought us strip malls and theme restaurants. There must exist some middle ground, a place where one was tortured on a daily basis but still allowed a few moments of pleasure, taken wherever one could find it. That place seemed to be Raleigh, North Carolina, so why the big fuss?" (*N* 249). He condemns the uniformity of U.S. culture and correspondingly extols the pleasures of regionalism, locating in Raleigh the ideal purgatory of trivial tortures and stolen pleasures. For Sedaris, cultural homogeneity threatens the distinctive characteristics of life throughout the United States, and the South's traditions merit respect for their contributions to cultural diversity—if also ridicule for their archaism.

As the agrarian South of yesteryear has mushroomed into a region of major metropolitan hubs, including Atlanta, Nashville, Charlotte, Orlando, Miami, New Orleans, Jacksonville, and, of course, Sedaris's childhood hometown, Raleigh, some of the South's historical character has faded, for these cities allow their denizens to distance themselves from the rural traditions of the past, while also facilitating mass migrations to the region. As Martyn Bone explains in *The Postsouthern Sense of Place in Contemporary Fiction:* "In the last few years, there has been much talk of a 'transnational turn' in American Studies. . . . I have noted (especially in my analysis of Atlanta and its literary representations) that there is compelling evidence that 'the South' is now comprehensively integrated into a globalized economy dominated by multinational corporations that have transcended or circumvented the physical boundaries of the nation-state."[6] Over the past several decades, numerous corporations (many lured by the region's long-standing hostility to unions) have relocated to or opened new branches in the South.[7] As part of the first wave of these corporate relocations, IBM transferred Lou, the father of the Sedaris clan, to Raleigh. Sedaris reports that this unexpected turn of events shocked his father:

> He was in his early forties when the company transferred our family to North Carolina.
>
> "You expect me to live *where?*" he'd asked.
>
> The Raleigh winters agreed with him, but he would have gladly traded the temperate climate for a decent radio station. (*MT* 18)

In this passage, which captures the tone of many of Sedaris's swipes at the South, Lou voices disbelief at his fate—as if Raleigh, North Carolina, in the 1960s, were some unheard-of outpost on the fringes of civilization. Sedaris also registers his father's regret for the inevitable loss of culture that will accompany their relocation, playing on regionalist visions of the North as a land of sophistication and culture, in contrast to the hillbilly South, where presumably radio stations play only country music.

However, as much as Sedaris uses the redneck South as the punchline for many of his jokes, he evinces his affinity for and allegiance to many aspects of southern identity. This affinity is congruent with his affection for regionalisms. As Jefferson Humphries explains in "The Discourse of Southernness," a southern sensibility relies not merely on geographical and other external factors but on a mindset that transcends the fictions of a purportedly postsouthern South: "Our cultural identity as southerners is not then, or not only, the logical expression of certain physical and circumstantial factors, but rather a hysterical and, one might even say, superstitious refusal to accommodate those physical and circumstantial factors, a refusal either to run away to some other reality or to attempt to confront the unruliness of circumstances honestly and directly."[8] Limning southernness as a hysterical, superstitious condition, one that refuses to accept the reality of a changing world, creates conditions ripe for humor, for the disjunctions between the South and perceptions of it render the region a contested space for comic conflicts to emerge. Although Sedaris presents himself as alienated from southern mores in many of his essays, he also describes his life in exaggerated terms reflective of Humphries's sense of "hysterical" southernness, in which one's frame of mind remains unconstrained by the realities of geography. Sedaris's essay "This Old House" tells of his experiences in a Chapel Hill boardinghouse: "An arthritic psychic, a ramshackle house, and either two or four crazy people, depending on your tolerance for hats. Harder to swallow is that each of us was such a cliché. It was as if you'd taken a Carson McCullers novel, mixed it with a Tennessee Williams play, and dumped all the sets and characters into a single box. I didn't add that Sister Sykes used to own a squirrel monkey, as it only amounted to overkill" (*EF* 47). With this final touch—that he does not mention Sister Sykes's monkey, only then to mention it in this disclaimer—Sedaris paints himself as yet another southern eccentric, a character taken from the pages of McCullers, Williams, or any other great writer of the decadent, gothic South.[9] Here, for Sedaris, the truth of the South must be remolded to make a convincing story, so the lies can then become the more acceptable "truths" that he presents in his essay.

Although Sedaris presents the vast majority of his narratives as memoirs, their status as such continually founders because his play with identity and regionalism creates divergent voices of self and other. Certainly, the question of individual and family identity percolates throughout his narratives. In creating semi-fictional characters from real people, including himself, Sedaris dissolves the ostensibly rigid borders between memoir and fiction. He divided the pieces in his first collection, *Barrel Fever* (1994), under the subheadings *stories* and *essays*. In a similar vein, the "Author's Note" in his sophomore effort *Naked* (1997) announces the veracity of all incidents recounted therein: "The events described in these stories are real. Other than the family members, the characters have fictitious names and identifying characteristics." *Me Talk Pretty One Day* (2000) does not include any such statement about the truth or falsity of its constituent chapters, but the author's note in *Dress Your Family in Corduroy and Denim* (2004) again proclaims the truthfulness of Sedaris's efforts: "The events described in these stories are real. Certain characters have fictitious names and identifying characteristics." However, in the front matter of *When You Are Engulfed in Flames* (2008), Sedaris concedes the ways in which fiction enhances the bare bones of his factual stories: "The events described in these stories are *realish.* Certain characters have fictitious names and identifying characteristics" (emphasis added).

A likely explanation for Sedaris's switch from *real* to *realish,* which tacitly admits that his work should not be considered nonfiction, emerges from the criticisms of such commentators as Alex Heard, who fact-checked several of his essays and determined that they contain numerous exaggerations and falsehoods, particularly in the characterizations of friends, family members, and acquaintances. Weighing the evidence, Heard concludes: "Still, his work is marketed as nonfiction, and there's a simple rule associated with that: Don't make things up."[10] Sedaris escaped the public castigation meted out to such quasi-factual fabulists as James Frey, who invented incidents for his memoir of addiction, *A Million Little Pieces,* and then received a public dressing-down from Oprah Winfrey for his falsehoods. This controversy alerted nonfiction writers that many of their readers expect only the unvarnished truth—with no embellishments for sensational or comic effect.[11] Within Sedaris's "realish" construction of the South and its characters, the nonfiction reader's demand for facts cedes to the humorist's need for comic material. Thus, Sedaris's stereotypes of the South perpetually confront the region's confused actuality—as evident in Sister Syke's pet monkey that bends the borders between fact and fiction. This example also demonstrates how true incidents from Sedaris's past may be presented as fictional when the facts, in their exaggerated play with southern tropes, are too unbelievable to be accepted as real. "I think autobiography is the last place you would look for truth," Sedaris states, and he also proclaims, "I just give the illusion of exposing myself, but really, I'm not exposed at all. There's a real me that lives inside my diary, and then there's a character of me."[12] The character that Sedaris creates for himself relies heavily on the variability of geography and southernness as markers of his identity, yet as Timothy Dow Adams argues, the purported lies in autobiographies sometimes reveal the truth of their authors' lives and perspectives: "All autobiographers are unreliable narrators, all humans are liars, and yet . . .

even those autobiographers with the most problematic approach to lying should be valued for telling the truth of their lives."[13] For Sedaris, such lies circle around his persona as a postsouthernist whose sense of regionalism fluctuates in response to the rhetorical demands of his writing rather than to the biographical truths of his past.

In this light, to identify Sedaris as a southern writer would oversimplify the complexity of the multiple personas he constructs throughout his essays, especially given that he introduced himself to national audiences as a New Yorker in the early 1990s. When National Public Radio aired his "SantaLand Diaries," which recall his experiences working as a holiday elf at Macy's, Sedaris was quickly acclaimed as one of the preeminent comic voices of the late twentieth century, yet in the essay's ensuing publication in *Barrel Fever,* only the most discerning readers would have noticed any hints of his southern roots. The dust-jacket biography succinctly introduces him through his vocations and his city of residence—"A playwright, radio commentator, and house cleaner, David Sedaris lives in New York City"—without mentioning his childhood years in North Carolina. The volume's essays clearly locate him as a New Yorker. "Diary of a Smoker" begins, "I rode my bike to the boat pond in Central Park" (*BF* 151), and "SantaLand Diaries" immediately invokes its New York setting: "I was in a coffee shop looking through the want ads when I read, 'Macy's Herald Square, the largest store in the world, has big opportunities for outgoing, fun-loving people of all shapes and sizes who want more than just a holiday job!'" (*BF* 167). Readers soon learn that Sedaris has recently transplanted himself to the metropolis: "I arrived in New York three weeks ago with high hopes, hopes that have been challenged. In my imagination I'd go straight from Penn Station to the offices of *One Life to Live,* where I would drop off my bags and spruce up before heading off for drinks with Cord Roberts and Victoria Buchanan, the show's greatest stars" (*BF* 169). This short vignette captures the clichéd storyline of an excited transplant to New York City who dreams of immediate fame and fortune, and while one can envision the small-town origins from which such a protagonist must flee, Sedaris mostly refrains from identifying his southern roots in *Barrel Fever.* Only in "The Curly Kind" does he briefly mention his childhood in Raleigh—"Five years after moving to Raleigh we still had Mayflower boxes in the living room" (*BF* 162)—but this essay is more concerned with the outrageous demands that homeowners place on their maids and cleaners than with the humor of southern living, and it pays little attention to the South or southern customs.[14]

Whereas *Barrel Fever* offers readers few clues about Sedaris's southern background, *Naked* and subsequent works discuss at length this aspect of his background. In many of Sedaris's comic jabs at the South, he characterizes himself as a little lost Yankee, confused by the cultural differences between his former and current homes. *Naked*'s opening pages recount his obsessive-compulsive tendencies—such as repeatedly touching telephone poles and pressing his nose against parked cars—and link them tacitly to his family's relocation: "I didn't remember things being this way back north. Our family had been transferred from Endicott, New York, to Raleigh, North Carolina" (*N* 9). While most of the family adapts to Raleigh with relative ease, Sedaris's mother Sharon despises it, as is evident in her curt appraisal of their new home: "'Our own little corner of hell,' my mother said, fanning herself with one of the shingles littering the front yard" (*N* 10). In a particularly biting passage, Sedaris riffs on southern stereotypes, creating a composite image of the ultimate fear for northern parents transferred below the Mason-Dixon line:

> IBM had relocated a great many northerners [to Raleigh], and together we made relentless fun of our new neighbors and their poky, backward way of life. Rumors circulated that the locals ran stills out of their toolsheds and referred to their house cats as "good eatin." Our parents discouraged us from using the titles "ma'am" or "sir" when addressing a teacher or shopkeeper. Tobacco was acceptable in the form of a cigarette, but should any of us experiment with plug or snuff, we would automatically be disinherited. Mountain Dew was forbidden, and our speech was monitored for the slightest hint of a Raleigh accent. Use the word "y'all," and before you knew it, you'd find yourself in a haystack French-kissing an underage goat. Along with grits and hush puppies, the abbreviated form of *you all* was a dangerous step on an insidious path leading straight to the doors of the Baptist church. (*MT* 60–61)

With this comically grotesque fantasia of the redneck South, Sedaris paints the region's population as the epitome of all its worst stereotypes: slow and lazy, with predilections for moonshine, chaw, bestiality, religious fundamentalism, and a lazy drawl (although it does leave one wondering who could possibly object to grits and hush puppies). This passage constructs southerners as the Others in their own land, a brash reimagining of the meaning of cultural traditions from the voice of the young Yankee in their midst, who fantasizes about destroying them all: "I remember only that at one time the story involved the citizens of Raleigh, North Carolina, being herded into a test balloon of my own design and making. It was rigged to explode once it reached the city limits, but the passengers were unaware of that fact" (*N* 22). Furthermore, Sedaris stresses that his parents resisted their children's assimilation into the very culture where they spent their formative years. When Sharon inherits a significant sum of money, she dedicates these funds to rescuing her children: "It went toward getting my mother's children out of the South, which, for her, spelled improvement" (*DF* 70).

Such passages illustrate Sedaris's propensity to mock key aspects of southern identity. Yet, as much as Sharon feared that her children would assimilate into the South, Sedaris depicts his brother Paul as fully southern, as the South's successful effort to subvert the Sedaris family's vision of themselves as distinct from their neighbors. For Sedaris, then, lineage is ultimately irrelevant to one's regional identity, for geographic affiliations can trump the training of kinship in the postsouthern South: "Our family remained free from outside influence until 1968, when my mother gave birth to my brother, Paul, a North Carolina native who has since grown to become my father's best ally and worst nightmare. Here was a child who, by the time he reached the second grade, spoke much like the toothless fishermen casting their nets into Albemarle Sound" (*MT* 61). With Paul infiltrating the family as its own outside influence, the structures of geographically inflected identity dissolve, for in the postsouthern South, an authentic southerner can intrude into a northern family still clinging to its sense of cultural separateness. Paul, who sports the countrified nickname of "The Rooster" (*MT* 61), embraces various aspects of southern culture many would find off-putting: "I've never tasted squirrel before. Hey, that sounds nice" (*N* 246). Many of the southern manners and mannerisms that Sedaris facetiously claimed would result in his and his siblings' disinheritance embellish his portrayals of Paul: "My brother politely ma'ams and sirs all strangers but refers to friends and family, his father included, as either 'bitch' or 'motherfucker.' . . . When my father complained about his aching feet, the Rooster set down his two-liter bottle of Mountain Dew . . . saying, 'Bitch, you need to have them ugly-ass bunions shaved down is what you need to do'" (*MT* 63–64). With his "ma'ams" and "sirs," his Mountain Dew, his nickname, and his crude speech, Paul incarnates the redneck South, which supplies Sedaris with an appropriate foil for several family episodes. "It often seems that my brother and I were raised in two completely different households" (*MT* 62), he concludes.

The stereotype of the southern redneck bears an extensive history, but Sedaris employs it in this instance to creates a postsouthern identity for Paul, who has integrated seamlessly into a version of the South alien to his family. He also epitomizes the ways in which the hillbilly stereotype, and thus the very meaning of southern identity, has shifted. Despite Lou's efforts to dissuade Paul from hanging out with his redneck friends—"Oh, Paul, those aren't the sort of people you need to be associating with. What are you doing with hayseeds like that? The goal is to better yourself. Meet some intellectuals. Read a book!" (*MT* 67)—his affiliations with southerners trump his northern family upbringing. While Paul cannot be considered a redneck according to blood, lineage, and family custom, as he was raised in an upper-middle-class family with the financial means to afford their children numerous educational and cultural opportunities, he incarnates and performs the redneck ideal in an ultimately postsouthern way, as an identity adopted in contrast to those of his family members. Sedaris also explores, in describing Paul's fiancée Kathy, how regional affiliations can just as easily be reversed in a postsouthern South: "Best of all, she was from the North, meaning that should she and Paul ever conceive a child, it stood a fifty-fifty chance of speaking understandable English" (*DF* 170). Paul's identity as a southerner, as with virtually any regional identity that Sedaris constructs, faces pressure from other family members, who might either embrace or spurn the regionalisms that define him. Sedaris further complicates his characterization of "The Rooster" when explaining his audiences' varying reactions toward his brother: "When I read a story about my brother in the South, he's everybody's brother. And then, if you read about it in another part of the country, people will say, 'Read the story about your white-trash brother.'" Sedaris bemoans how these audience members perceive his sibling—"Because [Paul] lives in North Carolina and he speaks a certain way, this is what they've decided"—notwithstanding the fact that his own postsouthern construction of his brother as a "hayseed" invites these interpretations.[15]

Thus, as his satirical treatment of his brother and the South as a whole shows, any sense of geographical identity for Sedaris is always mediated through the necessities of the experiences he is recounting. As Scott Romine argues of the meanings of geography, "Traditionally, 'place' has signified a nexus of *is* and *ought,* a describable outside metonymically associated with a network of imperatives, codes, norms, limitations, duties, obligations, and relationships. 'Place,' therefore, is both subject to representation and suggestive of things that resist representation—hence the 'texture' often associated with it."[16] Sedaris's mercurial sense of place shifts in response to the circumstances at hand, which further complicates his identity as a regionalist—southern, postsouthern, or otherwise. For example, Sedaris states, "I was never one of those easterners attracted by the romantic pull of California" (*N* 129). In this instance "easterners" both reveals and hides the truth of his geographical identity, for one can align oneself with New England, New York, and the rest of the Atlantic seaboard by referring to oneself with this term, whereas "southerner" would align North Carolinians with their Deep South neighbors along the Gulf of Mexico, including Louisianans, Mississippians, and Alabamans. In contrast, Sedaris recalls in "Day In, Day Out" his reaction to a frank discussion of sex on a radio program: "Coming from North Carolina, I couldn't believe that this was on the radio. And on a Sunday!" (*LE* 230). The mock naiveté of his voice—clutching for pearls at the shock of filthy talk defiling the Sabbath—relies on his southern roots to carry the humor. In many ways, Sedaris expresses such a multitude of regional sensibilities that he could be considered not merely postsouthern but postgeographic, such as when he realizes the fundamental sameness of his life, no matter his location: "Things wouldn't be any different in North Carolina than they'd been in Oregon. I thought of those people on the bus, going from one shitty place to the next, expecting nothing to change but the landscape" (*N* 180). Even his years in France and England do not contribute to his development of a cosmopolitan or otherwise antisouthern sensibility. Rather, he compares his relocation to France to his mother's journey below the Mason-Dixon line: "I wound up in Normandy the same way my mother wound up in North Carolina: you meet a guy, relinquish a tiny bit of control, and the next thing you know, you're eating a different part of the pig" (*MT* 153). As he mocks Raleigh and its environs, he also ridicules the French countryside, seeing it as a variant of the backwoods South: "I don't own a pair of sunglasses, or anything with writing on it, and I wear shorts only in Normandy, which is basically West Virginia without the possums" (*EF* 50). Celebrating his homeland, he proclaims, "Paris, it seems, is where I've come to dream about America" (*MT* 263). Denigrating France instead of celebrating her as the height of enlightened European sensibilities—a view that gay expatriates such as Gertrude Stein and James Baldwin expressed enthusiastically—Sedaris ridicules the possibility of geography allowing one to transcend oneself and one's roots. In a sense then, the prevailing factor of Sedaris's postsouthern identity is simply its utility—like a comfortable jacket, he wears it under the right conditions but discards it as necessary when other climates call or simply when he needs to crack a joke.

Homosexuality and Race in Sedaris's Postsouthern South

Although Sedaris barely mentions his southern roots in *Barrel Fever,* he frankly discusses his homosexuality in this work—despite the fact that queerness stood as the more controversial topic when the book was published in the early 1990s. "SantaLand Diaries" includes nonchalant accounts of the many gay flirtations among Macy's Santas and elves: "The overall cutest elf is a fellow from Queens named Snowball. . . . Snowball just leads elves on, elves and Santas. He is playing a dangerous game" (*BF* 184). Several of the stories in *Barrel Fever* feature gay narrators of breathtakingly comic narcissism, many of whom graphically discuss their sex lives. The narrator of "Parade" recounts his intimate affairs with such macho celebrities as Charlton Heston and Mike Tyson ("Mike said, What the hell, it wasn't like his teeth hadn't been up my ass before" [*BF* 8]), and Chad Holt, the narrator of "My Manuscript," outlines in ample detail his pornographic fantasies, including when "Chad and the studs headed toward the master bedroom to begin a ~~great fun filled sexy~~ sexsational orgy that none of them would soon forget!!!!" (*BF* 23). These stories lack any defined setting, southern or otherwise, as the narrators disgorge themselves of their queer desires, dishing out their dirt, hatred, and passion. As part of his candor about his sexuality, Sedaris, imagining himself winning an award, includes his long-term partner Hugh Hamrick as one of the loved ones and family members he would thank (*BF* 166), and his frankness about their relationship continues in *Naked* and subsequent works, such as when he details one of their spats: "Last night I was in a foul mood and provoked Hugh into a fight, goading him until he left the bedroom, shouting, 'You're a big, fat, hairy pig!'" (*N* 253). Considering *Barrel Fever* alone, it appears that, if anything, Sedaris was more closeted about his southern roots than his homosexuality in the early 1990s.

Sedaris's candor about homosexuality serves as a key part of his postsouthern ethos, for, in treating the subject as wholly unremarkable, he strips it of its ostensible shock value and reconfigures it as a part of the newly normative. Furthermore, Sedaris frequently links his considerations of homosexuality to issues of racial prejudice in the South, again forging a postsouthern perspective on a hidebound issue that has long dogged the region. While sexuality and race function differently in the construction of prejudice and discrimination, they overlap in key ways, as Richard Dyer notes: "All concepts of race are always concepts of the body and also of heterosexuality."[17] Raced bodies are also sexed bodies, in terms both of biological sex and of sexual orientation, for the social construction of minorities deemed Other does not halt at initial perceptions of differences in skin pigmentation. For Sedaris, then, the union of sexuality and race allows him to consider the conditions of postsouthern identity at the point where the South must move beyond its biases to confront desires, including homosexual and interracial ones, long ignored or denigrated.

To this end, and with his trademark blend of narcissism and self-deprecating humor, Sedaris imagines his perfect lover: "When I thought of sex, I pictured someone standing before me crying, 'I love you so much that . . . I don't even know who I am anymore.' My imaginary boyfriend was of no particular age or race, all that mattered was that he was crazy about me" (*N* 140). In a similar passage, he again presents himself as postracial in his erotic attractions, envisioning a boyfriend who would share his animosities, thus ensuring their lifelong compatibility: "Age, race, and weight were unimportant. In terms of mutual interests, I figured we could spend the rest of our lives discussing how much we hated the aforementioned characteristics" (*MT* 154). Further establishing his ethos as a postracial gay southerner, Sedaris recognizes the difficulties of discussing race in even a postsouthern South, for declarations of racial blindness, as he observes, often merely trumpet the progressive views of the speaker rather than any deeper commitment to racial integration:

> It always sounds false when white people talk about how gentle and color blind they are. "One thing I've learned from my many Asian, Latino, and African American friends is that we're all brothers under the skin." Statements like this make me queasy, but they're really no worse than the often heard, "How could I be racist when my first boyfriend was black?"
>
> My first boyfriend was black as well, but that doesn't prove I'm colorblind, just that I like big butts. . . . Does this make me rac*ist,* or simply race *conscious?* Either way, I'm more afraid of conservatives than I am of black people. (*LE* 152)

In reply to his rhetorical question, surely readers are meant to conclude that Sedaris is not racist but race conscious—aware of the difficulties of transcending race in civic and social discourse yet unhindered by racism in his personal interactions with African Americans. Sedaris dismantles the relevance of race to his personal life and politics while concurrently presenting an appropriate nemesis—namely, conservatives—who are demographically more likely to be white. Thus, race is tacitly registered as an area of concern, yet with its poles reversed.

Sedaris does not explicitly link his fear of conservatives to his homosexuality in this passage, but such a connection cannot be overlooked, given the hostility that social conservatives have long expressed toward gays. Still, homosexuality and race are experienced differently, as are homophobia and racism, and Sedaris's attempts to override their distinctions in pursuit of true egalitarianism frequently fall short of the mark, for he needs African American characters to function in the same way he needs characters of other races and geographies to function: as comic foils. As Charles Nero powerfully argues, "Liberal and nationalist politics has consistently been imagined as a union between black and white men. However, I challenge the idea that masculine sameness is, should be, or can be the basis for equality and justice. In a racist state, 'white tribalism' has always been a force for cohesiveness more powerful than masculine sameness."[18] Even as southerners of all races must deal with the legacy of racial discrimination, from the past continuing into the present, so too must gay men address the ways in which race functions in gay subcultures. The tribalism that Nero decries exposes the ways in which African Americans and gays experience discrimination differently, while also highlighting how white gay men's construction of race consciousness, no matter how laudable the intentions, can partially reestablish the barriers they aim to knock down.

A primary challenge Sedaris faces in his postsouthern treatment of race and homosexuality is to find humor in this material, for, as James Russell Lowell observes, social activism does not typically align with a comic worldview: "Men of one idea,—that is, who have one idea at a time,—men who accomplish great results, men of action, reformers, saints, martyrs, are inevitably destitute of humor; and if the idea that inspires them be great and noble, they are impervious to it."[19] A passionate treatise against racial injustice is not likely to be a humorous one, and while one does not criticize Martin Luther King Jr. for the gravity of tone evident throughout his "Letter from a Birmingham Jail," "I Have a Dream," and other rhetorical masterworks, Sedaris's postsouthern treatment of race finds humor in the prejudice directed against both African Americans and homosexuals. In a scene of self-mockery, Sedaris paints his interest in civil rights as another sign of his narcissism. He holds himself up as a model of progressive politics and racial sensitivity when, as a boy, he plans to date Delicia, a black girl, for the express purpose of shocking white people: "The part of my plan that made old people uncomfortable, that exposed them for the bigots they were—and on a Sunday!—still appealed to me. But the mechanics of it would have been a pain" (*LE* 51). At the conclusion of this episode, when Sedaris realizes he is using Delicia to advance his agenda, he wonders what his supposed girlfriend thought: "As for Delicia, what goes through a person's mind the first time they're patronized? Was she embarrassed? Enraged? Or perhaps this wasn't her first time. Maybe it happened so often she'd simply resigned herself to it" (*LE* 53). Empathizing with this young girl for the awkward position he put her in, Sedaris again presents himself as race conscious, not racist, yet the humor of the encounter depends on southern racism for Sedaris to be able to cast himself as the little white crusader for racial justice. Furthermore, Sedaris heightens the scene's comedy by threatening his mother with interracial progeny—"You're just afraid your grandchildren will be half black"—yet as he admits, the threat is a fairly ridiculous one: "How I'd jumped from dragging some poor girl to a senior citizens' apartment complex to dating her and then to fathering her children is beyond me now" (*LE* 50–51).

In establishing himself as a writer of the postsouthern South, Sedaris condemns racism and the region's legacy of racial hatred, yet he regularly uses the most offensive racial epithet—*nigger*—in his essays, despite the word's virulent history and the cultural baggage of a white man employing it. As Michael Eric Dyson argues of the word's use across racial lines, "most white folks attracted to black culture know better than to cross a line drawn in the sand of racial history. *Nigger* has never been cool when spit from white lips."[20] Sedaris clearly understands this point, for although he frequently employs the word as a writer, he never utters it as an essay's narrator, even when the resulting locutions sound forced. In describing the scarce snowfalls of southern winters, he explains, "What little snow there was would usually melt an hour or two after hitting the ground, and there you'd be in your windbreaker and unconvincing mittens, forming a lumpy figure made mostly of mud. Snow Negroes, we called them" (*DF* 13). "Snow Negroes" is an unlikely politically correct—or merely politically improved—variant for the offensive phrase more likely to be employed. Perhaps Sedaris and his family did say "Snow Negroes," or perhaps not, yet this instance is as close as he comes to letting the more offensive word slip from his lips.

Much of Sedaris's racial humor allows racists to convict themselves of their own failings through their word choice, which he merely reports to his readers, and several of his essays depict those who express racist sentiments as certifiably insane. "Get Your Ya-Ya's Out" details his grandmother's time in a retirement community, where "a spritely, white-haired lunatic named Mrs. Denardo" spouts such ramblings as, "I'm the stepsister of Jesus Christ sent back to earth to round up all the lazy, goddamned niggers and teach them to cook ribs the way they was meant to be cooked, goddamnit!" (*N* 32–33). Commenting on the Sedaris children's performance for the residents, Mrs. Denardo fulminates: "Your show was a piece of stinking shit. . . . You don't know fuck about shit, niggers" (*N* 33). The humor of Mrs. Denardo's tirades emerges in her virtuosic vulgarity, with Sedaris softening the offensiveness of the word through her utter irrationality, as well as through its application to a group of white children. Likewise, in the essay "Dix Hill," which recounts Sedaris's volunteer stint at a local mental hospital, an inmate claims his supernatural abilities while revealing his racism: "Tell the nigger I control all the music on his radio" (*N* 76). In addition to these lunatics, one of Sedaris's black characters, Lance, employs the word frequently—"You think I'm just some nigger you can shout at? Is that what you're saying, that I'm a nigger? Are you calling me a nigger?" (*DF* 100)—yet his identity as an African American absolves Sedaris of the responsibility of saying it himself. In Sedaris's postsouthern South, racism belongs in the past, and when characters speak this ultimate racist shibboleth in the present, it defines them as laughably unsympathetic because of the archaism of their language and beliefs.

By placing the word *nigger* in the mouths of insane and unlikable characters, Sedaris signals his postsouthern racial sensibilities, which he links as well to his treatment of whiteness and heterosexuality. To this end he denudes the word of its racial component in "C.O.G.," in a scene featuring his encounter with a pregnant woman retelling an argument with her boyfriend: "I told him, 'I'm through fucking around with a white-faced nigger too busy chasing bush pussy to get up off his fat fucking asshole and find his self a motherfucking job'" (*N* 154). In transcribing her words, Sedaris allows this young woman to condemn herself as uneducated through her grammar ("his self"), which she compounds through her torrent of profanity (of which this excerpt is merely a taste). More so, this young woman, and Sedaris's quotation of her, disproves the assumed correlation between race and *nigger,* for this "white-faced nigger" loses the assumed shield of his white skin and is degraded with the opprobrious term. She further proves her racism through the phrase "bush pussy," with which she denounces her white boyfriend for his interracial affairs. Again, Sedaris examines racism at its point of intersection with sexuality, for this vision of white heterosexuality—mired as it is in discord and vulgarity—questions the viability of whiteness and heterosexuality as privileged signifiers within discussions of race and sexual orientation.

Racism functions through its pervasiveness and its particularity, and Sedaris illustrates how race dictates both black and white people's performances of their identities. As Michael Omi and Howard Winant explain, "Racial ideology and social structure, therefore, mutually shape the nature of racism in a complex, dialectical, and overdetermined manner,"[21] for varieties of race and social class are perceived as mutually inflecting one another, with racism structuring their performances. In "Something for Everyone," the African American character Dupont knows he must perform his blackness and adapts as necessary for his white audiences: "To the landowning business woman, he was the grinning minstrel, standing upon an overturned bucket to deliver his hopeless State of the Union Address. To what he considered a sex-crazy homosexual, he was the indefatigable stud, roaming from haystack to canopied bed to serve his ever-expanding flock of enthusiastic bitches" (*N* 220). Dupont, although not a sympathetic character, embodies the ways in which African Americans have been forced to accommodate racist views. Sedaris escalates his treatment of race in this episode by depicting Uta, who has employed Dupont and Sedaris to strip and refinish woodwork for her apartments, as sympathetic to Dupont: "I understand it's very hard for your people. . . . You get all kinds of flak from southern rednecks and now I read in the paper where you're getting it from the Jews to boot" (*N* 222). Uta's words—condescendingly racist, starkly anti-southern and anti-Semitic—highlight the uniformity and particularity of prejudice, for her biased viewpoints range across skin tones to latch onto any insulting stereotype of a disparaged minority.[22]

Sedaris extends his observations of the social construction of race to his family, as he enjoys the humor of mocking the varieties of whiteness that he and his family perform. Whiteness, as a social concept, alleges that lighter skin pigmentation accords with many personal and social virtues, yet as numerous cultural commentators have unpacked, whiteness shifts in its construction, utility, and boundaries. When describing their errands to the residences his father rented primarily to African American families, Sedaris portrays the flimsy façade of his siblings' whiteness: "Alone in the car we were savages, but at The Empire we were ambassadors for our race, acting not like normal white people we'd grown up with but like the exceptional white people we vaguely remembered from random episodes of *Masterpiece Theatre*" (*DF* 94). Within a racist southern imaginary, African Americans are often denigrated as savages, yet in this passage white children act as savages until assuming the veneer of whiteness that they have learned to perform—one modeled not by southern adults but by British actors paid to impersonate the aristocracy on television.

In a particularly illustrative scene in which Sedaris encounters both southern racism and homophobia, he and his brother Paul, while on a quest to purchase marijuana, "found ourselves in a trailer twenty-odd miles outside of Raleigh" (*EF* 160). This incident's setting in a trailer alerts readers of its inhabitants' unrefined and unenlightened sensibilities, which become further evident when the drug dealer's wife Beth casually expresses her racist tendencies: "Then she turned back to the TV and glared at the screen, saying, 'This show's boring. Hand me the nigger'" (*EF* 161). Sedaris ignores his discomfort with her words—he wants the marijuana too much to risk enlightening her about her offensive views—yet, after Paul tells the drug dealer and Beth that Sedaris is gay, he uses this uncomfortable situation to muse on the connections between racial prejudice and homophobia:

> People I know, people who live in houses and do not call their remote control "the nigger," have often asked the same question, though usually in regard to lesbians, who are always either absent or safely out of earshot. "Which one's the man?"
>
> It's astonishing the amount of time that certain straight people devote to gay sex—trying to determine what goes where and how often. (*EF* 164)

Throughout this essay, Sedaris defines Beth by her racial and sexual ignorance—her racist language, her questions about the mechanics of gay sex—and thus posits her as an outsider to his postsouthern South. Because she lives outside the city limits, Sedaris is able to delineate Raleigh as the New South, in contrast to the Old South that lies just beyond its urban borders, where racism and homophobia flourish.

In other scenarios, Sedaris constructs southern race relations in light of how skin color and sexuality predetermine perceptions of events. Finding perverse humor in the story of his sister Gretchen's near rape, he laments the fact that her attacker is African American because of the complicated racial politics that will inevitably ensue: "Of all the possibilities, why did he have to be black, especially in North Carolina, where everything was so loaded? I think Gretchen was feeling the same way—not that she needed to let this slide but that she was caught up in some tiresome cliché. Now here was her father organizing a posse" (*LE* 109). Expanding his satire, Sedaris explores how southern society denigrates white women in interracial rape scenarios for their actions: "One thing the adults all seemed to agree on was that Gretchen was remiss in walking to the grocery store. So remiss, according to some, that you couldn't really blame the guy who attacked her, as what was he *supposed* to think, a young woman out on her own at that hour—a young woman in shorts, no less?" (*LE* 110). Interracial rape, as constructed within the southern discourses Sedaris mocks, casts black perpetrator and white victim as equally culpable, with the critical difference emerging in the ways in which all black men are seen as potential rapists while white women are seen as having the choice to behave in ways that either invite or avoid rape. It is a testament to the power of Sedaris's humor that this incident remains comic, couched as it is within his overarching assessment of the South and its mores, as he also tacitly contrasts his post-southern perspective on race and sexuality with the old-southern mores still in effect.

In "I Like Guys," Sedaris interweaves stories of racism and homophobia, detailing how both prejudices permeated his school years. While the title points to its attention to Sedaris's homosexuality, the essay begins with a discussion of race relations in the South, addressing his childhood memories of how "our county school system would adopt a policy of racial integration by way of forced busing" (*N* 81). Sedaris introduces readers to his school's racist and homophobic teachers, including one who patronizes African Americans ("'The thing to remember,' she said, 'is that more than anything in the world, those colored people wish they were white'" [*N* 82]) and another who mincingly performs as a queen: "Snatching a purse off the back of a student's chair, he would prance about the room, batting his eyes and blowing kisses at the boys seated in the front row. 'So fairy nice to meet you,' he'd say" (*N* 82). Sedaris characterizes Raleigh's school integration as relatively calm, noting that "There had been violence in other towns and counties, trouble as far away as Boston; but in Raleigh the transition was peaceful" (*N* 93).[23] More than a decade after the 1954 Supreme Court decision of *Brown v. Board of Education of Topeka,* conflicts surrounding the integration of U.S. public schools still roiled, crossing the perceived borders between North and South. With this nod to Boston, Sedaris paints the North as complicit in racial discrimination and, by so doing, challenges stereotypes of a uniformly racist South. Still, while he describes Raleigh's school integration as peaceful, he admits the racism of his instructors: "Several of my teachers, when discussing the upcoming school integration, would scratch at the damp stains beneath their arms, pulling back their lips to reveal every bit of tooth and gum" (*N* 85).[24] Given these teachers' hostility toward their new students, it is unlikely that African Americans found Raleigh's schools welcoming; Sedaris previously established in this essay that his teachers were inimical to any perceived deviation from their perceptions of southern cultural normativity—in all of its assumed whiteness and straightness.

Balancing the essay's examination of racial integration in Raleigh's schools, Sedaris tells the story of his summer-camp experiences in Athens, where he bonds with another boy, Jason, who later, to protect himself from accusations of homosexuality, publically denounces Sedaris for his sexual orientation. Jason pretends to find a piece of paper on which Sedaris has written, "I LIKE GUYS," but as Sedaris explains, these accusations rebound upon his accuser: "Presented as an indictment, the document was both pathetic and comic. . . . Touching such a foul document made him suspect and guilty by association. In attempting to discredit each other, we wound up alienating ourselves even further" (*N* 91–92). With these parallel storylines of racial discrimination in the schools and homophobic prejudice at summer camp, Sedaris paints the truly international scope of discrimination, for even a trip to Greece, a land historically hospitable to gay relationships, offers no respite from the blanket homophobia found in his southern school. Weaving together the narrative's threads of racism and homophobia, Sedaris concludes it by depicting the antigay bigotry of an African American teacher: "My new science teacher was a black man very adept at swishing his way across the room, mocking everyone from Albert Einstein to the dweebish host of a popular children's television program. Black and white, the teachers offered their ridicule as though it were an olive branch. 'Here,' they said, 'this is something we each have in common, proof that we're all brothers under the skin'" (*N* 94). It is a comically daring resolution to his essay, in which the South's postsouthern potential is somewhat achieved as black and white teachers unite to disparage gays. Sedaris's status as the denigrated Other in this man's classroom matches that of his African American classmates taught by racists, and so the South's construction of whiteness as a privileged signifier is shown to be a paltry façade for white gays, as it also points to the variability of individual identity under skins of any tone.

Finally, as much as Sedaris paints racism and homophobia as part of the South's enduring legacy, he also makes clear that this problem is not unique to the United States. Recalling the 2008 candidacy of Barack Obama for the U.S. presidency, Sedaris exposes how the international expectation that a white man would be prejudiced against a black man reveals the cultural biases of the person expressing such viewpoints: "'Being a white American, you wouldn't vote for a black man, would you?' the reporter asked. Though crudely phrased, the question was fairly common, and not just in backwater Normandy" (*LED* 150). With Normandy as the continental counterpoint to the American South, Sedaris universalizes discrimination and prejudice, which, as is typical with his acerbic style, does not erase racism through a saccharine vision of unity but instead insists upon its ubiquity. In its constructions of race and homosexuality, it appears, Sedaris's postsouthern South is just as good—or just as bad—as everywhere else.

Returning Home to the Postsouthern South

As much as Sedaris constructs himself as a postsouthern southerner who mocks the region's backward ways and criticizes its retrograde prejudices against African Americans and homosexuals, he balances his mockery of the South with mockery of himself. As Kevin Kopelson argues of Sedaris's construction of his narrative identity:

> Sedaris calls himself an asshole—not to mention scumbag, shithead, and son of a bitch. . . . Sedaris, however, is primarily autobiographical—not to mention hilarious, brutally honest, and painfully sad. By reviewing roles he's played in life as well as roles other have played with him, he reveals in alarming detail how he managed to become an asshole. Clearly though, and this has a lot to do with why most of us *like* Sedaris, he's trying to do something about that development—compensation made possible by the fact that some of those roles have shaped his work as an artist.[25]

From this perspective, as much as Sedaris denigrates the South and holds it accountable for its antediluvian attitudes towards African Americans and gays, he concomitantly holds himself up for ridicule—condemning himself, in Kopelson's terms, as an asshole precisely for his ridiculing of the South. Moreover, Sedaris delights in his outsider status, declaring in an interview, "There's something about not fitting in that I like," which hints that, no matter his geographical location, he will attempt to find a way not to adapt to its mores.[26]

Certainly, many of Sedaris's droll observations that ostensibly criticize the South boomerang back to mock him. "You know you're living in a small town when you can reach the ninth grade without ever having seen a mime" (*N* 95), he snipes, and though his words ridicule Raleigh on their surface, he is the one who ends up looking pretentious because of the faux superiority of this voice that assesses a city's cultural standing in relation to its mime population. In another incident, he apparently compliments himself and condemns southerners—"We were clearly ahead of our time but figured that, with enough drugs, the citizens of North Carolina would eventually catch up with us" (*MT* 50)—but in revealing that the populace of North Carolina would need hallucinogens and other pharmaceuticals to match his sense of cultural superiority, he again hoists himself on his own petard. One of the overarching themes of *Me Talk Pretty One Day* is, appropriately enough, speech and language communities. Recalling the speech therapy sessions meant to help him overcome his lisp, Sedaris ridicules his teacher for her accent: "The woman spoke with a heavy western North Carolina accent, which I used to discredit her authority. Here was a person for whom the word *pen* had two syllables. Her people undoubtedly drank from clay jugs and hollered for Paw when the vittles were ready—so who was she to advise me on anything?" (*MT* 7). Later in the book, when Sedaris studies French, he reverses positions with his former teacher and assumes the role of the hick from the sticks: "Things began to come together, and I went from speaking like an evil baby to speaking like a hillbilly. 'Is thems the thoughts of cows?' I'd ask the butcher, pointing to the calves' brains displayed in the front window. 'I want me some lamp chop with handles on 'em'" (*MT* 164). This thematic reversal—a postsouthern hillbilly, who once ridiculed the southern woman who helped him to improve his speech, now speaks garbled French and finds himself in the position of the linguistic Other—disproves the very meaning of geography, for the accents that ostensibly locate individuals on a spectrum of speech and class cannot hold. (Sedaris also disproves constructions of the South as a land of conservative sexuality versus the laissez-faire attitudes of the French in his jibe at the rigid rules policing the genders of French nouns: "Say what you like about southern social structures, but at least in North Carolina a hot dog is free to swing both ways" [*MT* 189]). The South, in these passages, allows Sedaris to hold a mirror to himself, thereby encouraging his readers to laugh at the arrogant voice he projects to expose his own failings.

Another theme running through many of Sedaris's essays concerns his gradual acceptance of his southern sensibilities, underlining that the regional distinctions between his brother Paul's redneck mannerisms and his own postsouthern pleasures are not intrinsically distinct. He confesses that not only does he like country music but that he formerly denied his appreciation of it to construct an appropriately antisouthern persona: "Here was the point where, without even trying, you could just be yourself and admit that you liked country music" (*DF* 85). Sedaris's affection for Dolly Parton could be attributed to her status as a gay icon, yet it stems as well from her southern childhood, the story of which Sedaris listens to on an audiobook while amid the sophistication of a French shopping excursion: "The grand department store felt significantly less intimidating when listening to *Dolly: My Life and Other Unfinished Business,* a memoir in which the busy author describes a childhood spent picking ticks out of her grandmother's scalp" (*MT* 184). He mentions as well listening to Merle Haggard's autobiography *My House of Memories,* and in a paean to his partner Hugh, he celebrates their mutual affections: "We both love bacon and country music, what more could you possibly want?" (*DF* 140). Relaxing into his southern identity as the years pass, Sedaris accentuates his fondness for country music to capture metonymically his relationship to the South: the young Yankee who would never touch a Mountain Dew or eat a hush puppy now embraces the cultural traditions of his childhood home.

Furthermore, the South, while it may evolve more slowly than other regions of the country, continues along its path to modernity. As Sedaris's stories span from his childhood in the mid 1960s to the current day, the South's evolution on homosexuality is registered in lives characterized first by sexual secrets and then by flagrant queer pride. In "Road Trips," Sedaris recalls his travels throughout the South, in particular his encounter with a closeted gay man who picks him up while hitchhiking and then repeatedly requests fellatio. The man's pick-up line—"Yessiree, good Old North Carolina . . . All I know is that if anyone wanted to give me a blow job, or have me give him one, I'd do it" (*EF* 68)—takes Sedaris by surprise: "This came out of nowhere, and what threw me was the way he'd attached it to his previous observation. North Carolina is temperate and populated with well-meaning people; therefore I will engage in oral sex with another man" (*EF* 68). Years later, during a return visit to the South, Sedaris is amazed to find a level of candor about sexuality absent during his childhood, and he contrasts this new attitude with his memories of the truck driver's furtive desires: "'My son is gay!' the boy's mother announced, as if none of us had figured this out yet. He may have attended one of those magnet schools for the arts, but still it floored me that a ninth grader in Raleigh, North Carolina—on the street where I grew up—could comfortably identify himself as a homosexual" (*EF* 64). "Road Trips" records the changing sexual mores of the South, with its emergence into a postsouthern sensibility causing Sedaris to reassess the region and his relationship to it.

On the border between fact and fiction throughout his memoirs, Sedaris's sense of geography expands his humor while also providing its regional foundations. In this light, his many returns to his southern home demonstrate the pull of family and long-familiar landscapes. At one point he decides North Carolina will serve as an ideal setting for a colonoscopy: "Once it was over, I planned on visiting my family, and, figuring I'd just be sitting around anyway, I called a North Carolina endoscopy center and made an appointment" (*LE* 264). North Carolina emerges as the literal butt of this episode's joke, yet at the same time, the satiric register shifts into an ode to his past, as his anesthesiologist instructs him to contemplate his "happy place" prior to the procedure:

> At first I thought my happy place would be a stage. I was walking from the wings to the podium, excited, like always, by all the attention I would soon be getting, when I changed my mind and revisited the house I grew up in. It was any night in the early 1970s and my sisters and I were sitting around the dining room table, trying to make our mother laugh. I could just see her, head cocked to one side, lighting a cigarette off a candle, when I jumped to a cottage my family rented one summer on the coast of North Carolina, and then to a September afternoon in Normandy. (*LE* 268)

Sedaris's "happy places"—his Raleigh home in the 1970s, a vacation on the North Carolina coast, and an idyllic day in Normandy—testify both to the strengths and variability of the places he calls home. This scene also tempers the performative narcissism he often projects, dismissing the glories of adulation for the pleasures of family.

His essay collections depict him living in Chicago, New York, France, England, Japan, and elsewhere, yet in one of his most recent pieces, "Now We Are Five," Sedaris returns to North Carolina for a family vacation and impulsively buys a beachfront home, fulfilling his childhood fantasy: "I told myself that one day *I* would buy a beach house and that it would be everyone's, as long as they followed my Draconian rules and never stopped thanking me for it."[27] Sedaris weaves this story of his return home with an elegiac account of his sister Tiffany's suicide, in which the family reunites in its southern homeland when it can no longer reunite as the family it once was. Sedaris finds comic potential in so many of life's bizarre and banal moments, but here the return home bespeaks the impossibility and the tragically inevitable impermanence of family, in a southern landscape of yesteryear creeping into the present. For Sedaris's humor, the old South—a land of hillbillies, racism, and homophobia—is the punchline, but then again, in the region's postsouthern potential to escape the past, so is he.

CONCLUSION

PRECIOUS PERVERSIONS AND THE SOUTHERN LITERARY CANON

The literary canon stirs up endless controversies. Its celebrants laud it as the repository of a culture's finest artistic expressions, one that provides moral and cultural elevation to its devotees, while its detractors lambast it as an archaic relic of conservative and hidebound values, luring readers into a false sense of aesthetic bliss predicated upon the dismissal of vast segments of the population. While the canon wars of the 1980s and 1990s have abated, the issues they raised remain relevant, and in this light it is instructive to remember Harold Bloom's lyrical suggestion that "when you read a canonical work for a first time you encounter a stranger, an uncanny startlement rather than a fulfillment of expectations."[1] It is also necessary to recall that his view of the Western canon circumscribes an insular heritage dismissive of other traditions—southern, queer, and otherwise. In contrast, as various scholars have demonstrated, to contest the canon's formation entails envisioning new paradigms of literature, its aesthetic worth, and its construction of cultures past, present, and future. In his classic study of African American literature's place in literary history, Henry Louis Gates Jr., argues for the necessity of opening the Western canon to black voices, to the mutual benefit of both traditions: "There can be no doubt that white texts inform and influence black texts (and vice versa), so that a thoroughly integrated canon of American literature is not only politically sound, it is *intellectually* sound as well."[2] With equal force, Nancy Walker details how the literary canon overlooks comic female voices and calls for readers to "reformulat[e] the canon of American humorous literature so that it represents both male and female humor," for women's humor opens up new perspectives on the past and its mores.[3] In these and other critiques of the canon, scholars insist that its boundaries be redrawn to include what has been excluded; without such provocative salvos, its parameters would remain uncontested.

Canons perform great cultural good in leading readers to some of the best texts their cultures have produced, but they can also cause great harm when they overlook swaths of people and their storylines. As with so many other tools, when used wisely canons build a better culture; when used indiscriminately or hegemonically they marginalize and destroy. Furthermore, as Carey Kaplan and Ellen Cronan Rose posit in *The Canon and the Common Reader,* the issue of the canon's formation intertwines with an equally fraught question: "Who speaks for the academy?"[4] Like the canon itself, the academy that defines it is monolithic yet individual, comprised of voices both sympathetic and resistant to the status quo. The canon is formed anew with each syllabus assigned, with each anthology published, with each essay and monograph written, and with each award bestowed, as these acts reinforce prevailing opinions that certain authors and texts are superior to others. Dorothy Allison aptly describes literature as "a conversation—a lively enthralling exchange that constantly challenges and widens our own imaginations,"[5] yet not every voice in this conversation is heard above the roar.

Canons, therefore, require constant tending and tweaking, so that established traditions do not drown out voices representing other genders, races, and sexualities and thereby promote a static future through continuous deference to the past. To this end, it is worthwhile to consider the place of gay southern authors in the regional and U.S. canon and to explore how their comic writings have been received. Simply put, do "precious perversions" merit esteem as some of the best literary artifacts the South has to offer? Or does the southern canon, despite notable shifts over the previous decades, remain an insular redoubt against queer voices?

In broaching these questions, it should be first noted that the literary canon's construction matters deeply to many gay readers, who see in its history an erasure of homosexuality and in its current reconstructions the possibility for inclusion. Many marginalized readers perceive canons not simply as lists of aesthetically sanctioned texts but also as a necessary means of providing cultural visibility. As John Guillory claims, even as he acknowledges the limitation of this viewpoint, "Canonical and noncanonical authors are supposed to *stand for* particular social groups, dominant or subordinate."[6] In a very real sense texts represent, quite simply, *representation*—the inclusion of viewpoints, desires, and lives as within the purview of the socially approved. In many anthologies forging a gay canon, one notes evidence of this desire for recognition among gay readers. Byrne Fone introduces his *Columbia Anthology of Gay Literature* with a call for the historical recognition of queer lives: "For most lesbians and gay people, writing has indeed been our history. What we wrote defined who we were and who we hoped to be. Our literature is therefore at once archive and the historical event."[7] In constructing his vision of a gay canon, Reed Woodhouse promotes certain texts to assist his readers in achieving the well-lived life, declaring, "My canon is not a mere list of good books or, despite its hubristic confidence, a prescription to authors of how or what they should write. It is rather an argument about how to be gay—how to lead a good life as a gay man."[8] Speaking to the canon's marginalization of lesbian experience, Lillian Faderman likewise expresses her ambition to find fiction representative of her experience: "I wanted 'real literature,' the kind I read in my English classes, to comment on the lifestyle I had just recently discovered with such enthusiasm, to reveal me to myself, to acknowledge the lesbian to the world."[9] Fone, Woodhouse, and Faderman collectively and singularly bestow canonicity upon various queer works in their volumes, yet—given the paradox of canon formation—even creating counter-canons reinforces the marginalization of some voices while creating space for others. No anthology has an endless page count.

Southern literature has witnessed unique vagaries within the overarching field of canon formation, with the regionalist designation *southern* delimiting these texts as simultaneously within yet outside the purview of U.S. literature. The question of what precisely defines southern literature exacerbates this problem, such that, in the introduction to his 1910 volume *The Literature of the South,* Montrose J. Moses observed that its parameters were amorphous to the point of meaninglessness: "Southern literature has, until recently, found itself handicapped through a deplorable lack of any discriminating standard by which to judge it."[10] Of course, no firm measures of a southern author's canonicity admit him or her into its ranks, nor does the canon clearly rank one author against another. (Is Twain or Faulkner the preeminent writer of the South?) The southern renaissance and the rise of southern modernism apparently clarified the status of various authors and texts. When surveying the field in 1996, almost a century after Moses, Fred Hobson claimed its well-marked parameters from the midcentury into approximately the 1970s: "A couple of decades ago, the boundaries of southern literature—and southern literary scholarship—appeared to be rather fixed and unchallenged. Simply stated, the major southern writers of this century were William Faulkner, Thomas Wolfe, Robert Penn Warren, Allen Tate, Eudora Welty, and perhaps Flannery O'Connor. The contemporary novelists to be reckoned with—besides Welty—were William Styron, Walker Percy, and perhaps John Barth."[11] In a 2006 essay Ed Piacentino identifies the canonical southern writers as Poe, Twain, Faulkner, O'Connor, McCullers, and Percy, which suggests that, as much as the ground may shift, certain totemic authors still preside over the rest.[12] Not surprisingly, advocates of gay inclusion have grown impatient with the lack of queer representation, as in Gary Richards's impassioned observation: "What has yet to be forcefully pointed out . . . is the comparative absence in this [southern literary] canon of gay and lesbian persons and/or writers centrally concerned with same-sex desire."[13] In studying the place of gay southern writers in the canon, one sees a gaping hole, and so the question then emerges of whether and with what to fill it.

Within the current contours of southern literature, the canon gravitates toward themes of history and tragedy, as well as toward a vision of humanity as constrained by wider social forces. To this end Farrell O'Gorman suggests in his analysis of the Agrarians: "The Southerner had a strong historical consciousness and a tragic sense of history; an awareness of human limitations and a particular suspicion of the Utopian promise of modern science."[14] These twin threads of southern canonicity—history blended with tragedy—do not readily align with comic sensibilities, nor necessarily with queer sensibilities that seek by their very expression to forge a new vision of human sexuality and thus to escape the tragic force of southern history. Still, in assessing the state of the southern literary canon, we are confronted with the opacity of aesthetics as a criterion for inclusion. Few of today's critics openly denounce gay or comic authors for their transgressions of southern gender (through their sexual orientations) or of literary form (through their humor), yet in constructing the canon critics rarely must justify their decisions beyond the ambiguous—and therefore obfuscating—realm of aesthetic judgment: one need only praise what is included, not disparage what is rejected, with the absence of these texts and authors speaking through their silence. Although several contemporary reviewers of Williams and Capote denigrated their work not due to its merits but simply because they were gay,[15] few scholars today attack gay authors for their sexuality, and few openly denigrate the comic as an inherently inferior literary mode.[16] It is nonetheless clear that relatively few queer southern humorists have joined the canon's fold.

Within this opaque realm of canon formation, certain signs indicate a given author's position in the field of southern literary studies. As a strategy of literary analysis, "bean-counting" does not usually elicit particularly impressive insights, yet it is relevant to mention that four common measures of literary reputation—academic journals dedicated to a single author,[17] citations in the Modern Language Association's International Bibliography,[18] publication in classroom anthologies,[19] and membership in the Fellowship of Southern Writers[20]—clearly elucidate the overarching marginalization of queer comic authors of the South. These observations illuminate the current construction of the southern literary canon in relation to precious perversions, yet the ground of literary studies forever shifts, with the likely possibility that various overlooked authors will find greater favor among new generations of readers.

Regarding the reception history of Williams, Capote, King, Brown, Allison, and Sedaris and their current positions in the southern literary canon, Williams stands above the rest in his canonicity, yet with his comic voice most muted. Quite simply, the lion's share of critical responses to Williams treat him as an outstanding dramatist, not as a camping wag, and so his status as an artist coincides in some degree with overlooking the comic subtexts of his corpus. In contrast, Capote's prominent position in popular culture is unquestioned, yet his place in the academy remains somewhat suspect. Cinematic biographies, including Bennett Miller's *Capote* (2005) and Douglas McGrath's *Infamous* (2006), have kept his tumultuous life in the public eye, but oddly, his celebrity overshadows his literary achievements in such tributes. Capote gained national attention early in his career for his precocious genius, winning awards for his short stories "Miriam" and "Shut a Final Door," yet later, at the height of his success, critical acclaim in the form of major awards eluded him. He was particularly disappointed that his masterpiece *In Cold Blood* failed to win the Pulitzer Prize for fiction or the National Book Award. Monographs on his corpus mostly provide overviews and introductory studies or consider his relation to cinema, Hollywood, and celebrity; to date, his fiction has not received the sustained critical inquiry given Twain, Faulkner, O'Connor, or others of their stature.[21]

The evidence suggests that King and Brown have not joined the southern literary canon and will not join its ranks in the future. King's *Confession of a Failed Southern Lady* and Brown's *Rubyfruit Jungle* stand as their most critically and commercially successful texts, yet these appear to offer insufficient ballast to support their authors' reputations. Furthermore, King has primarily written essays, and Brown moved from literary fiction to genre fiction. Again, such moves should not necessarily prohibit authors from the canon: essayists including Michel de Montaigne, Joseph Addison and Richard Steele, and Virginia Woolf were not debarred from admission for their belle-lettristic efforts. For the most part, however, canonical authors write serious literary fiction rather than essays, whether amusing or somber in tone. Genre fiction is even more widely disparaged, and I do not argue for Brown's inclusion in the southern literary canon based on her mystery novels. Still, it appears evident that part of King's and Brown's rejections as writers hinges on their political viewpoints—conservatism for King, and the irony of being insufficiently feminist for Brown—with little consideration paid to the merits of their most praiseworthy texts.

In contrast to King and Brown, Allison, with her breakthrough novel *Bastard Out of Carolina,* achieved an astonishing critical and commercial success, as well as, so it appears, a lasting place in the southern literary canon. *Bastard Out of Carolina* was a finalist for the 1992 National Book Award and won the Publishing Triangle's Ferro-Grumley Award for Lesbian Fiction; upon its twentieth anniversary, Penguin Books proclaimed it a Modern Classic and republished it in this influential series. The *New York Times* named her subsequent novel *Cavedweller* a Notable Book of 1998, and this book also received a Lambda Literary Award for Lesbian Fiction. Allison's critical success, however, appears pinned to a steadfast desire among readers to focus on the traumas of her fictions rather than on their pleasures, to overlook the bravado and laughter that provide a steady backdrop to the pain.

Sedaris's place in the annals of southern literature remains, in large part, to be written. To the best of my knowledge, this study is the first to place him within the field of southern literary studies, and his oscillating depictions of his geographic identity complicate his status as a southern writer, for he varyingly portrays himself as a transplanted northerner, as a southerner either despising or embracing his surroundings, and as a nomad traveling the globe to such destinations as England, France, Japan, and Australia. It further remains to be seen whether, as much as Sedaris stands as one of the most popular writers of the 1990s through the 2010s, he will ever be taken seriously. Comedy may be a disparaged form, but comic authors do not advance their cause when they dismiss their own efforts as fundamentally juvenile. Sedaris himself denies any meaning in his work beyond its humor: "My writing is just a desperate attempt to get laughs. If you get anything else out of it, it's an accident."[22] When wags disavow their art, it is challenging to disagree with them ("No, you're wrong! You're a serious artist!"), but Sedaris's account of his growth as an artist argues strongly against his cavalier presentation of his writings as being written solely to provoke laughter. For example, he now cringes at the thought of "SantaLand Diaries," his breakthrough essay that sparked his career: "In terms of the writing, it's probably the weakest writing I've ever done. I can't say enough bad things about it. I really can't."[23] It is ironic (yet not humorously so) that Sedaris derides the prose style of one of his undeniably funniest essays yet claims that laughter is his sole objective as a writer.

Any conclusions about the canon's formation and the future of southern literature must remain conjectural, but contradictions can be observed and questions posed. Foremost, one cannot simply suggest that comic authors are excluded, for, in assessing the role of humor in the formation of the southern literary canon, we find that comedic talents lie safely within its confines. Mark Twain's and Flannery O'Connor's comic voices did not preclude them from entry, and John Kennedy Toole's masterpiece *A Confederacy of Dunces* points to the tradition's embrace of a flagrantly queer and comic voice; his own precious perversions did not debar his entry into the canon (even if they did cost him his life).[24] In the Western tradition writ large, numerous voices are revered for their comic brio: Aristophanes, Chaucer, Molière, Pope, Austen, and Dickens, to name a few. The South's relationship to comic voices, however, is intertwined with the very necessity of creating a southern renaissance, in which the region's authors demanded respect for their talent and their literary sophistication. Thus, the South's sometimes hesitant embrace of comic literature bespeaks a regional need to define itself as an intellectual equal vis-à-vis the rest of the United States.

In this admittedly conjectural conclusion, recurring themes arise. The comic remains an aesthetically suspicious category when assessing literary merit, and the history of homosexuality in twentieth-century America coincides with a "coming out" of literary queerness. While Williams and Capote candidly discussed their sexualities throughout their careers, their texts in many ways encode issues of homosexuality and of camp humor, such that only knowing readers can decipher the inside jokes of queer culture. With fierce and fearless humor King and Brown spoke openly about women's homoerotic desire in the 1970s and 1980s, when even feminist circles largely rejected lesbianism as counterproductive to the advancement of women's equality. Allison and Sedaris, writing in the 1990s and beyond, address same-sex desire openly, yet Allison wins laurels for speaking of abuse, poverty, and trauma, with most critics simply ignoring her comic voice. Sedaris garners little respect within the academy as a subject of serious inquiry. By denigrating his writing as mere jokes, rather than by describing his artistry in weaving together complementary comic storylines that puncture the pretenses of southern and other culture, he apparently endorses his marginalization

In appraising the role of the comic in U.S. culture, William Faulkner, certainly one of the most canonical of twentieth-century southern authors, noted and regretted its absence: "We have one priceless universal trait, we Americans. That trait is our humor. What a pity it is that it is not more prevalent in our art."[25] As canons define cultures, however, people create canons, and the rich history of the South's creation is implicated within its literary roots, as Richard Gray persuasively intones: "Generations of Southerners have, I believe, been engaged not so much in writing about the South as in writing the South; they have, whether they have known it or not (and, as a matter of fact, many have known it) been busy reimagining and remaking their place in the act of seeing and describing it."[26] Williams, Capote, King, Brown, Allison, and Sedaris have written the queer South and thus have re-created it through their own imaginations. My own simple prescriptions for their admission into the southern literary canon are as follows: embrace Williams not merely for his dramas but for his campy humor, and recognize Capote as the major talent he is—both in relation to his comic voice and in his magpie style. King's *Confessions of a Failed Southern Lady* and Brown's *Rubyfruit Jungle* are underappreciated masterworks, detailing with joie de vivre the pleasures of lesbianism in literary romps rich in allusion and a keen awareness of their place in the annals of Western comedy; they also speak to their cultural moment in the women's movement. The southern literary canon has embraced Allison but for her trauma rather than for her humor, thus rehashing the stereotype of the lesbian as a victim of the South rather than as one of its comic victors. Southerners should recruit Sedaris into the fold as one of the region's defining voices, not merely in recognition of his comic talents but to maintain the vitality of its storytelling traditions as it moves into this new "postsouthern" phrase. I offer these endorsements not as a lone prophetic voice crying out in the wilderness but as a devoted reader of a rich southern literary legacy, one whose vitality dims without queer humor as one of its myriad defining features. The South offers a raucous legacy of queer laughter, yet one that is, for the most part, silenced within its overarching canon. Some people, it seems, just can't—or won't—take a joke.

Notes

INTRODUCTION

1. These rulings shifted the legal status of gay marriage across the nation, but before such judicial intervention, the prospects for advancing marital equality in the South looked bleak. Statistician Nate Silver, analyzing the region's demographic trends, predicted that the former Confederate States would be the last to grant marriage rights to their gay citizens ("How Opinion on Same Sex Marriage Is Changing, And What It Means," fivethirtyeight .blogs.nytimes.com, 26 Mar. 2013).

2. Carlos Dews, "Afterword," *Out in the South,* ed. Carlos Dews and Carolyn Leste Law (Philadelphia: Temple University Press, 2001), 236–40, at 238.

3. John Howard, *Men Like That: A Southern Queer History* (Chicago: University of Chicago Press, 1999); E. Patrick Johnson, *Sweet Tea: Black Gay Men of the South* (Chapel Hill: University of North Carolina Press, 2008); and Bernadette Barton, *Pray the Gay Away: The Extraordinary Lives of Bible Belt Gays* (New York: New York University Press, 2012). Additional such studies include Brock Thompson, *The Un-Natural State: Arkansas and the Queer South* (Fayetteville: University of Arkansas Press, 2010); Reta Ugena Whitlock, ed., *Queer South Rising: Voices of a Contested Place* (Charlotte: Information Age, 2013); and Angelia R. Wilson, *Below the Belt: Sexuality, Religion, and the American South* (London: Cassell, 2000), 125–56.

4. James T. Sears, *Rebels, Rubyfruits, and Rhinestones: Queering Space in the Stonewall South* (New Brunswick: Rutgers University Press, 2001), 4. See also his *Lonely Hunters: An Oral History of Lesbian and Gay Southern Life, 1948–1968* (Boulder, CO: Westview, 1997), as well as *Edwin and John: A Personal History of the American South* (New York: Routledge, 2009)—a fascinating study of a southern gay couple's life over the twentieth century.

5. Jennifer Rae Greeson, *Our South: Geographic Fantasy and the Rise of National Literature* (Cambridge, MA: Harvard University Press, 2010), 1. See also Tara McPherson, *Reconstructing Dixie: Race, Gender, and Nostalgia in the Imagined South* (Durham, NC: Duke University Press, 2003). On southern literature and its construction as a discourse of regionalism, see Richard Gray, *Southern Aberrations: Writers of the American South and the Problems of Regionalism* (Baton Rouge: Louisiana State University Press, 2000).

6. Stephen A. Smith, *Myth, Media, and the Southern Mind* (Fayetteville: University of Arkansas Press, 1985), 62.

7. Richard Dyer, *The Culture of Queers* (London: Routledge, 2002), 97.

8. John Howard, *Men Like That,* 5.

9. James R. Keller, "Tennessee Williams Doesn't Live Here Anymore: Hypocrisy, Paradox, and Homosexual Panic in the New/Old South," *Studies in Popular Culture* 19.2 (1996): 303–18.

10. Walker Percy, *Love in the Ruins* (New York: Picador, 1971), 19. For further analysis of Percy's treatment of homosexuality, see my *Queer Chivalry: Medievalism and the Myth of White Masculinity in Southern Literature* (Baton Rouge: Louisiana State University Press, 2013), 138–75. See also William Armstrong Percy III, "William Alexander Percy (1885–1942): His Homosexuality and Why It Matters," *Carryin' On in the Lesbian and Gay South,* ed. John Howard (New York: New York University Press, 1997), 75–92, for an exploration of Walker Percy's uncle, William Alexander Percy, and how his homosexuality affected the family.

11. Flannery O'Connor, *The Violent Bear It Away,* in *Three by Flannery O'Connor* (New York: Signet, 1983), 121–267, at 261.

12. In a letter to Elizabeth Fenwick Way, O'Connor writes, "That voice you object to is the Tempter, the Devil . . . and he becomes actualized as the man who gives Tarwater the lift toward the end" (*The Habit of Being,* ed. Sally Fitzgerald [New York: Farrar, Straus, & Giroux, 1979], 375).

13. James Dickey, *Deliverance* (Boston: Houghton Mifflin, 1970), 114. Pamela Barnett concludes in her study of the gender and sexual dynamics of *Deliverance* that the protagonist Ed "is threatened by his own femininity and by homosexuality" and that he "must vanquish the two if he is to live into the 1970s with his manhood intact" ("James Dickey's *Deliverance:* Southern, White, Suburban Male Nightmare or Dream Come True?" *Forum for Modern Language Studies* 40.2 [2004]: 145–59, at 145). Her analysis points to the ways in which authors frequently depict homosexuality as a narrative obstacle that their protagonists must overcome.

14. While this monograph focuses on issues of queer representation, one could also query Dickey's treatment of whiteness in *Deliverance,* in which "redneck" southerners represent an uncivilized savagery, in contrast to the button-down respectability of white, urban, southern masculinity. See Duane Carr's *A Question of Class: The Redneck Stereotype in Southern Fiction* (Bowling Green, OH: Bowling Green State University Popular Press, 1996), for a probing study of the ways in which stereotypical portrayals of "rednecks" prop up southern social codes of white normativity.

15. For Faulkner's elliptical treatment of homosexuality, see such representative studies as Betina Entzminger, "Passing as Miscegenation: Whiteness and Homoeroticism in Faulkner's *Absalom, Absalom!,*" *Faulkner Journal* 22.1–2 (2006–2007): 90–105; Nathan Tipton, "Rope and Faggot: The Homoerotics of Lynching in William Faulkner's *Light in August,*" *Mississippi Quarterly* 64.3–4 (2011): 369–91; and Christopher Peterson, "The Haunted House of Kinship: Miscegenation, Homosexuality, and Faulkner's *Absalom, Absalom!,*" *New Centennial Review* 4.1 (2004): 227–65. An insistent absence, Faulkner's queer themes weave throughout many of his narratives, imbuing them with much depth while hiding same-sex desire from plain view.

16. Michael Bibler, *Cotton's Queer Relations: Same-Sex Intimacy and the Literature of the Southern Plantation, 1936–1968* (Charlottesville: University of Virginia Press, 2009), 182–88.

17. Jaime Harker, "'And you too, sister, sister?': Lesbian Sexuality, *Absalom, Absalom!*, and the Reconstruction of the Southern Family," *Faulkner's Sexualities: Faulkner and Yoknapatawpha, 2007,* ed. Annette Trefzer and Ann Abadie (Jackson: University Press of Mississippi, 2010), 38–53, at 38.

18. See Francis Hutcheson, *Thoughts on Laughter, and Observations on the Fable of the Bees, in Six Letters* (Glasgow: Robert and Andrew Foults, 1758); Henri Bergson, *Laughter: An Essay on the Meaning of the Comic,* trans. Cloudesley Brereton and Fred Rothwell (London: Macmillan, 1921); and Sigmund Freud, *The Joke and Its Relation to the Unconscious,* trans. Joyce Crick (1905; New York: Penguin, 2003).

19. Sigmund Freud, "On Humour," *Collected Papers,* ed. James Strachey, vol. 5 (New York: Basic Books, 1959), 215–21, at 217.

20. Estimates of the Civil War dead vary. The prevailing wisdom counts their number at 620,000, but in a recent study, J. David Hacker posits that, based on an analysis of census data, the actual number ranges somewhere between 650,000 to 850,000 ("A Census-Based Count of the Civil War Dead," *Civil War History* 57.4 [2011]: 307–48, at 348). Despite this gruesome bloodshed, the Civil War has generated much humor, both during the years of the conflict and throughout its aftermath. See the studies of Wade Hall, *Reflections of the Civil War in Southern Humor* (Gainesville: University of Florida Press, 1962), and Cameron C. Nickels, *Civil War Humor* (Jackson: University of Mississippi Press, 2010). As Nickels postulates of the intersection of war and humor, "the point is not that this war, or any war, is laughable, but that humor provides a way of dealing with something so literally and figuratively devastating, even horrific" (ix).

21. Quintilian, *The Institutio Oratoria of Quintilian,* trans. H. E. Butler (Cambridge, MA: Harvard University Press, 1986), 9.2.44, at 401.

22. Søren Kierkegaard, *The Concept of Irony, with Constant Reference to Socrates,* trans. Lee Capel (Bloomington: Indiana University Press, 1965), 339. Various theorists have addressed the many ancillary topics surrounding irony, including its rhetorical tropes, semantics, ideological investments, and audiences. See such pivotal studies as D. C. Muecke, *The Compass of Irony* (London: Methuen, 1969); Wayne C. Booth, *A Rhetoric of Irony* (Chicago: University of Chicago Press, 1974); and Linda Hutcheon, *Irony's Edge: The Theory and Politics of Irony* (London: Routledge, 1994).

23. C. Vann Woodward, "The Irony of Southern History," *Journal of Southern History* 19.1 (1953): 3–19, at 7.

24. Mab Segrest, *My Mama's Dead Squirrel: Lesbian Essays on Southern Culture* (Ithaca, NY: Firebrand, 1985), 57.

25. Florence King, *Confessions of a Failed Southern Lady* (New York: St. Martin's, 1985), 232.

26. Robert Higgs, "Southern Humor: The Light and the Dark," *Thalia: Studies in Literary Humor* 6.2 (1983): 17–27. Higgs identifies ten primary tropes of southern humor, focusing in particular on the mountain humor of the Appalachians: love of tricks; delight in language; narrative form; oral delivery; comedy as opposed to satire; Calvinism; emphasis on irony as opposed to sentiment; deprecation; the absurd and the grotesque; and moral or theological enlightenment.

27. C. G. Parsons, *Inside View of Slavery: or, a Tour among the Planters* (Boston: Jewett, 1855), 135. This passage is quoted in Grady McWhiney, *Cracker Culture: Celtic Ways in the Old South* (Tuscaloosa: University of Alabama Press, 1988); see his chapter "Pleasures" (105–45) for further aspersions against the South's character.

28. Wade Hall, *The Smiling Phoenix: Southern Humor from 1865 to 1914* (Gainesville: University of Florida Press, 1965), 24.

29. Andrew Silver, *Minstrelsy and Murder: The Crisis of Southern Humor, 1835–1925* (Baton Rouge: Louisiana State University Press, 2006), 1–2.

30. Arthur Palmer Hudson, ed., *Humor of the Old Deep South* (New York: Macmillan, 1936), 4.

31. Simon Critchley, *On Humour* (London: Routledge, 2002), 68.

32. Roy Blount Jr., introduction to *Roy Blount's Book of Southern Humor,* ed. Roy Blount Jr. (New York: Norton, 1994), 19–35, at 23.

33. Blount includes in his anthology of southern humor Poe's "X-ing a Paragraph" (305–11), excerpts from Hurston's *Dust Tracks on a Road* (55–58) and *Mules and Men* (277–86), and Warren's "Last Laugh" (645–47) to exemplify these writers' interest in comic tones and themes.

34. Joseph Goodwin, *More Man Than You'll Ever Be: Gay Folklore and Acculturation in Middle America* (Bloomington: Indiana University Press, 1989), 20. For the use of humor in lesbian communities, see Chapter 4, which addresses Rita Mae Brown's comic sensibility and her engagement with lesbian and majoritarian communities.

35. Rod Martin, *The Psychology of Humor: An Integrative Approach* (Burlington, MA: Elsevier, 2007), 118.

36. Charles Flowers, ed., *Out, Loud, and Laughing: A Collection of Gay and Lesbian Humor* (New York: Anchor, 1995), ix.

37. Gloria Kaufman, ed., *In Stitches: A Patchwork of Feminist Humor and Satire* (Bloomington: Indiana University Press, 1991), viii.

38. Andrew Britton, "For Interpretation: Notes against Camp," *Camp: Queer Aesthetics and the Performing Subject: A Reader,* ed. Fabio Cleto (Ann Arbor: University of Michigan Press, 1999), 136–42, at 138.

39. Ralph Ellison, "An Extravagance of Laughter," *The Collected Essays of Ralph Ellison,* ed. John F. Callahan (New York: Modern Library, 1995), 613–58, at 614–15.

40. Janet Winn, "Capote, Mailer, and Miss Parker," *New Republic* 9 Feb. 1959: 27–28, at 27. Capote used this barb earlier, in a 1957 interview, when discussing writers who lack a distinct style: "But yes, there *is* such an animal as a nonstylist. Only they're not writers. They're typists" (Pati Hill, "The Art of Fiction XVII: Truman Capote," *Paris Review* 16 [1957]: 34–51, at 47).

41. Florence King, *Confessions of a Failed Southern Lady,* 119.

42. Florence King, *Lump It or Leave It* (New York: St. Martin's, 1990), 162. Italics original. All italics included in quoted material throughout this book are those of the cited author.

43. In this study's foundational irony, I do not address a definitive work of twentieth-century queer southern humor: John Kennedy Toole's *A Confederacy of Dunces.* This novel's carnivalesque humor and play with southern codes of masculinity inspired a chapter in my previous monograph in southern literary studies: "'It's prolly fulla dirty stories': Queer Masculinity and Masturbatory Allegory in John Kennedy Toole's *A Confederacy of Dunces*" (*Queer Chivalry,* 83–111). Contemplating Toole's humor and the cultural conditions that motivated his suicide spurred me to undertake this project.

44. Donna Jo Smith, "Queering the South: Constructions of Southern/Queer Identity," in Howard, *Carryin' On in the Lesbian and Gay South,* 370–85, at 380.

45. George Whitmore, "George Whitmore Interviews Tennessee Williams," *Gay Sunshine Interviews,* ed. Winston Leyland, vol. 1 (San Francisco: Gay Sunshine Press, 1978), 309–25, at 320.

46. Rochelle Girson, "'48's Nine," *Saturday Review of Literature* 12 Feb. 1949: 12–14, at 14.

47. Florence King, *STET, Damnit! The Misanthrope's Corner, 1991 to 2002* (New York: National Review, 2003), 41.

48. Florence King, *Reflections in a Jaundiced Eye* (New York: St. Martin's, 1989), 47. She further explained, "Of all the benefits of spinsterhood, the greatest is carte blanche. Once a woman is called 'that crazy old maid' she can get away with anything" (50).

49. Patricia Holt, "Rita Mae Brown," *Publishers Weekly* 2 Oct. 1978: 16–17.

50. Lania Knight, "A Conversation with David Sedaris," *Missouri Review* 30.1 (2007): 72–89, at 81.

51. Dorothy Allison, *Skin: Talking about Sex, Class, and Literature* (Ithaca, NY: Firebrand, 1994), 212.

52. E. B. White and Katherine S. White, eds., *A Subtreasury of American Humor* (New York: Coward-McCann, 1941), xvii.

53. Roy Blount Jr., introduction to *Roy Blount's Book of Southern Humor,* 21.

CHAPTER ONE

Note to epigraphs: Quotations from *A Streetcar Named Desire* (563) and *Cat on a Hot Tin Roof* (903) are taken from *Tennessee Williams: Plays,* vol. 1, *1937–1955* (New York: Library of America, 2000). Quotation from *Suddenly, Last Summer* (140) is from *Tennessee Williams: Plays,* vol. 2, *1957–1980* (New York: Library of America, 2000). All quotations from Williams's plays in this chapter are from these two volumes. Italics are Williams's own.

1. Susan Sontag, "Notes on 'Camp,'" *Against Interpretation and Other Essays* (New York: Delta, 1966), 275–92, at 275.

2. David Savran, *A Queer Sort of Materialism: Recontextualizing American Theater* (Ann Arbor: University of Michigan Press, 2003), 171.

3. Charles Brooks, "Williams' Comedy," *Tennessee Williams: A Tribute,* ed. Jac Tharpe (Jackson: University Press of Mississippi, 1977), 720–35, at 720.

4. Christopher Isherwood, *The World in the Evening* (1952; Minneapolis: University of Minnesota Press, 1999), 110.

5. Susan Sontag, "Notes on 'Camp,'" 279.

6. Susan Sontag, "Notes on 'Camp,'" 284.

7. Mark Booth, "*Campe-Toi!* On the Origins and Definitions of Camp," *Camp: Queer Aesthetics and the Performing Subject,* ed. Fabio Cleto (Ann Arbor: University of Michigan Press, 1999), 66–79, at 69.

8. Moe Meyer, "Reclaiming the Discourse of Camp," *The Politics and Poetics of Camp,* ed. Moe Meyer (Routledge: London: 1994), 1–22, at 5.

9. Kathryn Conrad, "The Politics of Camp," *Deviant Acts: Essays on Queer Performance,* ed. David Cregan (Dublin: Carysfort, 2009), 25–36, at 33.

10. Tennessee Williams, *Memoirs* (1972; New York: New Directions, 2006), 50.

11. Tennessee Williams, *Memoirs,* 50.

12. George Whitmore, "George Whitmore Interviews Tennessee Williams," *Gay Sunshine Interviews,* ed. Winston Leyland, vol. 1 (San Francisco: Gay Sunshine Press, 1978), 309–25, at 315.

13. Donald Spoto, *The Kindness of Strangers: The Life of Tennessee Williams* (Boston: Little Brown, 1985), 51–52. For Smith's account of his friendship with Williams, see his *My Friend Tom: The Poet-Playwright Tennessee Williams* (Jackson: University Press of Mississippi, 2012).

14. George Whitmore, "George Whitmore Interviews Tennessee Williams," 318.

15. Tennessee Williams, *Memoirs,* 83.

16. Moe Meyer, *An Archaeology of Posing: Essays on Camp, Drag, and Sexuality* (United States: Macater, 2010), 39.

17. George Whitmore, "George Whitmore Interviews Tennessee Williams," 315.

18. Lyle Leverich, *Tom: The Unknown Tennessee Williams* (New York: Crown, 1995), 554.

19. George Whitmore, "George Whitmore Interviews Tennessee Williams," 312.

20. George Whitmore, "George Whitmore Interviews Tennessee Williams," 322.

21. Kate Davy, "Fe/Male Impersonation: The Discourse of Camp," in Meyer, *The Politics and Poetics of Camp,* 130–48, at 141.

22. Arthur B. Waters, "Tennessee Williams: Ten Years Later," *Theater Arts* July 1955: 72–73+, at 73. In another interview, Williams qualified his assessment of Brick's sexuality: "Was Brick homosexual? He probably—no, I would even say quite certainly—went no further in physical expression than clasping Skipper's hand across the space between their twin beds in hotel rooms —and yet his sexual nature was not innately 'normal'" (Tennessee Williams, *Where I Live: Selected Essays,* ed. Christine Day and Bob Woods [New York: New Directions, 1978], 72). Williams rightly refused to give pat answers to such questions about his plays, preferring for their ambiguity to encourage audiences to reflect further on the mysteries of the human condition.

23. Philippe Sollers, "Lettre de Sade," *Tel Quel* 61 (Spring 1975): 14–20, at 20.

24. Leopold von Sacher-Masoch, *Venus in Furs,* in *Masochism,* ed. Gilles Deleuze (New York: Zone, 1991), 141–293, at 255 and 266.

25. Gilles Deleuze, *Coldness and Cruelty,* in Deleuze, *Masochism,* 9–138, at 89. It should be noted as well that Deleuze argues against the very concept of sadomasochism, deriding it as "pseudomasochism" (124) and as a "semiological howler" (134). He is, of course, correct that Sade and Sacher-Masoch write from contrasting perspectives, as he also delineates the shaky psychological foundations of this concept. Sadomasochism nonetheless exists within the wider cultural imaginary, and Williams depicts the union of these psychic and sexual drives as complementary. Artists need not strictly adhere to the psychoanalytic paradigms of literary scholars to facilitate the seamless application of these theories to their works.

26. Tennessee Williams, *Collected Stories* (New York: New Directions, 1985); citations of this story are indicated parenthetically.

27. Nathan Tipton, "What's Eating Anthony Burns? Dismembering the Bodies That Matter in Tennessee Williams's 'Desire and the Black Masseur,'" *Southern Literary Journal* 43.1 (2010): 39–58, at 40.

28. Annette Saddik, "The (Un)Represented Fragmentation of the Body in Tennessee Williams's 'Desire and the Black Masseur' and *Suddenly, Last Summer,*" *Modern Drama* 41 (1998): 347–54, at 348.

29. For additional studies of "Desire and the Black Masseur," see Brian Peters, "Queer Semiotics of Expression: Gothic Language and Homosexual Destruction in Tennessee Williams's 'One Arm' and 'Desire and the Black Masseur,'" *Tennessee Williams Annual Review* 8 (2006): 109–21; Paul Hurley, "Williams' 'Desire and the Black Masseur': An Analysis," *Studies in Short Fiction* 2 (1964): 51–55; and David Savran's chapter "Eat Me," from *A Queer Sort of Materialism* (170–79). None of these essays comment on the story's farcical humor.

30. It is possible that in these lines Williams refers to Burns's ejaculation rather than to his erection, especially with the reference to the "feeling of pleasure" that "swept as a liquid

from either end of his body." Still, this pleasure travels "into the tingling hollow of his groin"—not out of it. Whether these lines refer to an erection or an ejaculation, the humor of the story persists.

31. William Shakespeare, *Titus Andronicus, The Riverside Shakespeare: The Complete Works,* ed. G. Blakemore Evans, 2nd ed. (Boston: Houghton Mifflin, 1997), 1065–100, at Act 3, sc. 1, l. 233.

32. Edward Gordon Craig, *Index to the Story of My Days* (London: Hulton, 1957), 125.

33. Carol Warren, *Madwives: Schizophrenic Women in the 1950s* (New Brunswick, NJ: Rutgers University Press, 1987), 17.

34. For the foundational study of erotic triangles, see Eve Sedgwick, *Between Men: English Literature and Male Homosocial Desire* (New York: Columbia University Press, 1985).

35. Tennessee Williams, *Memoirs,* 170.

36. John Waters, *Role Models* (New York: Farrar, Straus, & Giroux, 2010), 36.

37. Nick Mansfield, *Masochism: The Art of Power* (Westport, CT: Praeger, 1997), 25.

38. Walter Braun, *The Cruel and the Meek: Aspects of Sadism and Masochism,* trans. N. Meyer (New York: Lyle Stuart, 1967), 122.

39. Kathryn Lee Seidel, *The Southern Belle in the American Novel* (Tampa: University of South Florida Press, 1985), 169.

40. On the relationship between the two plays, see Lyle Leverich, *Tom: The Unknown Tennessee,* 437.

41. William Free, "Camp Elements in the Plays of Tennessee Williams," *Southern Quarterly* 21.2 (1983): 16–23, at 18–19; cf. Sontag, "Notes on 'Camp,'" 279.

42. Slavoj Žižek, *The Metastases of Enjoyment: Six Essays on Women and Causality* (1994; London: Verso, 2005), 91. Žižek further explains, "Masochism, on the contrary, is made to the measure of the victim: it is the victim (the servant in the masochistic relationship) who initiates a contract with the Master (woman), authorizing her to humiliate him in any way she considers appropriate (within the terms defined by the contract) and binding himself to act 'according to the whims of the sovereign lady'" (92). Contracts are recurring themes in Williams's plays, as evident in such scenes as Chicken's plan in *Kingdom of Earth* to inherit his brother's land: "You remember that agreement between us, witnessed, signed, notarized, giving the place to me when you take the one-way trip to the kingdom of heaven?" (2:650). Likewise, in *Sweet Bird of Youth,* Chance repeatedly mentions his legal obligations: "But I guess the contract we signed is full of loopholes?" (2:175), he hopes, but later admits, "I am now under personal contract to her" (2:213).

43. For exemplary readings of Brick's ambiguous sexuality, see John Bak, "'Sneakin' and Spyin' from Broadway to the Beltway: Cold War Masculinity, Brick, and Homosexual Existentialism," *Theatre Journal* 56 (2004): 225–49, and Mark Royden Winchell, "Come Back to the Locker Room Ag'in, Brick Honey," *Mississippi Quarterly* 48.4 (1995): 701–12.

44. Alan Sinfield, *Out on Stage: Lesbian and Gay Theatre in the Twentieth Century* (New Haven, CT: Yale University Press, 1999), 192.

45. Kevin Ohi, "Devouring Creation: Cannibalism, Sodomy, and the Scene of Analysis in *Suddenly, Last Summer,*" *Cinema Journal* 38.3 (1999): 27–49, at 39. Ohi focuses on the film in this essay, yet most of his points apply to the play as well.

46. Italo Calvino, *The Literature Machine: Essays,* trans. Patrick Creagh (1982; London: Secker & Warburg, 1987), 66–67.

CHAPTER TWO

1. E. B. White and Katherine S. White, eds., *A Subtreasury of American Humor* (New York: Coward-McCann, 1941), xviii.

2. For example, in *Truman Capote* (New York: Frederick Ungar, 1980), Helen S. Garson mentions *Beat the Devil* only in passing (8), and Kenneth T. Reed, in his *Truman Capote* (Boston: Twayne, 1981), describes the madcap writing process of the film rather than how it illuminates Capote's oeuvre (27). In *Truman Capote—Enfant Terrible* (New York: Continuum, 2008), Robert Emmet Long offers a brief review of the film, reading it as a parody, a "sendup of Huston's earlier work" (61–64, at 62).

3. Cynthia Morrill, "Revamping the Gay Sensibility," *The Politics and Poetics of Camp,* ed. Moe Meyer (London: Routledge, 1994), 110–29, at 119.

4. Donald Windham, *Lost Friendships: A Memoir of Truman Capote, Tennessee Williams, and Others* (New York: Morrow, 1987), 32.

5. Tennessee Williams, *Memoirs* (1972; New York: New Directions, 2006), 150.

6. Tennessee Williams, *Memoirs,* 151.

7. Capote's nickname "Tiny Terror" resonates as a core part of his persona, as evident in such publications as Patricia Burstein, "Tiny, Yes, But a Terror? Do Not Be Fooled by Truman Capote in Repose," *People* 10 May 1976: 12–17.

8. Gerald Clarke, "Petronus Americanus: The Ways of Gore Vidal," *Atlantic* Mar. 1972: 44–51, at 46.

9. Mary Vespa, "Sued by Gore Vidal and Stung by Lee Radziwill, A Wounded Truman Capote Lashes Back at the Dastardly Duo," *People* 25 June 1979: 34–36, at 35.

10. Gerald Clarke, ed., *Too Brief a Treat: The Letters of Truman Capote* (New York: Vintage, 2004), 441.

11. Lawrence Grobel, *Conversations with Capote* (New York: New American Library, 1985), 172.

12. C. Robert Jennings, "Truman Capote Talks, Talks, Talks," *New York* 13 May 1968: 53–55, at 53 and 55.

13. Truman Capote, *The Dogs Bark: Public People and Private Places* (New York: Random House, 1973), 353.

14. Gloria Steinem, "'Go right ahead and ask me anything': And So She Did," *McCall's* Nov. 1967: 76+, at 148.

15. Truman Capote, *The Grass Harp and A Tree of Night and Other Stories* (1952; New York: Vintage, 1993).

16. Truman Capote, *Breakfast at Tiffany's and Three Stories* (1950; New York: Vintage, 1986).

17. Northrop Frye, *Anatomy of Criticism: Four Essays* (Princeton, NJ: Princeton University Press, 1957), 180.

18. The film is based on James Helvick's novel *Beat the Devil* (Philadelphia: Lippincott, 1951); Helvick is the pen name of Claud Cockburn. For Capote's work with Selznick and De Sica on *Indiscretion of an American Wife* and for the state of *Beat the Devil* prior to his hire, see my *Truman Capote: A Literary Life at the Movies* (Athens: University of Georgia Press, 2014), 45–61. I briefly consider camp elements of *Beat the Devil* in *Truman Capote*; this chapter expands the previous discussion and extends it to an analysis of how camp humor influences interpretations of Capote's literature.

19. Don Lee Keith, "An Interview with Truman Capote," *Contempora* Oct.–Nov. 1970: 36–40, at 38.

20. For John Huston's account of this wrestling match, see his autobiography *An Open Book* (New York: Knopf, 1980), 247; for Capote's version, see Gloria Steinem, "Go right ahead," 149.

21. Roger Ebert, "Beat the Devil," rogerebert.com, 26 Nov. 2000. Ebert's defense of *Beat the Devil*'s campiness contrasts with Susan Sontag's critique. In her groundbreaking 1964 essay "Notes on Camp," she derides *Beat the Devil* for "want[ing] so badly to be campy that [it is] continually losing the beat," positing that "intending to be campy is always harmful" (*Against Interpretation and Other Essays* [New York: Delta, 1966], 275–92, at 282).

22. Peter Barnes, "The Director on Horseback," *Quarterly of Film, Radio, and Television* 10.3 (1956): 281–87, at 281 and 285.

23. B. G. Marple, review of *Beat the Devil, Films in Review* Mar. 1953: 143–44, at 144.

24. Lindsay Anderson, "In Brief: *Beat the Devil,*" *Sight & Sound* 23 (Jan.–Mar. 1954): 147–48, at 148.

25. "Review of *Beat the Devil,*" *Film Society Review* Jan. 1966: 13.

26. Roger Ebert, "Beat the Devil."

27. Susan Sontag, "Notes on 'Camp,'" 280.

28. Fabio Cleto, "Introduction: Queering the Camp," *Camp: Queer Aesthetics and the Performing Subject: A Reader,* ed. Fabio Cleto (Ann Arbor: University of Michigan Press, 1999), 1–48, at 25.

29. As mentioned in Chapter 1, Sontag saw Lollobrigida as an incarnation of excessive—and thus campy—femininity, citing "the corny flamboyant femaleness of Jayne Mansfield, Gina Lollobrigida, Jane Russell, Virginia Mayo; the exaggerated he-man-ness of Steve Reeves, Victor Mature" (Sontag, "Notes on 'Camp,'" 279).

30. Neil Bartlett, *Who Was That Man? A Present for Oscar Wilde* (Bristol, England: Serpent's Tongue, 1988), 171.

31. Pati Hill, "The Art of Fiction XVII: Truman Capote," *Paris Review* 16 (1957): 34–51, at 45.

32. Gerald Clarke, *Too Brief a Treat,* 215 and 217; cf. John Malcolm Brinnin, *Truman Capote: Dear Heart, Old Buddy* (New York: Delacourte, 1981), 83.

33. Rudolph Elie Jr., "*Other Voices* a Very Fine First Novel," *Boston Herald* 25 Feb. 1948: 15.

34. According to the *Oxford English Dictionary,* an ancillary definition of *lavender* is "effeminacy; homosexuality or homosexual tendencies."

35. Richard Boulton, "Lavender Pastiche: Review of *Other Voices, Other Rooms,*" *Hartford Courant Magazine* 15 Feb. 1948: 12.

36. R. J. D., review of *Other Voices, Other Rooms, Boston Daily Globe* 21 Jan. 1948: 15.

37. Charles Rolo, "The South and the Psyche," *Atlantic* Mar. 1948: 108–10, at 109.

38. Jesse Cross, review of *Other Voices, Other Rooms, Library Journal* 1 Dec. 1947: 1685.

39. Carlos Baker, "Deep-South Guignol: Review of *Other Voices, Other Rooms,*" *New York Times Book Review* 18 Jan. 1948: L 5.

40. Truman Capote, *Other Voices, Other Rooms* (1948; New York: Vintage, 1975).

41. Jerry Leath Mills, "The Dead Mule Rides Again," *Southern Cultures* 6.4 (2000): 11–34, at 23.

42. Avril Horner and Sue Zlosnik, *Gothic and the Comic Turn* (Hampshire: Palgrave Macmillan, 2005), 15.

43. Selma Robinson, "The Legend of 'Little T,'" *PM Picture News* 14 Mar. 1948: 6–8, at 8.

44. Review of *Other Voices, Other Rooms, Newsweek* 26 Jan. 1948: 9.

45. Martin Bucco, "Truman Capote and the Country below the Surface," *Four Quarters* Nov. 1957: 22–25, at 22.

46. Rochelle Girson, "'48's Nine," *Saturday Review of Literature* 12 Feb. 1949: 12–14, at 13; cf. Martin Bucco, "Truman Capote and the Country below the Surface," 22.

47. Roy Newquist, *Counterpoint* (Chicago: Rand McNally, 1964), 80.

48. Eric Norden, "*Playboy* Interview: Truman Capote," *Playboy* Mar. 1968: 51+, at 53.

49. Harold Beaver, "Homosexual Signs (In Memory of Roland Barthes)," *Camp: Queer Aesthetics and the Performing Subject,* 160–78, at 165.

50. Richard Spears documents the symbolic connection between *bird* and *penis,* as in the common vulgarity "to flip the bird"; he dates this usage to the 1800s (*Slang and Euphemism* [Middle Village, NY: Jonathan David, 1981], 29).

51. Richard Spears, *Slang and Euphemism,* 70.

52. It should be noted that the *OED* dates this use to 1977, from Eric James Trimmer, *A Visual Dictionary of Sex:* "A ring through the glans . . . is known as the Prince Albert or dressing ring. This type, according to tradition, was used in Victorian times to secure the penis in the right or left trouser leg." Although nearly thirty years span between Capote's use of the term "Prince Albert" in *Other Voices, Other Rooms* and Trimmer's definition of it, it must have circulated prior to 1977. Trimmer does not claim his definition ex nihilo; rather, he simply labels it as commonly known. Elayne Angel, while not specifying a date for the origin of the Prince Albert, states: "In the world of modern body piercing, the Prince Albert is a historic piercing, not because Queen Victoria's consort wore one—he didn't. It is because during the early years of modern body piercing, the PA was the most popular male genital piercing. Many heavily pierced men describe the Prince Albert as their favorite" (*The Piercing Bible: The Definitive Guide to Safe Body Piercing* [Berkeley, CA: Crossing Press, 2009], 156). Prince Albert piercings circulated in the underground world of gay culture long before Trimmer's definition, and it stretches credulity to think that Capote used this term without understanding its relevance to his storyline. I am indebted to Christina Guillén, who first brought to my attention the relevance of piercing culture to Capote's novel.

53. Diana Trilling, "Fiction in Review," *Nation* 31 Jan. 1949: 133–34, at 134.

54. Leslie Fiedler, "The Profanation of the Child," *New Leader* 23 June 1958: 26–29, at 27. With an odd and backhanded compliment that questions the author's sanity, Fiedler praised Capote's treatment of children in *A Tree of Night and Other Stories:* "Capote has . . . an honest tenderness toward those of his characters he can understand (children and psychotics)" ("Capote's Tales," *Nation* 2 Apr. 1949: 395–96, at 395).

55. Andre Leon Talley, "An Afternoon with Truman Capote," *W* 23–30 July 1976: 8

56. Gerald Clarke, "Checking in with Truman Capote," *Esquire* Nov. 1972: 136+, at 137 and 187.

57. Truman Capote, *Answered Prayers: The Unfinished Novel* (New York: Random House, 1987).

58. Andrew Britton, "For Interpretation: Notes against Camp," in Cleto, *Camp: Queer Aesthetics and the Performing Subject,* 136–42, at 138. Among the controversies of camp, however, is the very question of its potential variability, with some camp theorists arguing that it is inherently a static, conservative mode, as Quentin Crisp himself explains: "The

strange thing about 'camp' is that it has become fossilized. The mannerisms have never changed. If I were now to see a woman sitting with her knees clamped together, one hand on her hip and the other lightly touching her back hair, I should think, 'Either she scored her last social triumph in 1926 or it is a man in drag'" (*The Naked Civil Servant* [1968; New York: Penguin, 1997], 21).

59. Gordon Merrick, "How to Write Lying Down," *New Republic* 8 Dec. 1958: 23–24, at 23.

60. Linda Mizejewski, "Camp among the Swastikas: Isherwood, Sally Bowles, and 'Good Heter Stuff,'" in Cleto, *Camp: Queer Aesthetics and the Performing Subject*, 237–53, at 238.

61. Gerald Clarke, "Checking in with Truman Capote," 188.

62. Eric Norden, "*Playboy* Interview: Truman Capote," 56.

63. Andy Warhol, "Sunday with Mister C.: An Audiodocumentary by Andy Warhol Starring Truman Capote," *Truman Capote: Conversations*, ed. M. Thomas Inge (Jackson: University Press of Mississippi, 1987), 236–95, at 260–61.

64. Truman Capote, *The Dogs Bark*, 417.

65. Truman Capote, *The Dogs Bark*, 411.

CHAPTER THREE

1. Quotations of Florence King's writings are taken from the following editions: *Southern Ladies and Gentleman* (1975; New York: St. Martin's Griffin, 1993); *WASP, Where Is Thy Sting?* (New York: Stein & Day, 1977); *He: An Irreverent Look at the American Male* (New York: Stein & Day, 1978); *When Sisterhood Was in Flower* (New York: Viking, 1982); *Confessions of a Failed Southern Lady* (New York: St. Martin's, 1985); *Reflections in a Jaundiced Eye* (New York: St. Martin's, 1989); *Lump It or Leave It* (New York: St. Martin's, 1990); *With Charity toward None: A Fond Look at Misanthropy* (New York: St. Martin's, 1992); *STET, Damnit! The Misanthrope's Corner, 1991 to 2002* (New York: National Review, 2003); and *Deja Reviews: Florence King All Over Again: Selections from* National Review *and* The American Spectator*, 1990–2001* (Wilmington, DE: Intercollegiate Studies Institute, 2006). Quotations of King's texts are cited parenthetically, with the following abbreviations—*SL, WW, H, SF, CF, RJ, LI, WC, SD,* and *DR*—aligning with the above titles. All italics in quotations of King are her own.

2. Kenneth Cimino, *Gay Conservatives: Group Consciousness and Assimilation* (New York: Harrington Park, 2007), 6.

3. For example, many queers have pointed out the bias latent in scientific attempts to discover the root causes of homosexuality: because few complementary efforts seek to pinpoint heterosexuality's origins, studies of homosexuality's roots, in effect, stigmatize queerness as unnatural, as an aberration from the assumed normativity of heterosexuality. See Timothy Murphy, *Gay Science: The Ethics of Sexual Orientation Research* (New York: Columbia University Press, 1997).

4. Because gay conservatives desire the tax cuts invariably promised by the political right, this line of thinking proposes, they vote for their financial interests rather than for sexual equality. Even commentators who rebut this "filthy lucre" hypothesis of queer conservatism indulge in other ad hominem attacks. Paul Robinson, in discussing the conservatism of various gay cultural commentators, concludes, "If they are guilty of any sin, it is not grubby materialism but a perhaps understandable historical shortsightedness and ingratitude to-

ward the achievements of the men and women of the Stonewall generation who made their very existence possible" (*Queer Wars: The New Gay Right and Its Critics* [Chicago: University of Chicago Press, 2005], 8). Absolving queer conservatives of greed while accusing them of ingratitude, Robinson's otherwise intriguing analysis glosses over the possibility of any deeply held philosophical convictions behind their political beliefs.

5. Determining the percentage of gay people who identify as conservative is challenging, but in reviewing data from the 2012 presidential election the *New York Times* reports, "Exit polls showed that 76 percent of voters who identified as gay supported Mr. Obama last week, and that 22 percent supported Mr. Romney" (Micah Cohen, "Gay Vote Proved a Boon for Obama," *New York Times,* 15 Nov. 2012). These figures roughly match those of a Gallup poll of October 2012, which concludes that whereas "45% of LGBT individuals describe their political views as liberal or very liberal, one in five (20%) describe themselves as conservative or very conservative" (Gary Gates and Frank Newport, "Gallup Special Report: The LGBT Vote in the 2012 Presidential Election," The Williams Institute of UCLA Law School, Oct. 2012, williamsinstitute.law.ucla.edu).

6. Michel Foucault, *The History of Sexuality: An Introduction,* trans. Robert Hurley (1976; New York: Vintage, 1990), 157.

7. Milton Friedman, "Defining Principles: Capitalism and Freedom," *Conservatism in America since 1930,* ed. Gregory Schneider (New York: New York University Press, 2003), 69–90, at 70.

8. F. A. Hayek, "Resurrecting the Abandoned Road," *Conservatism in America since 1930,* 53–65, at 60.

9. José Esteban Muñoz, *Disidentifications: Queers of Color and the Performance of Politics* (Minneapolis: University of Minnesota Press, 1999), 97. It should be noted that Muñoz's analysis focuses on, as his subtitle indicates, queers of color, including such performers as African American drag queen Vaginal Creme Davis. Applying his ideas to a defiantly Wasp figure such as King thus redirects them to the hegemonic culture against which such performers are reacting. Nonetheless, Muñoz recognizes that majoritarian subjects also employ disidentificatory strategies (5), and his model of a triangulation of identity, in which identification and counteridentification fail and identity is constructed in reaction to and through appropriations of mainstream culture, is certainly in play in King's humor.

10. Stephen A. Smith, "The Rhetoric of Southern Humor," *The Future of Southern Letters,* ed. Jefferson Humphries and John Lowe (New York: Oxford University Press, 1996), 170–85, at 180.

11. Nancy Walker and Zita Dresner, eds., *Redressing the Balance: American Women's Literary Humor from Colonial Times to the 1980s* (Jackson: University Press of Mississippi, 1988), xxii.

12. Regina Barreca, ed., *Last Laughs: Perspectives on Women and Comedy* (New York: Gordon & Breach, 1988), 15.

13. Margaret Cho, *I Have Chosen to Stay and Fight* (New York: Riverhead, 2005), 93.

14. Many critics dismiss essentialism as indicative of lax analysis, such as Stephan Fuchs's position that "Essentialism makes either/or distinctions, rather than variable distinctions in degree. It posits polar opposites, instead of gradations and empirical continua" (*Against Essentialism: A Theory of Culture and Society* [Cambridge, MA: Harvard University Press, 2001], 13). Diana Fuss's powerful analysis of essentialism—"in and of itself, essentialism is

neither good nor bad, progressive nor reactionary, beneficial nor dangerous"—creates a space for its rigorous study, which is particularly relevant for studies of women and humor (*Essentially Speaking: Feminism, Nature, and Difference* [New York: Routledge, 1989], xi).

15. Sean Zwagerman, *Wit's End: Women's Humor as Rhetorical and Performative Strategy* (Pittsburgh, PA: University of Pittsburgh Press, 2010), 6

16. Nancy Walker, *A Very Serious Thing: Women's Humor and American Culture* (Minneapolis: University of Minnesota Press, 1988), 7–8.

17. King's publications in *Ms.* include "Sex and the Good Ole Boy," July 1975: 53+, and "Benched: Life after Sex," May 1989: 43–45.

18. In her analyses of gender and performativity, Judith Butler argues that the enactments of gender codes, through their repeated citations, accrete into cultural meaning. As she states, "If gender is performative, then it follows that the reality of gender is itself produced as an effect of that performance. Although there are norms that govern what will and will not be real, and what will and will not be intelligible, they are called into question and reiterated at the moment in which performativity begins its citational practice" (*Undoing Gender* [New York: Routledge, 2004], 218).

19. See Laura Buchanan, *The Barbarian Princess* (New York: Berkley, 1978); the novel's front matter identifies King as the copyright holder.

20. For more on the Feminist Sex Wars, see the discussion in Chapter 5 of Dorothy Allison's defense of her sexual desires and practices.

21. Andrea Dworkin, *Right-Wing Women* (New York: Coward-McCann, 1982), 83–84.

22. Robin Morgan, *The Word of a Woman: Feminist Dispatches, 1968–1992* (New York: Norton, 1991), 88; italics in original.

23. Pat Califia, "Gay Men, Lesbians, and Sex: Doing It Together," *The Columbia Reader on Lesbians and Gay Men in Media, Society, and Politics,* ed. Larry Gross and James D. Woods (New York: Columbia University Press, 1999), 92–96, at 95.

24. Joan Nestle, "My Mother Liked to Fuck," in Gross and Woods, *The Columbia Reader on Lesbians and Gay Men in Media, Society, and Politics,* 505–06, at 506, 505.

25. Jaime Harker, "'And you too, sister, sister?' Lesbian Sexuality, *Absalom, Absalom!,* and the Reconstruction of the Southern Family," *Faulkner's Sexualities: Faulkner and Yoknapatawpha, 2007,* ed. Annette Trefzer and Ann Abadie (Jackson: University of Mississippi Press, 2010), 38–53, at 38.

26. It should be noted that King does not use the term "a little funny" only to describe gay men, such as in her account of one of her heterosexual lovers: "Being an introvert also gives him time to think, to explore the facets of his personality and to plumb the depths of his sexuality—things that are impossible to do on the golf course. Sometimes he is 'a little funny' when measured against the Regular Guy norm, but he is also lots of fun" (*H* 162). Nonetheless, in the preponderance of King's uses of the phrase, as in the reference to Bonnie Prince Charlie, she clearly refers to homosexuality.

27. In King's satire of southerners seeking to ascertain their queerly aristocratic lineage, it matters little whether Charles Edward Stuart (a.k.a. Bonnie Prince Charlie) was indeed homosexual, for her perception of him as "a little funny" inflects with queerness both him and the southern women who venerate him. This chapter focuses on King's construction of the South and its sexual hysterics, not on the possible homosexuality of members of the Stuart clan or the

legitimacy of their claims to the English throne. It is nonetheless relevant to mention that the historical record attests that Stuart fathered an illegitimate child with Clementina Walkinshaw in 1753 and married Princess Louise of Stolberg-Gedern in 1772. While acknowledging these heteroerotic endeavors, Margaret Forster paints a queer picture of the Bonnie Prince, affirming that "Charles' attitude toward marriage had always been unconventional in that he never seemed to find it inevitable. Neither did he find it attractive. . . . [M]ore important, his total lack of wenching had not gone unnoticed. It was all very well for him to say all that could wait, but would any normal man in his twenties have forsworn attendant pleasures while he waited?" (*The Rash Adventurer: The Rise and Fall of Charles Edward Stuart* [London: Secker & Warburg, 1973], 226). Also, when fleeing the Hanoverian forces after his failed rebellion, the Bonnie Prince disguised himself as Betty Burke, the maid of Flora McDonald. Such situational transvestism need not detract from the Bonnie Prince's masculine puissance, but nor does such gender play bolster it. For Stuart's flight as Betty Burke, see Hugh Douglas and Michael Stead, *The Flight of Bonnie Prince Charlie* (Gloucestershire, England: Sutton, 2000), 90–100.

28. King does not specify where this anecdote from *He* occurs geographically, but she describes the landlady Ma Perkins as the type who "can be found in small cities like Worcester, Mobile, and Boise, whenever resourceful widows inherit huge houses" (*H* 157). Thus, although readers cannot be certain that this encounter transpired in the South, it adheres to King's portrayals of southern women and their overwrought reactions to sexuality.

29. Although the location of Washington, D.C., near the border between North and South complicates its relationship to southern culture, King clearly depicts her grandmother as fully southern in her sensibilities, such as in her assessment of various regions of the South: "Granny's theology had been enervated by her superiority complex. A lifetime of looking down on the Bible Belt South as only a Virginian can had driven her into a bizarre form of heresy: Christianity reminded her of places like Georgia" (*CF* 37).

30. Margo Jefferson, "Scarlett Women: *Southern Ladies and Gentlemen* by Florence King," *Newsweek* 30 June 1975: 66.

31. Mab Segrest, *My Mama's Dead Squirrel: Lesbian Essays on Southern Culture* (Ithaca, NY: Firebrand, 1985), 117.

CHAPTER FOUR

1. Brown's lesbian comic novels are cited parenthetically from the following editions: *Rubyfruit Jungle* (1973; New York: Bantam, 1977), *In Her Day* (1976; New York: Bantam, 1988), *Southern Discomfort* (1982; New York: Bantam, 1988), *Sudden Death* (1983; New York: Bantam, 1988), *Venus Envy* (1993; New York: Bantam, 1994), *Riding Shotgun* (1996; New York: Bantam, 1997), and *Alma Mater* (New York: Ballantine, 2002). For the Hunsenmeier novels, *Six of One* (1978; New York: Bantam, 2008), *Bingo* (1988; New York: Bantam, 2008), *Loose Lips* (1999; New York: Bantam, 2008), and *The Sand Castle* (New York: Grove, 2008). The following abbreviations aligning with the above titles—*RJ, HD, SoD, SuD, VE, RS, AM,* and *SO, B, LL, SC*—are used for in-text citations. All italics in quotations appear in the author's original, including quotations of secondary sources.

2. Brown's poetry is collected in *The Hand That Cradles the Rock* (New York: New York University Press, 1971) and *Songs to a Handsome Woman* (Oakland, CA: Diana Press, 1973). To

date, Brown has written over thirty mystery novels in three primary series: the "Mrs. Murphy" series, for which she impishly credits coauthorship to her cat Sneaky Pie; the "'Sister' Jane Arnold" series, which revolves around a Virginia fox-hunting club; and the "Mags Rogers" series, which features Rogers's pet dachshund Baxter. Her historical fiction consists of *High Hearts* (1986; New York: Bantam, 1988) and *Dolley: A Novel of Dolley Madison in Love and War* (1994; New York: Bantam, 1995). Brown's autobiography is entitled *Rita Will: Memoir of a Literary Rabble-Rouser* (New York: Bantam, 1997), abbreviated *RW,* and her memoir of life with pets and other animals is *Animal Magnetism: My Life with Creatures Great and Small* (New York: Ballantine, 2009). Brown's writing advice appears in *Starting from Scratch: A Different Kind of Writer's Manual* (Toronto: Bantam, 1988), abbreviated *SS,* and her political writings are compiled in *A Plain Brown Rapper* (Oakland, CA: Diana Press, 1976), abbreviated *BR.* Brown's screenplays include, among others, *The Slumber Party Massacre* (1982) and *The Long Hot Summer* (1985), which adapts William Faulkner's work.

3. For an overview of autobiographical moments in Brown's fiction, see Barbara Ladd, "Rita Mae Brown," *Contemporary Fiction Writers of the South: A Bio-Bibliographical Sourcebook,* ed. Joseph Flora and Robert Bain (Westport, CT: Greenwood, 1993), 67–75.

4. Andrea Sachs, "Rita Mae Brown: Loves Cats, Hates Marriage," *Time* 18 Mar. 2008, time.com. Brown also mentions in this interview that Friedan apologized to her approximately twenty years later.

5. Martha Gever and Nathalie Magnan, "The Same Difference: On Lesbian Representation," *Stolen Glances,* ed. Tessa Boffin and Jean Fraser (London: Pandora, 1991), 67–75, at 67.

6. Janet Bing and Dana Heller, "How Many Lesbians Does It Take to Screw in a Light Bulb?" *Humor* 16.2 (2003): 157–82, at 176.

7. Dorothy Painter, "Lesbian Humor as a Normalization Device," *Communication, Language, and Sex: Proceedings of the First Annual Conference,* ed. Cynthia Berryman, Virginia Eman, and Cheris Kramarae (Rowley, MA: Newbury, 1980), 132–48, at 146.

8. Gary Alan Fine, "Humour in Situ: The Role of Humour in Small Group Culture," *It's a Funny Thing, Humour,* ed. A. J. Chapman and H. C. Foot (Oxford: Pergamon, 1977), 315–18, at 315.

9. John Morreall, *Comic Relief: A Comprehensive Philosophy of Humor* (Malden, MA: Wiley-Blackwell, 2009), 116.

10. Matthew Hurley, Daniel Dennett, and Reginald Adams, *Inside Jokes: Using Humor to Reverse-Engineer the Mind* (Cambridge, MA: MIT Press, 2011), 291.

11. Judy Klemesrud, "Underground Book Brings Fame to a Lesbian Author," *New York Times* 26 Sept. 1977: 42.

12. Martha Chew, "Rita Mae Brown: Feminist Theorist and Southern Novelist," *Southern Quarterly* 22.1 (1983): 61–80, at 63.

13. Daniel Levine, "Uses of Classical Mythology in Rita Mae Brown's *Southern Discomfort,*" *Classical and Modern Literature* 10.1 (1989): 63–70, at 65.

14. Lillian Faderman, *Surpassing the Love of Men: Romantic Friendship and Love between Women from the Renaissance to the Present* (New York: Quill, 1981), 406.

15. Leonore Fleischer, "Leonore Fleischer Talks with Rita Mae Brown," *Washington Post Book World* 15 Oct. 1978: 16. On Brown's passion for Aristophanes, see *BR* 12.

16. Carolyn Horn, "Rita Mae Brown: Being Different Really Isn't So Different," *Washington Post* 24 Oct. 1977: C1, 13, at 13.

17. Brown balances Molly Bolt's critique of Stoppard's *Rosencrantz and Guildenstern Are Dead* by including it in her list of recommended reading in *Starting from Scratch* (252).

18. Louise Kawada, "Liberating Laughter: Comedic Form in Some Lesbian Novels," *Sexual Practice / Textual Theory: Lesbian Cultural Criticism,* ed. Susan Wolfe and Julia Penelope (Cambridge, MA: Blackwell, 1993), 251–62, at 252.

19. Brown's interest in classical authors extends beyond her debts to Aristophanes, Euripides, and Aeschylus, and she frequently compares her characters to classical gods and goddesses, likening Cig Blackwood to Artemis and her friend Margaret to Hera, who ironically declares, "I hope I have a more faithful husband" (*RS* 156–57). Also, Brown often cites classical philosophers, such as her references to Seneca ("Scorn pain. Either it goes away or you do" [*RS* 53]) and Heraclitus ("You never step into the same river twice" [*RS* 123]). For a study of Brown's debt to the classical tradition, see Daniel Levine, "Uses of Classical Mythology in Rita Mae Brown's *Southern Discomfort.*"

20. Mikhail Bakhtin, *Rabelais and His World,* trans. Hélène Iswolsky (Bloomington: Indiana University Press, 1984), 21

21. Leslie Fishbein, "*Rubyfruit Jungle:* Lesbianism, Feminism, and Narcissism," *International Journal of Women's Studies* 7.2 (1984): 155–59, at 159.

22. W. C. Harris, "Dr. Molly Feelgood; or, How I Can't Learn to Stop Worrying and Love *Rubyfruit Jungle,*" *EAPSU Online: A Journal of Critical and Creative Work* 1 (2004): 23–41, at 37.

23. James Mandrell, "Questions of Genre and Gender: Contemporary American Versions of the Feminine Picaresque," *Novel* 20.2 (1987): 149–70, at 163.

24. Jonathan Dollimore, "The Dominant and the Deviant: A Violent Dialectic," *Homosexual Themes in Literary Studies,* ed. Wayne Dynes and Stephen Donaldson (New York: Garland, 1992), 87–100, at 94.

25. Martha Chew, "Rita Mae Brown: Feminist Theorist and Southern Novelist," 63.

26. Jan Clausen, *A Movement of Poets: Thoughts on Poetry and Feminism* (Brooklyn, NY: Long Haul, 1982), 14.

27. Sharon Boyle, "Rita Mae Brown," *Lesbian Writers of the United States: A Bio-Bibliographical Critical Sourcebook,* ed. Sandra Pollack, Denise Knight, and Tucker Farley (Westport, CT: Greenwood, 1993), 94–105, at 102 and 104.

28. Kathleen Martindale, "Rita Mae Brown's *Six of One* and Anne Cameron's *The Journey:* Fictional Contributions to the Ethics of Feminist Nonviolence," *Atlantis* 12.1 (1986): 103–10, at 103.

29. Lillian Faderman, *Odd Girls and Twilight Lovers: A History of Lesbian Life in Twentieth-Century America* (New York: Penguin, 1991), 230.

30. D. B. Atcheson, "Lovely Rita," *Advocate* 15 June 1993: 68–69, at 69.

31. As Judith Butler outlines in her groundbreaking study of gender and performativity: "the substantive effect of gender is performatively produced and compelled by the regulatory practices of gender coherence. Hence, within the inherited discourse of the metaphysics of substance, gender proves to be performative—that is, constituting the identity it is purported to be" (*Gender Trouble: Feminism and the Subversion of Identity* [New York: Routledge, 1990], 24–25).

32. For an overview of chivalric traditions in the South, see John Fraser, *America and the Patterns of Chivalry* (Cambridge: Cambridge University Press, 1982), esp. 3–14. In *Queer Chivalry: Medievalism and the Myth of White Masculinity in Southern Literature* (Baton Rouge: Louisiana State University Press, 2013), I explore the queer edges to the chivalric

tradition (1–25) and Ellen Gilchrist's reimagining of chivalry as a woman's tradition in her corpus (176–84).

33. Dolores Alexander, "Rita Mae Brown: The Issue for the Future Is Power," *Ms.* Sept. 1973: 110–13, at 110.

34. Carolyn Horn, "Rita Mae Brown: Being Different Really Isn't So Different," 13.

35. On the utility of queer theory for interrogating heterosexuality, see Calvin Thomas, ed., *Straight with a Twist: Queer Theory and the Subject of Heterosexuality* (Urbana: University of Illinois Press, 2000).

36. Patricia Holt, "Rita Mae Brown," *Publishers Weekly* 2 Oct. 1978: 16–17.

37. Alice Turner, "Fall Preview: Rita Mae Brown," *New York* 18 Sept. 1978: 60.

38. Gail Shister, "Rita Mae Brown: A Nice Southern Girl Makes Good as a Chronicler of Unconventional Love," *Philadelphia Inquirer* 12 May 1983: D12.

39. Scott Herring, *Another Country: Queer Anti-Urbanism* (New York: New York University Press, 2010), 4.

40. Joseph Addison, *Essays in Criticism and Literary Theory,* ed. John Loftis (Northbrook, IL: AHM, 1975), 67, for the 10 May 1711 edition of *The Spectator.*

41. In Wilde's words, "My wallpaper and I are fighting a duel to the death. One or the other of us has to go," as recorded in Richard Ellman, *Oscar Wilde* (Ontario: Viking, 1987), 546.

CHAPTER FIVE

1. Dorothy Allison's works include *Trash* (1988; New York: Plume, 2002); *The Women Who Hate Me: Poetry, 1980–1990* (Ithaca, NY: Firebrand, 1991); *Bastard Out of Carolina* (1992; London: Penguin, 2012); *Skin: Talking about Sex, Class, and Literature* (Ithaca, NY: Firebrand, 1994); *Two or Three Things I Know for Sure* (New York: Plume, 1996); and *Cavedweller* (New York: Dutton, 1998). In-text citations align with the following abbreviations: *T, WW, BC, S, TT,* and *C.*

2. Cathy Caruth, ed., *Trauma: Explorations in Memory* (Baltimore, MD: Johns Hopkins University Press, 1995), 11.

3. Kelly L. Thomas, "White Trash Lesbianism: Dorothy Allison's Queer Politics," *Gender Reconstructions: Pornography and Perversions in Literature and Culture,* ed. Cindy Carlson, Robert Mazzola, and Susan Benardo (Aldershot, England: Ashgate, 2002), 167–88, at 175.

4. Carolyn E. Megan, "Moving toward Truth: An Interview with Dorothy Allison," *Kenyon Review* 16.4 (1994): 71–83, at 73, 74.

5. Michael LeMahieu, "An Interview with Dorothy Allison," *Contemporary Literature* 54.1 (2010): 651–76, at 655.

6. Ann Cvetkovich, *An Archive of Feelings: Trauma, Sexuality, and Lesbian Public Cultures* (Durham, NC: Duke University Press, 2003), 4.

7. Michael LeMahieu, "An Interview with Dorothy Allison," 657.

8. Carolyn E. Megan, "Moving toward Truth," 81.

9. Allison describes Morton Thompson's *Not as a Stranger* (1954) as a key text of her childhood. Also, notwithstanding her words of praise for O'Connor, her character Toni, in the story "Monkeybites," expresses her exasperation with the southern gothic tradition: "Shit girl, it's just too much, too Southern Gothic—catfish and monkeys and chewed-off fingers.

Throw in a little red dirt and chicken feathers, a little incest and shotgun shells, and you join the literary tradition" (*T* 87).

10. Michael LeMahieu, "An Interview with Dorothy Allison," 656. Allison concedes that "*Two or Three Things I Know for Sure* is a memoir," yet she couples this admission with the caveat that "truly it is a meditation on storytelling" (656).

11. Connie Griffin, "'I will not wear that coat': Cross-Dressing in the Works of Dorothy Allison," *He Said, She Says: An RSVP to the Male Text,* ed. Mica Howe and Sarah Appleton Aguiar (Madison, NJ: Fairleigh Dickinson University Press, 2001), 143–57, at 144.

12. For further discussion of the Feminist Sex Wars of the 1970s and 1980s, see Chapter 4 and Florence King's treatment of rape humor.

13. The title page does not include ellipses between "the women who hate" and ME."; instead, white space signifies this distance. The period after "ME" is included in the title's design, which further underscores the speaker's emphatic sense of self.

14. For an example of such denigration, see the discussion of David Sedaris, grits, and hush puppies in Chapter 6. Sedaris, of course, writes with tongue in cheek in these passages, yet his parents' resistance to southern culture appears to represent their true feelings, if exaggerated for comic effect.

15. Joanna Russ, *Magic Mommas, Trembling Sisters, Puritans, and Perverts: Feminist Essays* (Trumansburg, NY: Cross Press, 1985), 94.

16. Leigh Gilmore, "Limit-Cases: Trauma, Self-Representation, and the Jurisdictions of Identity," *Biography* 24.1 (2001): 128–39, at 129.

17. Soyoung Park, "'Survival is the least of my desires': Testimony, Shame, and Desire in Dorothy Allison's *Bastard Out of Carolina," Feminist Studies in English Literature* 18.2 (2010): 57–85, at 60.

18. Tamara Lea Spira, "Remembering Trauma, Refusing Disappearance: *Corregidora, Bastard Out of Carolina,* and the Transnational Labors of Memory," *Transnationalism and Resistance: Experience and Experiment in Women's Writing,* ed. Adele Parker and Stephanie Young (Amsterdam: Rodopi, 2013), 113–37, at 115.

19. Suzette Henke, "'A Child Is Being Beaten': Dorothy Allison's Testimony of Trauma and Abuse in *Bastard Out of Carolina," Critical Essays on the Works of American Author Dorothy Allison,* ed. Christine Blouch and Laurie Vickroy (Lewiston, NY: Mellen, 2004), 9–28, at 9.

20. Conrad Hyers, "The Dialectic of the Sacred and the Comic," *Holy Laughter: Essays on Religion in the Comic Perspective,* ed. Conrad Hyers (New York: Seabury, 1969), 208–40, at 232–33; qtd. in John Morreall, *Comic Relief: A Comprehensive Philosophy of Humor* (Malden, MA: Wiley-Blackwell, 2009), 119. See Morreall's insightful discussion of humor and the Holocaust (119–24), in which he proposes that a primary function of humor during the Holocaust was to help "oppressed people cope with suffering without going insane" (123).

21. Roseanne Barr, *Roseanne: My Life as a Woman* (New York: Harper & Row, 1989), 45.

22. Roseanne Barr, *Rosannearchy: Dispatches from the Nut Farm* (New York: Gallery Books, 2011), 59–60.

23. Carolyn Kraus, "The Road from Illegitimacy to Art: Dorothy Allison's *Bastard Out of Carolina," North Dakota Quarterly* 71.3 (2004): 127–43, at 130.

24. With these words Bone updates Augustine's prayerful one-liner of religious aspiration: "Grant me chastity and self-control, but please not yet" (*Confessions,* ed. John Rotelle, trans. Maria Boulding [Hyde Park, NY: New City, 1997], 8.7, at p. 198). With this allusion Allison

embeds a deeper context for her storyline of Shannon Pearl and the gospel singers in the pleasures of the fallen amid the struggle for salvation. These pages contain some of the novel's sharpest barbs, like the reaction of fellow churchgoers to Shannon: "I don't care. The Lord didn't intend me to get nauseous in the middle of Sunday services. That child is a shock to the digestion" (*BC* 156). Bone recounts as well her family's response to Shannon: "I laughed back, remembering what Aunt Raylene had said about Mrs. Pearl—'If she'd been fucked right just once, she'd have never birthed that weird child'" (*BC* 161). An earlier version of the story of Shannon Pearl appears in *Trash* as "Gospel Song," and in *Skin* Allison explains how she built this character: "The historical truth about the child on whom I based my character Shannon Pearl is that she went on, a child of her culture, and lives that life still, as far as I know, back in Greenville, though the child I remember knew nothing about gospel music. I gave her that life to make a larger story" (*S* 217).

25. Mary Wiles, "The Fascination of the Lesbian Fetish: A Perverse Possibility across the Body of Dorothy Allison's *Bastard Out of Carolina*," *Straight with a Twist: Queer Theory and the Subject of Heterosexuality*, ed. Calvin Thomas (Urbana: University of Illinois Press, 2000), 152–62, at 155.

26. Barbara Bennett, *Comic Visions, Female Voices: Contemporary Women Novelists and Southern Humor* (Baton Rouge: Louisiana State University Press, 1998), 27. Bennett is one of the few critics who reads Allison's novel through a comic lens (24–27).

27. Anthony Dyer Hoefer, *Apocalypse South: Judgment, Cataclysm, and Resistance in the Regional Imaginary* (Columbus: Ohio State University Press, 2012), 152–53.

CHAPTER SIX

1. Quotations of Sedaris's essay collections are taken from *Barrel Fever* (Boston: Little, Brown, 1994); *Naked* (Boston: Little, Brown, 1997); *Holidays on Ice* (Boston: Little, Brown, 1997); *Me Talk Pretty One Day* (Boston: Little, Brown, 2000); *Dress Your Family in Corduroy and Denim* (Boston: Little, Brown, 2004); *When You Are Engulfed in Flames* (Boston: Little, Brown, 2008); *Squirrel Seeks Chipmunk: A Modest Bestiary* (Boston: Little, Brown, 2010); and *Let's Explore Diabetes with Owls: Essays, Etc.* (Boston: Little, Brown, 2013). The following abbreviations are used for in-text citations: *BF, N, HI, MT, DF, EF, SS,* and *LE.*

2. Robert Penn Warren and Albert Erskine, eds., *A New Southern Harvest: An Anthology* (New York: Bantam, 1957), viii–ix.

3. Florence King, *Southern Ladies and Gentlemen* (1975; New York: St. Martin's Griffin, 1993), 218.

4. Florence King, *Southern Ladies and Gentlemen,* 212.

5. Ellen Degeneres, *My Point . . . And I Do Have One* (New York: Bantam, 1995), 135. Degeneres also defends "y'all" for its convenience: "'Y'all going?' is so much easier to say than, 'Are you presently considering departing?'" (*The Funny Thing Is . . .* [New York: Simon & Schuster, 2003], 116).

6. Martyn Bone, *The Postsouthern Sense of Place in Contemporary Fiction* (Baton Rouge: Louisiana State University Press, 2005), 250–51. Additional key studies of the South's postsouthern turn include Michael Kreyling, *The South That Wasn't There: Postsouthern Memory and History* (Baton Rouge: Louisiana State University Press, 2010), and Scott Romine, "Where Is Southern Literature? The Practice of Place in a Postsouthern Age," *South to a New*

Place: Region, Literature, Culture, ed. Suzanne W. Jones and Sharon Monteith (Baton Rouge: Louisiana State University Press, 2002), 23–43.

7. For example, Boeing's decision to open a plant in South Carolina has been widely viewed as an effort by the company to enjoy lower labor costs and to send a message to its unionized workers in the Seattle area; see Dean Foust and Justin Bachman, "Boeing's Flight from Union Labor," *BusinessWeek* 16 Nov. 2009: 34, as well as Robert H. Zieger's *Life and Labor in the New New South* (Gainesville: University Press of Florida, 2012) and his *Organized Labor in the Twentieth-Century South* (Knoxville: University of Tennessee Press, 1991).

8. Jefferson Humphries, "The Discourse of Southernness, or How We Know There Will Still Be Such a Thing as the South and Southern Literature in the Twenty-First Century," *The Future of Southern Letters,* ed. Jefferson Humphries and John Lowe (New York: Oxford University Press, 1996), 119–33, at 130–31.

9. Sedaris rarely alludes directly to southern authors and southern literature in his essays, which further establishes the uniqueness of his voice as a postsouthern regionalist. An exception to this overriding tendency appears in his story "After Malison," in which the narrator, an obsessive undergraduate stalking a famous writer visiting her campus, expresses her strong dislike for "O'Flannery," an amusing epithet for Flannery O'Connor: "I think Malison hates O'Flannery for the same reasons I do, because she's a fascist, a typical bourgeois racist, a judgmental Christian right-wing parrot, and a timid writer who relies on grammar to carry her through the page. I hate O'Flannery, I really do" (*BF* 115). One cannot distill Sedaris's personal opinion on O'Connor from this passage, yet it is clear that this narrator should receive the reader's ridicule because of her distaste for grammatically correct constructions.

10. Alex Heard, "This American Lie," *New Republic* 19 Mar. 2007: 35–38, at 38. Beyond his play with personal identity in his memoirs, Sedaris adopts outrageous personas in many of his fictional narratives, including the ones collected under the heading "Stories" in *Barrel Fever,* in which he voices such characters as the murderous mother of the Dunbar clan ("Seasons Greetings to Our Friends and Family!!!") and a vengeful suicide-note writer ("The Last You'll Hear from Me"). His disclaimer in *Let's Explore Diabetes with Owls: Essays, Etc.* explains, "To that end, as part of the 'Etc.' in this book's subtitle, I have written six brief monologues that young people might deliver before a panel of judges. I believe these stories should be self-evident. They're the pieces in which I am a woman, a father, and a sixteen-year-old girl with a fake British accent" (ix). Sedaris's decision to clearly identify these pieces as fictional, returning to his strategy in *Barrel Fever,* attests to the ways in which debates about the line between memoir and fiction have influenced the presentation of his essays.

11. For a brief account of the James Frey scandal, see David Carr, "How Oprah Trumped Truthiness," *New York Times* 30 Jan. 2006.

12. Lania Knight, "A Conversation with David Sedaris," *Missouri Review* 30.1 (2007): 72–89, at 80 and 89.

13. Timothy Dow Adams, *Telling Lies in Modern American Autobiography* (Chapel Hill: University of North Carolina Press, 1990), ix.

14. Some of Sedaris's fictional narratives in *Barrel Fever* briefly mention a southern setting. "Glen's Homophobic Newsletter" takes place in Carteret County (61). The narcissistic narrator of "Don's Story" describes himself as a "just a guy from Cumberland County, North Carolina" (68) and mentions his past employment at a mainstay of southern dining, K&W Cafeterias (71). The narrator of "Barrel Fever," who has relocated from Piedmont, finds an-

other hometown émigré in his high-school acquaintance Trudy Chase (146). These stories lack any attention to local color, and readers would need to be rather knowledgeable of North Carolina's counties and towns to identify their location.

15. Lania Knight, "A Conversation with David Sedaris," 79.

16. Scott Romine, "Where Is Southern Literature?" 24.

17. Richard Dyer, *White* (London: Routledge, 1997), 20.

18. Charles Nero, "Black Gay Men and White Gay Men: A Less Than Perfect Union," *Out in the South,* ed. Carlos L. Dews and Carolyn Leste Law (Philadelphia: Temple University Press, 2001), 115–26, at 115.

19. James Russell Lowell, "Humor, Wit, Fun, and Satire," *Century* Nov. 1893: 124–31, at 126.

20. Michael Eric Dyson, "Nigger Gotta Stop," *Source* June 1999; qtd. in Randall Kennedy, *Nigger: The Strange Career of a Troublesome Word* (New York: Pantheon, 2002), 51.

21. Michal Omi and Howard Winant, "Racial Formation," *Race Critical Theories: Text and Context,* ed. Philomena Essed and David Theo Goldberg (Malden, MA: Blackwell, 2002), 123–45, at 138.

22. Toward the essay's end, however, it is also apparent that Uta perceives that Dupont's performances of race camouflage his underlying personality: "It's not all that difficult to see through you, Dupont . . . Take my word for it, the hard part is listening to you" (*N* 224)

23. The regional variability of school desegregation requires virtually a city-by-city analysis, as evident in the numerous scholarly studies of desegregation addressing a particular urban area, such as Howell S. Baum, *Brown in Baltimore: School Desegregation and the Limits of Liberalism* (Ithaca, NY: Cornell University Press, 2010); Christopher Bonastia, *Southern Stalemate: Five Years without Public Education in Prince Edward County, Virginia* (Chicago: University of Chicago Press, 2012); and William Bagwell, *School Desegregation in the Carolinas: Two Case Studies* (Columbia: University of South Carolina Press, 1972). As Leon Jones documents, many municipalities throughout North Carolina enforced only token integration in the decade following the *Brown* decision (*From Brown to Boston: Desegregation in Education,* 2 vols. [Metuchen, NJ: Scarecrow, 1979], 1:612). On the tokenism of many North Carolina school districts' efforts to integrate and on their strategies for resisting integration, see also Christina Greene, *Our Separate Ways: Women and the Black Freedom Movement in Durham, North Carolina* (Chapel Hill: University of North Carolina Press, 2005), 209–15.

24. Certainly, the Raleigh / Durham / Chapel Hill area was not immune to racial controversies surrounding desegregation. The 1958 case *Holt v. The Raleigh City Board of Education* involved an African American student and his parents suing for his right to attend an all-white high school closer to their home than the one to which he was assigned. See Leon Jones, *From Brown to Boston,* 2:1181.

25. Kevin Kopelson, *Sedaris* (Minneapolis: University of Minnesota Press, 2007), 1–2.

26. Philip Gambone, *Travels in a Gay Nation: Portraits of LGBTQ Americans* (Madison: University of Wisconsin Press, 2010), 247.

27. David Sedaris, "Now We Are Five," *New Yorker* 23 Oct. 2013.

CONCLUSION

1. Harold Bloom, *The Western Canon: The Books and School of the Ages* (New York: Harcourt Brace, 1994), 3.

2. Henry Louis Gates Jr., *Loose Canons: Notes on the Culture Wars* (New York: Oxford University Press, 1992), 39; his italics.

3. Nancy Walker, *A Very Serious Thing: Women's Humor and American Culture* (Minneapolis: University of Minnesota Press, 1988), 182.

4. Carey Kaplan and Ellen Cronan Rose, *The Canon and the Common Reader* (Knoxville: University of Tennessee Press, 1990), 128.

5. Dorothy Allison, *Trash* (1988; New York: Plume, 2002), xv.

6. John Guillory, *Cultural Capital: The Problem of Literary Canon Formation* (Chicago: University of Chicago Press, 1993), 7; his italics.

7. Byrne Fone, ed., *The Columbia Anthology of Gay Literature: Readings from Western Antiquity to the Present Day* (New York: Columbia University Press, 1998), xxxii.

8. Reed Woodhouse, *Unlimited Embrace: A Canon of Gay Fiction, 1945–1995* (Amherst: University of Massachusetts Press, 1998), 13. See also Robert Drake, *The Gay Canon: Great Books Every Gay Man Should Read* (New York: Anchor, 1998), who aligns himself with Harold Bloom's perspective and seeks "to isolate the qualities that made these gay authors canonical—that is, authoritative—in gay culture" (xv–xvi).

9. Lillian Faderman, *Chloe Plus Olivia: An Anthology of Lesbian Literature from the Seventeenth Century to the Present* (New York: Viking, 1994), vii.

10. Montrose J. Moses, "Introduction to *The Literature of the South* (1910)," *Defining Southern Literature: Perspectives and Assessments, 1831–1952,* ed. John E. Bassett (Madison, NJ: Fairleigh Dickinson University Press, 1997), 274–77, at 274. Bassett's anthology cites a diverse array of attempts to define the character of the South and its literature.

11. Fred Hobson, "Of Canons and Cultural Wars: Southern Literature and Literary Scholarship after Midcentury," *The Future of Southern Letters,* ed. Jefferson Humphries and John Lowe (New York: Oxford University Press, 1996), 72–86, at 72. Hobson expounds further upon the vagaries of the canon, suggesting that Wolfe has lost ground while Ralph Ellison has gained attention.

12. Ed Piacentino, "Challenging the Canon: Other Southern Literary Lives," *Southern Literary Journal* 38.2 (2006): 145–49, at 145. In this review essay, Piacentino advocates expanding the southern literary canon's range and uses these six names to demonstrate its apparent rigidity.

13. Gary Richards, *Lovers and Beloveds: Sexual Otherness in Southern Fiction, 1936–1961* (Baton Rouge: Louisiana State University Press, 2005), 12.

14. Farrell O'Gorman, "The Fugitive-Agrarians and the Twentieth-Century Southern Canon," *A Companion to the Regional Literature of America,* ed. Charles Crow (Malden, MA: Blackwell, 2003), 286–305, at 294.

15. For contemporary reviewers hostile to Williams and Capote, see the sections called "Camp" in Chapter 1 and "Camp Gothic in *Other Voices, Other Rooms*" in Chapter 2, respectively.

16. Fred Hobson dismisses the potential for comic fiction to enter the southern literary canon, positing that the "new, largely comic southern novel of manners . . . does not lend itself to th[e] kind of force" that would warrant its inclusion ("Of Canons and Cultural Wars," 85). While I disagree with his conclusion, I applaud his candor.

17. Several southern authors serve as the subjects of scholarly journals dedicated solely to their lives and literature, including *Mark Twain Journal, Faulkner Journal, Eudora Welty Review,* and *Flannery O'Connor Review.* Of the authors analyzed in this study, only Williams,

with the *Tennessee Williams Annual Review*, receives sufficient critical attention to merit his own journal; there is also an annual New Orleans literary festival in his honor. It appears unlikely that Capote, King, Brown, Allison, and Sedaris will accrue similar accolades.

18. In a search of the MLA International Bibliography conducted 1 May 2014, Tennessee Williams generated 1,299 hits, Capote 260, Florence King 5, Rita Mae Brown 18, Dorothy Allison 113, and David Sedaris 11. Such results again suggest William's primacy among these writers in terms of canonicity, yet he is overshadowed by Faulkner (6,937), Twain (2,206), and O'Connor (1,662). King's and Brown's results show that they barely register in the field of southern literary studies, in contrast to Allison, whose 113 hits bespeak a serious interest in her work within the roughly twenty years since the publication of *Bastard Out of Carolina*. Sedaris's eleven hits could betoken either a coalescing scholarly interest in his work or simply an accurate assessment of his marginal position in the field.

19. Anthologies introduce new generations of students to the finest authors of various traditions, yet as Michael Kreyling wryly notes, "No literature anthology, southern included, is innocent of political gamesmanship" (*Inventing Southern Literature* [Jackson: University Press of Mississippi, 1998], 57). Kreyling's chapter "Southern Literature Anthologies and the Invention of the South" (56–75) invaluably charts varying currents in the formation of the southern literary canon. Three of the most influential and best-selling anthologies of southern literature—Edward Ayers and Bradley Mittendorf's *The Oxford Book of the American South: Testimony, Memory, and Fiction* (New York: Oxford University Press, 1997), William Andrews, Minrose Gwin, Trudier Harris, and Fred Hobson's *The Literature of the American South: A Norton Anthology* (New York: Norton, 1998), and Edward Francisco, Robert Vaughan, and Linda Francisco's *The South in Perspective: An Anthology of Southern Literature* (Upper Saddle River, NJ: Prentice Hall, 2001) illustrate the marginalization of Capote, King, Brown, and Sedaris, and the primacy of Williams and Allison. King, Brown, and Sedaris do not appear in any of these anthologies; Capote appears only in *The South in Perspective* with his short story "A Diamond Guitar." Williams and Allison appear in both *The Literature of the American South* (*A Streetcar Named Desire* and two stories from *Trash*, respectively) and *The South in Perspective* (*Portrait of a Madonna* and an excerpt from *Bastard Out of Carolina*). Williams, Capote, King, Brown, Allison, and Sedaris share the dubious distinction of being shut out of the pages of Ayers and Mittendorf's *The Oxford Book of the American South*, as well as of Suzanne Jones's *Growing Up in the South: An Anthology of Modern Southern Literature* (New York: Mentor, 1991). (However, this anthology was published in 1991, which would make Allison's and Sedaris's inclusion unlikely). To the best of my knowledge, Sedaris has not been published in any anthology of southern literature, although his work is included in such composition and nonfiction textbooks as Lex Williford and Michael Martone's *Touchstone Anthology of Contemporary Creative Nonfiction* (New York: Touchstone, 2007).

20. The Fellowship of Southern Writers, established in 1987, proclaims in its mission statement, "The Fellowship of Southern Writers (FSW) seeks to recognize and encourage literature in the South." Its Web site outlines its procedures for electing new members:

> The Fellowship is composed of 50 active members. New members are nominated by current members and elected by majority vote, and are drawn from among writers of fiction, poetry, drama, criticism, and history. To be considered for membership a writer must have been born and raised, or have resided for a significant part of his or her life

in the South, or have written works that in character and spirit embody aspects of the Southern experience. (The Fellowship of Southern Writers: About Us," thefsw.org, 2014)

Williams and Capote died prior to the organization's inception, and to date only Allison has been elected to its ranks, with King, Brown, and Sedaris failing to measure up to its standards. Sedaris is young enough for this oversight to be rectified, but it appears unlikely that King and Brown will be issued invitations at the very twilight of their careers. Again, however, one cannot make blanket arguments about the place of homosexuality and humor in the southern literary canon, for the Fellowship of Southern Writers includes humorists such as Roy Blount Jr. and gay members such as Allan Gurganus.

21. General studies of Capote's fiction include Helen S. Garson, *Truman Capote* (New York: Frederick Ungar, 1980); Kenneth T. Reed, *Truman Capote* (Boston: Twayne, 1981); Robert Emmet Long, *Truman Capote—Enfant Terrible* (New York: Continuum, 2008); and Thomas Fahy, *Understanding Truman Capote* (Columbia: University of South Carolina Press, 2014). Examinations of Capote's film career include Ralph Voss, *Truman Capote and the Legacy of* In Cold Blood (Tuscaloosa: University of Alabama Press, 2011) and my *Truman Capote: A Literary Life at the Movies* (Athens: University of Georgia Press, 2014). These books are all illuminating about Capote's literary and cinematic career, yet, as overviews and film studies, they ironically testify to the lack of critical attention that Capote's literature warrants, given its full range of styles, genres, and aesthetic concerns.

22. Kathie Bergquist, "David Sedaris: La Maison de mes dents," *Publishers Weekly* 19 June 2000: 54–55, at 55.

23. Kathie Bergquist, "David Sedaris: La Maison de mes dents," 55.

24. On Toole's suicide, see Rene Pol Nevils and Deborah George Hardy, *Ignatius Rising: The Life of John Kennedy Toole* (Baton Rouge: Louisiana State University Press, 2005), and Cory MacLauchlin, *Butterfly in the Typewriter: The Tragic Life of John Kennedy Toole and the Remarkable Story of* A Confederacy of Dunces (New York: Da Capo, 2013).

25. William Faulkner, foreword to *Sherwood Anderson and Other Famous Creoles,* William Spratling and William Faulkner (1926; Austin: University of Texas Press, 1966), 25–26, at 26. Wade Hall cites this quotation of Faulkner in his *The Smiling Phoenix: Southern Humor from 1865 to 1914* (Gainesville: University of Florida Press, 1965), 354.

26. Richard Gray, *Writing the South: Ideas of an American Region* (Cambridge: Cambridge University Press, 1986), xii.

Works Cited

Adams, Timothy Dow. *Telling Lies in Modern American Autobiography.* Chapel Hill: University of North Carolina Press, 1990.

Addison, Joseph. *Essays in Criticism and Literary Theory.* Ed. John Loftis. Northbrook, IL: AHM, 1975.

Alexander, Dolores. "Rita Mae Brown: The Issue for the Future Is Power." *Ms.* Sept. 1973: 110–13.

Allison, Dorothy. *Bastard Out of Carolina.* 1992. London: Penguin, 2012.

———. *Cavedweller.* New York: Dutton, 1998.

———. *Skin: Talking about Sex, Class, and Literature.* Ithaca, NY: Firebrand, 1994.

———. *Trash.* 1988. New York: Plume, 2002.

———. *Two or Three Things I Know for Sure.* New York: Plume, 1996.

———. *The Women Who Hate Me: Poetry, 1980–1990.* Ithaca, NY: Firebrand, 1991.

Anderson, Lindsay. "In Brief: *Beat the Devil.*" *Sight & Sound* 23 (Jan.–Mar. 1954): 147–48.

Andrews, William, Minrose Gwin, Trudier Harris, and Fred Hobson, eds. *The Literature of the American South: A Norton Anthology.* New York: Norton, 1998.

Angel, Elayne. *The Piercing Bible: The Definitive Guide to Safe Body Piercing.* Berkeley, CA: Crossing Press, 2009.

Atcheson, D. B. "Lovely Rita." *Advocate* 15 June 1993: 68–69.

Augustine. *Confessions.* Ed. John Rotelle. Trans. Maria Boulding. Hyde Park, NY: New City, 1997.

Ayers, Edward, and Bradley Mittendorf, eds. *The Oxford Book of the American South: Testimony, Memory, and Fiction.* New York: Oxford University Press, 1997.

Bagwell, William. *School Desegregation in the Carolinas: Two Case Studies.* Columbia: University of South Carolina Press, 1972.

Bak, John. "'Sneakin' and Spyin' from Broadway to the Beltway: Cold War Masculinity, Brick, and Homosexual Existentialism." *Theatre Journal* 56 (2004): 225–49.

Baker, Carlos. "Deep-South Guignol: Review of *Other Voices, Other Rooms.*" *New York Times Book Review* 18 Jan. 1948: L5.

Bakhtin, Mikhail. *Rabelais and His World.* Trans. Hélène Iswolsky. Bloomington: Indiana University Press, 1984.

Barnes, Peter. "The Director on Horseback." *Quarterly of Film, Radio, and Television* 10.3 (1956): 281–87.

Barnett, Pamela. "James Dickey's *Deliverance:* Southern, White, Suburban Male Nightmare or Dream Come True?" *Forum for Modern Language Studies* 40.2 (2004): 145–59.

Barr, Roseanne. *Roseanne: My Life as a Woman.* New York: Harper & Row, 1989.

———. *Rosannearchy: Dispatches from the Nut Farm.* New York: Gallery Books, 2011.

Barreca, Regina, ed. *Last Laughs: Perspectives on Women and Comedy.* New York: Gordon & Breach, 1988.

Bartlett, Neil. *Who Was That Man? A Present for Oscar Wilde.* Bristol, England: Serpent's Tongue, 1988.

Barton, Bernadette. *Pray the Gay Away: The Extraordinary Lives of Bible Belt Gays.* New York: New York University Press, 2012.

Baum, Howell S. *Brown in Baltimore: School Desegregation and the Limits of Liberalism.* Ithaca, NY: Cornell University Press, 2010.

Beaver, Harold. "Homosexual Signs (In Memory of Roland Barthes)." Cleto 160–78.

Beat the Devil. Dir. John Huston. Perf. Humphrey Bogart, Jennifer Jones, and Gina Lollobridgida. Screenplay by Truman Capote and John Huston. Romulus Films, 1953.

Bennett, Barbara. *Comic Visions, Female Voices: Contemporary Women Novelists and Southern Humor.* Baton Rouge: Louisiana State University Press, 1998.

Bergquist, Kathie. "David Sedaris: La Maison de mes dents." *Publishers Weekly* 19 June 2000: 54–55.

Bergson, Henri. *Laughter: An Essay on the Meaning of the Comic.* Trans. Cloudesley Brereton and Fred Rothwell. London: Macmillan, 1921.

Bibler, Michael. *Cotton's Queer Relations: Same-Sex Intimacy and the Literature of the Southern Plantation, 1936–1968.* Charlottesville: University of Virginia Press, 2009.

Bing, Janet, and Dana Heller. "How Many Lesbians Does It Take to Screw in a Light Bulb?" *Humor* 16.2 (2003): 157–82.

Bloom, Harold. *The Western Canon: The Books and School of the Ages.* New York: Harcourt Brace, 1994.

Blount, Roy, Jr., ed. *Roy Blount's Book of Southern Humor.* New York: Norton, 1994.

Bonastia, Christopher. *Southern Stalemate: Five Years without Public Education in Prince Edward County, Virginia.* Chicago: University of Chicago Press, 2012.

Bone, Martyn. *The Postsouthern Sense of Place in Contemporary Fiction.* Baton Rouge: Louisiana State University Press, 2005.

Booth, Mark. "*Campe-Toi!* On the Origins and Definitions of Camp." Cleto 66–79.

Booth, Wayne C. *A Rhetoric of Irony.* Chicago: University of Chicago Press, 1974.

Boulton, Richard. "Lavender Pastiche: Review of *Other Voices, Other Rooms.*" *Hartford Courant Magazine* 15 Feb. 1948: 12.

Boyle, Sharon. "Rita Mae Brown." *Lesbian Writers of the United States: A Bio—Bibliographical Critical Sourcebook.* Ed. Sandra Pollack, Denise Knight, and Tucker Farley. Westport, CT: Greenwood, 1993. 94–105.

Braun, Walter. *The Cruel and the Meek: Aspects of Sadism and Masochism.* Trans. N. Meyer. New York: Lyle Stuart, 1967.

Brinnin, John Malcolm. *Truman Capote: Dear Heart, Old Buddy.* New York: Delacorte, 1981.

Britton, Andrew. "For Interpretation: Notes against Camp." Cleto 136–42.

Brooks, Charles. "Williams' Comedy." *Tennessee Williams: A Tribute.* Ed. Jac Tharpe. Jackson: University Press of Mississippi, 1977. 720–35.

Brown, Rita Mae. *Alma Mater.* New York: Ballantine, 2002.

———. *Bingo.* 1988. New York: Bantam, 2008.

———. *In Her Day.* 1976. New York: Bantam, 1988.

———. *Loose Lips.* 1999. New York: Bantam, 2008.

———. *A Plain Brown Rapper.* Oakland, CA: Diana Press, 1976.

———. *Riding Shotgun.* 1996. New York: Bantam, 1997.

———. *Rita Will: Memoir of a Literary Rabble-Rouser.* New York: Bantam, 1997.

———. *Rubyfruit Jungle.* 1973. New York: Bantam, 1977.

———. *The Sand Castle.* New York: Grove, 2008.

———. *Six of One.* 1978. New York: Bantam, 2008.

———. *Southern Discomfort.* 1982. New York: Bantam, 1988.

———. *Starting from Scratch: A Different Kind of Writer's Manual.* Toronto: Bantam, 1988.

———. *Sudden Death.* 1983. New York: Bantam, 1988.

———. *Venus Envy.* 1993. New York: Bantam, 1994.

Bucco, Martin. "Truman Capote and the Country below the Surface." *Four Quarters* Nov. 1957: 22–25.

Buchanan, Laura [Florence King]. *The Barbarian Princess.* New York: Berkley, 1978.

Burstein, Patricia. "Tiny, Yes, But a Terror? Do Not Be Fooled by Truman Capote in Repose." *People* 10 May 1976: 12–17.

Butler, Judith. *Gender Trouble: Feminism and the Subversion of Identity.* New York: Routledge, 1990.

———. *Undoing Gender.* New York: Routledge, 2004.

Califia, Pat. "Gay Men, Lesbians, and Sex: Doing It Together." Gross and Woods 92–96.

Calvino, Italo. *The Literature Machine: Essays.* Trans. Patrick Creagh. 1982. London: Secker & Warburg, 1987.

Capote, Truman. *Answered Prayers: The Unfinished Novel.* New York: Random House, 1987.

———. *Breakfast at Tiffany's and Three Stories.* 1950. New York: Vintage, 1986.

———. *The Dogs Bark: Public People and Private Places.* New York: Random House, 1973.

———. *The Grass Harp and A Tree of Night and Other Stories.* 1952. New York: Vintage, 1993.

———. *Other Voices, Other Rooms.* 1948. New York: Vintage, 1975.

Carr, David. "How Oprah Trumped Truthiness." *New York Times* 30 Jan. 2006.
Carr, Duane. *A Question of Class: The Redneck Stereotype in Southern Fiction.* Bowling Green, OH: Bowling Green State University Popular Press, 1996.
Caruth, Cathy, ed. *Trauma: Explorations in Memory.* Baltimore, MD: Johns Hopkins University Press, 1995.
Chew, Martha. "Rita Mae Brown: Feminist Theorist and Southern Novelist." *Southern Quarterly* 22.1 (1983): 61–80.
Cho, Margaret. *I Have Chosen to Stay and Fight.* New York: Riverhead, 2005.
Cimino, Kenneth. *Gay Conservatives: Group Consciousness and Assimilation.* New York: Harrington Park, 2007.
Clarke, Gerald. "Checking In with Truman Capote." *Esquire* Nov. 1972: 136+.
———. "Petronus Americanus: The Ways of Gore Vidal." *Atlantic* Mar. 1972: 44–51.
———, ed. *Too Brief a Treat: The Letters of Truman Capote.* New York: Vintage, 2004.
Clausen, Jan. *A Movement of Poets: Thoughts on Poetry and Feminism.* Brooklyn, NY: Long Haul, 1982.
Cleto, Fabio, ed. *Camp: Queer Aesthetics and the Performing Subject: A Reader.* Ann Arbor: University of Michigan Press, 1999.
Cohen, Micah. "Gay Vote Proved a Boon for Obama." *New York Times* 15 Nov. 2012.
Conrad, Kathryn. "The Politics of Camp." *Deviant Acts: Essays on Queer Performance.* Ed. David Cregan. Dublin: Carysfort, 2009. 25–36.
Craig, Edward Gordon. *Index to the Story of My Days.* London: Hulton, 1957.
Crisp, Quentin. *The Naked Civil Servant.* 1968. New York: Penguin, 1997.
Critchley, Simon. *On Humour.* London: Routledge, 2002.
Cross, Jesse. Review of *Other Voices, Other Rooms. Library Journal* 1 Dec. 1947: 1685.
Cvetkovich, Ann. *An Archive of Feelings: Trauma, Sexuality, and Lesbian Public Cultures.* Durham, NC: Duke University Press, 2003.
Davy, Kate. "Fe/Male Impersonation: The Discourse of Camp." Meyer, *Politics and Poetics of Camp* 130–48.
Degeneres, Ellen. *The Funny Thing Is . . .* New York: Simon & Schuster, 2003.
———. *My Point . . . And I Do Have One.* New York: Bantam, 1995.
Deleuze, Gilles. "Coldness and Cruelty." Deleuze, *Masochism* 9–138.
———, ed. *Masochism.* New York: Zone, 1991.
Dews, Carlos, and Carolyn Leste Law, eds. *Out in the South.* Philadelphia: Temple University Press, 2001.
Dickey, James. *Deliverance.* Boston: Houghton Mifflin, 1970.
Dollimore, Jonathan. "The Dominant and the Deviant: A Violent Dialectic." *Homosexual Themes in Literary Studies.* Ed. Wayne Dynes and Stephen Donaldson. New York: Garland, 1992. 87–100.
Douglas, Hugh, and Michael Stead. *The Flight of Bonnie Prince Charlie.* Gloucestershire, England: Sutton, 2000.
Drake, Robert, ed. *The Gay Canon: Great Books Every Gay Man Should Read.* New York: Anchor, 1998.

Dworkin, Andrea. *Right-Wing Women*. New York: Coward-McCann, 1982.
Dyer, Richard. *The Culture of Queers*. London: Routledge, 2002.
———. *White*. London: Routledge, 1997.
Dyson, Michael Eric. "Niggas Gotta Stop." *Source* June 1999: 182.
Ebert, Roger. "Beat the Devil." rogerebert.com. 26 Nov. 2000.
Elie, Rudolph, Jr. "*Other Voices* a Very Fine First Novel." *Boston Herald* 25 Feb. 1948: 15.
Ellison, Ralph. "An Extravagance of Laughter." *The Collected Essays of Ralph Ellison*. Ed. John F. Callahan. New York: Modern Library, 1995. 613–58.
Ellman, Richard. *Oscar Wilde*. Ontario: Viking, 1987.
Entzminger, Betina. "Passing as Miscegenation: Whiteness and Homoeroticism in Faulkner's *Absalom, Absalom!*" *Faulkner Journal* 22.1–2 (2006–2007): 90–105.
Faderman, Lillian, ed. *Chloe Plus Olivia: An Anthology of Lesbian Literature from the Seventeenth Century to the Present*. New York: Viking, 1994.
———. *Odd Girls and Twilight Lovers: A History of Lesbian Life in Twentieth-Century America*. New York: Penguin, 1991.
———. *Surpassing the Love of Men: Romantic Friendship and Love between Women from the Renaissance to the Present*. New York: Quill, 1981.
Fahy, Thomas. *Understanding Truman Capote*. Columbia: University of South Carolina Press, 2014.
Faulkner, William. Foreword to *Sherwood Anderson and Other Famous Creoles*. Drawings by William Spratling and text by William Faulkner. 1926. Austin: University of Texas Press, 1966. 25–26.
The Fellowship of Southern Writers. "The Fellowship of Southern Writers: About Us." 2014. thefsw.org.
Fiedler, Leslie. "Capote's Tales." *Nation* 2 Apr. 1949: 395–96.
———. "The Profanation of the Child." *New Leader* 23 June 1958: 26–29.
Film Society Review. Review of *Beat the Devil*. Jan. 1966: 13.
Fine, Gary Alan. "Humour in Situ: The Role of Humour in Small Group Culture." *It's a Funny Thing, Humour*. Ed. A. J. Chapman and H. C. Foot. Oxford: Pergamon, 1977. 315–18.
Fishbein, Leslie. "*Rubyfruit Jungle:* Lesbianism, Feminism, and Narcissism." *International Journal of Women's Studies* 7.2 (1984): 155–59.
Fleischer, Leonore. "Leonore Fleischer Talks with Rita Mae Brown." *Washington Post Book World* 15 Oct. 1978: 16.
Flowers, Charles, ed. *Out, Loud, and Laughing: A Collection of Gay and Lesbian Humor*. New York: Anchor, 1995.
Fone, Byrne, ed. *The Columbia Anthology of Gay Literature: Readings from Western Antiquity to the Present Day*. New York: Columbia University Press, 1998.
Forster, Margaret. *The Rash Adventurer: The Rise and Fall of Charles Edward Stuart*. London: Secker & Warburg, 1973.
Foucault, Michel. *The History of Sexuality: An Introduction*. Trans. Robert Hurley. 1976. New York: Vintage, 1990.

Foust, Dean, and Justin Bachman. "Boeing's Flight from Union Labor." *BusinessWeek* 16 Nov. 2009: 34.

Francisco, Edward, Robert Vaughan, and Linda Francisco, eds. *The South in Perspective: An Anthology of Southern Literature.* Upper Saddle River, NJ: Prentice Hall, 2001.

Fraser, John. *America and the Patterns of Chivalry.* Cambridge: Cambridge University Press, 1982.

Free, William. "Camp Elements in the Plays of Tennessee Williams." *Southern Quarterly* 21.2 (1983): 16–23.

Freud, Sigmund. *The Joke and Its Relation to the Unconscious.* Trans. Joyce Crick. 1905. New York: Penguin, 2003.

———. "On Humour." *Collected Papers.* Ed. James Strachey. Vol. 5. New York: Basic Books, 1959. 215–21.

Friedman, Milton. "Defining Principles: Capitalism and Freedom." Schneider 69–90.

Frye, Northrop. *Anatomy of Criticism: Four Essays.* Princeton, NJ: Princeton University Press, 1957.

Fuchs, Stephan. *Against Essentialism: A Theory of Culture and Society.* Cambridge, MA: Harvard University Press, 2001.

Fuss, Diana. *Essentially Speaking: Feminism, Nature, and Difference.* New York: Routledge, 1989.

Gambone, Philip. *Travels in a Gay Nation: Portraits of LGBTQ Americans.* Madison: University of Wisconsin Press, 2010.

Garson, Helen S. *Truman Capote.* New York: Frederick Ungar, 1980.

Gates, Gary, and Frank Newport. "Gallup Special Report: The LGBT Vote in the 2012 Presidential Election." Williams Institute of UCLA Law School. October 2012. http://williamsinstitute.law.ucla.edu.

Gates, Henry Louis, Jr. *Loose Canons: Notes on the Culture Wars.* New York: Oxford University Press, 1992.

Gever, Martha, and Nathalie Magnan. "The Same Difference: On Lesbian Representation." *Stolen Glances.* Ed. Tessa Boffin and Jean Fraser. London: Pandora, 1991. 67–75.

Gilmore, Leigh. "Limit-Cases: Trauma, Self-Representation, and the Jurisdictions of Identity." *Biography* 24.1 (2001): 128–39.

Girson, Rochelle. "'48's Nine." *Saturday Review of Literature* 12 Feb. 1949: 12–14.

Goodwin, Joseph. *More Man Than You'll Ever Be: Gay Folklore and Acculturation in Middle America.* Bloomington: Indiana University Press, 1989.

Gray, Richard. *Southern Aberrations: Writers of the American South and the Problems of Regionalism.* Baton Rouge: Louisiana State University Press, 2000.

———. *Writing the South: Ideas of an American Region.* Cambridge: Cambridge University Press, 1986.

Greene, Christina. *Our Separate Ways: Women and the Black Freedom Movement in Durham, North Carolina.* Chapel Hill: University of North Carolina Press, 2005.

Greeson, Jennifer Rae. *Our South: Geographic Fantasy and the Rise of National Literature.* Cambridge, MA: Harvard University Press, 2010.

Griffin, Connie. "'I will not wear that coat': Cross-Dressing in the Works of Dorothy Allison." *He Said, She Says: An RSVP to the Male Text.* Ed. Mica Howe and Sarah Appleton Aguiar. Madison, NJ: Fairleigh Dickinson University Press, 2001. 143–57.

Grobel, Lawrence. *Conversations with Capote.* New York: New American Library, 1985.

Gross, Larry, and James D. Woods, eds. *The Columbia Reader on Lesbians and Gay Men in Media, Society, and Politics.* New York: Columbia University Press, 1999.

Guillory, John. *Cultural Capital: The Problem of Literary Canon Formation.* Chicago: University of Chicago Press, 1993.

Hacker, J. David. "A Census-Based Count of the Civil War Dead." *Civil War History* 57.4 (2011): 307–48.

Hall, Wade. *Reflections of the Civil War in Southern Humor.* Gainesville: University of Florida Press, 1962.

———. *The Smiling Phoenix: Southern Humor from 1865 to 1914.* Gainesville: University of Florida Press, 1965.

Harker, Jaime. "'And you too, sister, sister?': Lesbian Sexuality, *Absalom, Absalom!,* and the Reconstruction of the Southern Family." *Faulkner's Sexualities: Faulkner and Yoknapatawpha, 2007.* Ed. Annette Trefzer and Ann Abadie. Jackson: University Press of Mississippi, 2010. 38–53.

Harris, W. C. "Dr. Molly Feelgood; or, How I Can't Learn to Stop Worrying and Love *Rubyfruit Jungle.*" *EAPSU Online: A Journal of Critical and Creative Work* 1 (2004): 23–41.

Hayek, F. A. "Resurrecting the Abandoned Road." Schneider 53–65.

Heard, Alex. "This American Lie." *New Republic* 19 Mar. 2007: 35–38.

Helvick, James [Claud Cockburn]. *Beat the Devil.* Philadelphia: Lippincott, 1951.

Henke, Suzette. "'A Child Is Being Beaten': Dorothy Allison's Testimony of Trauma and Abuse in *Bastard Out of Carolina.*" *Critical Essays on the Works of American Author Dorothy Allison.* Ed. Christine Blouch and Laurie Vickroy. Lewiston, NY: Mellen, 2004. 9–28.

Herring, Scott. *Another Country: Queer Anti-Urbanism.* New York: New York University Press, 2010.

Higgs, Robert. "Southern Humor: The Light and the Dark." *Thalia: Studies in Literary Humor* 6.2 (1983): 17–27.

Hill, Pati. "The Art of Fiction XVII: Truman Capote." *Paris Review* 16 (1957): 34–51.

Hobson, Fred. "Of Canons and Cultural Wars: Southern Literature and Literary Scholarship after Midcentury." Humphries and Lowe 72–86.

Hoefer, Anthony Dyer. *Apocalypse South: Judgment, Cataclysm, and Resistance in the Regional Imaginary.* Columbus: Ohio State University Press, 2012.

Holt, Patricia. "Rita Mae Brown." *Publishers Weekly* 2 Oct. 1978: 16–17.

Horn, Carolyn. "Rita Mae Brown: Being Different Really Isn't So Different." *Washington Post* 24 Oct. 1977: C1, 13.

Horner, Avril, and Sue Zlosnik. *Gothic and the Comic Turn.* Hampshire: Palgrave Macmillan, 2005.

Howard, John, ed. *Carryin' On in the Lesbian and Gay South.* New York: New York University Press, 1997.

———. *Men Like That: A Southern Queer History.* Chicago: University of Chicago Press, 1999.

Hudson, Arthur Palmer, ed. *Humor of the Old Deep South.* New York: Macmillan, 1936.

Humphries, Jefferson. "The Discourse of Southernness, or How We Know There Will Still Be Such a Thing as the South and Southern Literature in the Twenty-First Century." Humphries and Lowe 119–33.

Humphries, Jefferson, and John Lowe, eds. *The Future of Southern Letters.* New York: Oxford University Press, 1996.

Hurley, Matthew, Daniel Dennett, and Reginald Adams. *Inside Jokes: Using Humor to Reverse-Engineer the Mind.* Cambridge, MA: MIT Press, 2011.

Hurley, Paul. "Williams' 'Desire and the Black Masseur': An Analysis." *Studies in Short Fiction* 2 (1964): 51–55.

Huston, John. *An Open Book.* New York: Knopf, 1980.

Hutcheon, Linda. *Irony's Edge: The Theory and Politics of Irony.* London: Routledge, 1994.

Hutcheson, Francis. *Thoughts on Laughter, and Observations on the Fable of the Bees, in Six Letters.* Glasgow: Robert and Andrew Foults, 1758.

Hyers, Conrad. "The Dialectic of the Sacred and the Comic." *Holy Laughter: Essays on Religion in the Comic Perspective.* Ed. Conrad Hyers. New York: Seabury, 1969. 208–40.

Isherwood, Christopher. *The World in the Evening.* 1952. Minneapolis: University of Minnesota Press, 1999.

Jefferson, Margo. "Scarlett Women: *Southern Ladies and Gentlemen* by Florence King." *Newsweek* 30 Jun. 1975: 66.

Jennings, C. Robert. "Truman Capote Talks, Talks, Talk." *New York* 13 May 1968: 53–55.

Johnson, E. Patrick. *Sweet Tea: Black Gay Men of the South.* Chapel Hill: University of North Carolina Press, 2008.

Jones, Leon. *From Brown to Boston: Desegregation in Education.* 2 vols. Metuchen, NJ: Scarecrow, 1979.

Jones, Suzanne W., ed. *Growing Up in the South: An Anthology of Modern Southern Literature.* New York: Mentor, 1991.

Jones, Suzanne W., and Sharon Monteith, eds. *South to a New Place: Region, Literature, Culture.* Baton Rouge: Louisiana State University Press, 2002.

Kaplan, Carey, and Ellen Cronan Rose. *The Canon and the Common Reader.* Knoxville: University of Tennessee Press, 1990.

Kaufman, Gloria, ed. *In Stitches: A Patchwork of Feminist Humor and Satire.* Bloomington: Indiana University Press, 1991.

Kawada, Louise. "Liberating Laughter: Comedic Form in Some Lesbian Novels." *Sexual Practice / Textual Theory: Lesbian Cultural Criticism.* Ed. Susan Wolfe and Julia Penelope. Cambridge, MA: Blackwell, 1993. 251–62.

Keith, Don Lee. "An Interview with Truman Capote." *Contempora* Oct.–Nov. 1970: 36–40.

Keller, James R. "Tennessee Williams Doesn't Live Here Anymore: Hypocrisy, Paradox, and Homosexual Panic in the New/Old South." *Studies in Popular Culture* 19.2 (1996): 303–18.

Kennedy, Randall. *Nigger: The Strange Career of a Troublesome Word.* New York: Pantheon, 2002.

Kierkegaard, Søren. *The Concept of Irony, with Constant Reference to Socrates.* Trans. Lee Capel. Bloomington: Indiana University Press, 1965.

King, Florence. "Benched: Life after Sex." *Ms.* May 1989: 43–45.

———. *Confessions of a Failed Southern Lady.* New York: St. Martin's, 1985.

———. *Deja Reviews: Florence King All Over Again: Selections from* National Review *and* The American Spectator, *1990–2001.* Wilmington, DE: Intercollegiate Studies Institute, 2006.

———. *He: An Irreverent Look at the American Male.* New York: Stein & Day, 1978.

———. *Lump It or Leave It.* New York: St. Martin's, 1990.

———. *Reflections in a Jaundiced Eye.* New York: St. Martin's, 1989.

———. "Sex and the Good Ole Boy." *Ms.* July 1975: 53+.

———. *Southern Ladies and Gentleman.* 1975. New York: St. Martin's Griffin, 1993.

———. *STET, Damnit! The Misanthrope's Corner, 1991 to 2002.* New York: National Review, 2003.

———. *WASP, Where Is Thy Sting?* New York: Stein & Day, 1977.

———. *When Sisterhood Was in Flower.* New York: Viking, 1982.

———. *With Charity toward None: A Fond Look at Misanthropy.* New York: St. Martin's, 1992.

Klemesrud, Judy. "Underground Book Brings Fame to a Lesbian Author." *New York Times* 26 Sept. 1977: 42.

Knight, Lania. "A Conversation with David Sedaris." *Missouri Review* 30.1 (2007): 72–89.

Kopelson, Kevin. *Sedaris.* Minneapolis: University of Minnesota Press, 2007.

Kraus, Carolyn. "The Road from Illegitimacy to Art: Dorothy Allison's *Bastard Out of Carolina.*" *North Dakota Quarterly* 71.3 (2004): 127–43.

Kreyling, Michael. *Inventing Southern Literature.* Jackson: University Press of Mississippi, 1998.

———. *The South That Wasn't There: Postsouthern Memory and History.* Baton Rouge: Louisiana State University Press, 2010.

Ladd, Barbara. "Dismantling the Monolith: Southern Places—Past, Present, and Future." Jones and Monteith 44–57.

———. "Rita Mae Brown." *Contemporary Fiction Writers of the South: A Bio-Bibliographical Sourcebook.* Ed. Joseph Flora and Robert Bain. Westport, CT: Greenwood, 1993. 67–75.

LeMahieu, Michael. "An Interview with Dorothy Allison." *Contemporary Literature* 54.1 (2010): 651–76.

Leverich, Lyle. *Tom: The Unknown Tennessee Williams.* New York: Crown, 1995.

Levine, Daniel. "Uses of Classical Mythology in Rita Mae Brown's *Southern Discomfort.*" *Classical and Modern Literature* 10.1 (1989): 63–70.

Long, Robert Emmet. *Truman Capote—Enfant Terrible.* New York: Continuum, 2008.

Lowell, James Russell. "Humor, Wit, Fun, and Satire." *Century* Nov. 1893: 124–31.

MacLauchlin, Cory. *Butterfly in the Typewriter: The Tragic Life of John Kennedy Toole and the Remarkable Story of* A Confederacy of Dunces. New York: Da Capo, 2013.

Mandrell, James. "Questions of Genre and Gender: Contemporary American Versions of the Feminine Picaresque." *Novel* 20.2 (1987): 149–70.

Mansfield, Nick. *Masochism: The Art of Power.* Westport, CT: Praeger, 1997.

Marple, B. G. Review of *Beat the Devil. Films in Review* Mar. 1953: 143–44.

Martin, Rod. *The Psychology of Humor: An Integrative Approach.* Burlington, MA: Elsevier, 2007.

Martindale, Kathleen. "Rita Mae Brown's *Six of One* and Anne Cameron's *The Journey:* Fictional Contributions to the Ethics of Feminist Nonviolence." *Atlantis* 12.1 (1986): 103–10.

McPherson, Tara. *Reconstructing Dixie: Race, Gender, and Nostalgia in the Imagined South.* Durham, NC: Duke University Press, 2003.

McWhiney, Grady. *Cracker Culture: Celtic Ways in the Old South.* Tuscaloosa: University of Alabama Press, 1988.

Megan, Carolyn E. "Moving toward Truth: An Interview with Dorothy Allison." *Kenyon Review* 16.4 (1994): 71–83.

Merrick, Gordon. "How to Write Lying Down." *New Republic* 8 Dec. 1958: 23–24.

Meyer, Moe. *An Archaeology of Posing: Essays on Camp, Drag, and Sexuality.* United States: Macater, 2010.

———. "Reclaiming the Discourse of Camp." Meyer, *Politics and Poetics of Camp* 1–22.

———, ed. *The Politics and Poetics of Camp.* Routledge: London: 1994.

Mills, Jerry Leath. "The Dead Mule Rides Again." *Southern Cultures* 6.4 (2000): 11–34.

Mizejewski, Linda. "Camp among the Swastikas: Isherwood, Sally Bowles, and 'Good Heter Stuff.'" Cleto 237–53.

Morgan, Robin. *The Word of a Woman: Feminist Dispatches, 1968–1992.* New York: Norton, 1991.

Morreall, John. *Comic Relief: A Comprehensive Philosophy of Humor.* Malden, MA: Wiley-Blackwell, 2009.

Morrill, Cynthia. "Revamping the Gay Sensibility." Meyer, *Politics and Poetics of Camp* 110–29.

Moses, Montrose J. "Introduction to *The Literature of the South* (1910)." *Defining Southern Literature: Perspectives and Assessments, 1831–1952.* Ed. John E. Bassett. Madison, NJ: Fairleigh Dickinson University Press, 1997. 274–77.

Muecke, D. C. *The Compass of Irony.* London: Methuen, 1969.

Muñoz, José Esteban. *Disidentifications: Queers of Color and the Performance of Politics.* Minneapolis: University of Minnesota Press, 1999.

Murphy, Timothy. *Gay Science: The Ethics of Sexual Orientation Research.* New York: Columbia University Press, 1997.

Nero, Charles. "Black Gay Men and White Gay Men: A Less Than Perfect Union." Dews and Law 115–26.

Nestle, Joan. "My Mother Liked to Fuck." Gross and Woods 505–6.

Nevils, Rene Pol, and Deborah George Hardy. *Ignatius Rising: The Life of John Kennedy Toole.* Baton Rouge: Louisiana State University Press, 2005.

Newquist, Roy. *Counterpoint.* Chicago: Rand McNally, 1964.

Newsweek. Review of *Other Voices, Other Rooms.* 26 Jan. 1948: 9.

Nickels, Cameron C. *Civil War Humor.* Jackson: University of Mississippi Press, 2010.

Norden, Eric. "*Playboy* Interview: Truman Capote." *Playboy* Mar. 1968: 51+.

O'Connor, Flannery. *The Habit of Being.* Ed. Sally Fitzgerald. New York: Farrar, Straus, & Giroux, 1979.

———. *The Violent Bear It Away. Three by Flannery O'Connor.* New York: Signet, 1983. 121–267.

O'Gorman, Farrell. "The Fugitive-Agrarians and the Twentieth-Century Southern Canon." *A Companion to the Regional Literature of America.* Ed. Charles Crow. Malden, MA: Blackwell, 2003. 286–305.

Ohi, Kevin. "Devouring Creation: Cannibalism, Sodomy, and the Scene of Analysis in *Suddenly, Last Summer.*" *Cinema Journal* 38.3 (1999): 27–49.

Omi, Michael, and Howard Winant. "Racial Formation." *Race Critical Theories: Text and Context.* Ed. Philomena Essed and David Theo Goldberg. Malden, MA: Blackwell, 2002. 123–45.

Painter, Dorothy. "Lesbian Humor as a Normalization Device." *Communication, Language, and Sex: Proceedings of the First Annual Conference.* Ed. Cynthia Berryman, Virginia Eman, and Cheris Kramarae. Rowley, MA: Newbury, 1980. 132–48.

Park, Soyoung. "'Survival is the least of my desires': Testimony, Shame, and Desire in Dorothy Allison's *Bastard Out of Carolina.*" *Feminist Studies in English Literature* 18.2 (2010): 57–85.

Parsons, C. G. *Inside View of Slavery: or, a Tour among the Planters.* Boston: Jewett, 1855.

Percy, Walker. *Love in the Ruins.* New York: Picador, 1971.

Percy, William Armstrong, III. "William Alexander Percy (1885–1942): His Homosexuality and Why It Matters." Howard, *Carryin' On* 75–92.

Peters, Brian. "Queer Semiotics of Expression: Gothic Language and Homosexual Destruction in Tennessee Williams's 'One Arm' and 'Desire and the Black Masseur.'" *Tennessee Williams Annual Review* 8 (2006): 109–21.

Peterson, Christopher. "The Haunted House of Kinship: Miscegenation, Homosexuality, and Faulkner's *Absalom, Absalom!*" *New Centennial Review* 4.1 (2004): 227–65.

Piacentino, Ed. "Challenging the Canon: Other Southern Literary Lives." *Southern Literary Journal* 38.2 (2006): 145–49.

Pugh, Tison. *Queer Chivalry: Medievalism and the Myth of White Masculinity in Southern Literature.* Baton Rouge: Louisiana State University Press, 2013.

———. *Truman Capote: A Literary Life at the Movies.* Athens: University of Georgia Press, 2014.
Quintilian. *The Institutio Oratoria of Quintilian.* Trans. H. E. Butler. Cambridge, MA: Harvard University Press, 1986.
Reed, Kenneth T. *Truman Capote.* Boston: Twayne, 1981.
Richards, Gary. *Lovers and Beloveds: Sexual Otherness in Southern Fiction, 1936–1961.* Baton Rouge: Louisiana State University Press, 2005.
R. J. D. Review of *Other Voices, Other Rooms. Boston Daily Globe* 21 Jan. 1948: 15.
Robertson, Pamela. *Guilty Pleasures: Feminist Camp from Mae West to Madonna.* Durham, NC: Duke University Press, 1996.
Robinson, Paul. *Queer Wars: The New Gay Right and Its Critics.* Chicago: University of Chicago Press, 2005.
Robinson, Selma. "The Legend of 'Little T.'" *PM Picture News* 14 Mar. 1948: 6–8.
Rolo, Charles. "The South and the Psyche." *Atlantic* Mar. 1948: 108–10.
Romine, Scott. "Where Is Southern Literature? The Practice of Place in a Postsouthern Age." Jones and Monteith 23–43.
Russ, Joanna. *Magic Mommas, Trembling Sisters, Puritans, and Perverts: Feminist Essays.* Trumansburg, NY: Cross Press, 1985.
Sachs, Andrea. "Rita Mae Brown: Loves Cats, Hates Marriage." *Time* 18 Mar. 2008.
Saddik, Annette. "The (Un)Represented Fragmentation of the Body in Tennessee Williams's 'Desire and the Black Masseur' and *Suddenly, Last Summer.*" *Modern Drama* 41 (1998): 347–54.
Savran, David. *A Queer Sort of Materialism: Recontextualizing American Theater.* Ann Arbor: University of Michigan Press, 2003.
Schneider, Gregory, ed. *Conservatism in America since 1930.* New York: New York University Press, 2003.
Sears, James T. *Edwin and John: A Personal History of the American South.* New York: Routledge, 2009.
———. *Lonely Hunters: An Oral History of Lesbian and Gay Southern Life, 1948–1968.* Boulder, CO: Westview, 1997.
———. *Rebels, Rubyfruits, and Rhinestones: Queering Space in the Stonewall South.* New Brunswick, NJ: Rutgers University Press, 2001.
Sedaris, David. *Barrel Fever.* Boston: Little, Brown, 1994.
———. *Dress Your Family in Corduroy and Denim.* Boston: Little, Brown, 2004.
———. *Holidays on Ice.* Boston: Little, Brown, 1997.
———. *Let's Explore Diabetes with Owls: Essays, Etc.* Boston: Little, Brown, 2013.
———. *Me Talk Pretty One Day.* Boston: Little, Brown, 2000.
———. *Naked.* Boston: Little, Brown, 1997.
———. "Now We Are Five." *New Yorker* 23 Oct. 2013.
———. *Squirrel Seeks Chipmunk: A Modest Bestiary.* Boston: Little, Brown, 2010.
———. *When You Are Engulfed in Flames.* Boston: Little, Brown, 2008.

Sedgwick, Eve. *Between Men: English Literature and Male Homosocial Desire.* New York: Columbia University Press, 1985.

Segrest, Mab. *My Mama's Dead Squirrel: Lesbian Essays on Southern Culture.* Ithaca, NY: Firebrand, 1985.

Seidel, Kathryn Lee. *The Southern Belle in the American Novel.* Tampa: University of South Florida Press, 1985.

Shakespeare, William. *Titus Andronicus. The Riverside Shakespeare: The Complete Works.* Ed. G. Blakemore Evans. 2nd ed. Boston: Houghton Mifflin, 1997. 1065–1100.

Shister, Gail. "Rita Mae Brown: A Nice Southern Girl Makes Good as a Chronicler of Unconventional Love." *Philadelphia Inquirer* 12 May 1983: D12.

Silver, Andrew. *Minstrelsy and Murder: The Crisis of Southern Humor, 1835–1925.* Baton Rouge: Louisiana State University Press, 2006.

Silver, Nate. "How Opinion on Same Sex Marriage Is Changing, And What It Means." 26 Mar. 2013. fivethirtyeight.blogs.nytimes.com.

Sinfield, Alan. *Out on Stage: Lesbian and Gay Theatre in the Twentieth Century.* New Haven, CT: Yale University Press, 1999.

Smith, Donna Jo. "Queering the South: Constructions of Southern/Queer Identity." Howard, *Carryin' On* 370–85.

Smith, Stephen A. *Myth, Media, and the Southern Mind.* Fayetteville: University of Arkansas Press, 1985.

———. "The Rhetoric of Southern Humor." Humphries and Lowe 170–85.

Smith, William Jay. *My Friend Tom: The Poet-Playwright Tennessee Williams.* Jackson: University Press of Mississippi, 2012.

Sollers, Philippe. "Lettre de Sade." *Tel Quel* 61 (Spring 1975): 14–20.

Sontag, Susan. "Notes on 'Camp.'" *Against Interpretation and Other Essays.* New York: Delta, 1966. 275–92.

Spears, Richard. *Slang and Euphemism.* Middle Village, NY: Jonathan David, 1981.

Spira, Tamara Lea. "Remembering Trauma, Refusing Disappearance: *Corregidora, Bastard Out of Carolina,* and the Transnational Labors of Memory." *Transnationalism and Resistance: Experience and Experiment in Women's Writing.* Ed. Adele Parker and Stephanie Young. Amsterdam: Rodopi, 2013. 113–37.

Spoto, Donald. *The Kindness of Strangers: The Life of Tennessee Williams.* Boston: Little Brown, 1985.

Steinem, Gloria. "'Go right ahead and ask me anything': And So She Did." *McCall's* Nov. 1967: 76+.

Talley, Andre Leon. "An Afternoon with Truman Capote." *W* 23–30 July 1976: 8.

Thomas, Calvin, ed. *Straight with a Twist: Queer Theory and the Subject of Heterosexuality.* Urbana: University of Illinois Press, 2000.

Thomas, Kelly L. "White Trash Lesbianism: Dorothy Allison's Queer Politics." *Gender Reconstructions: Pornography and Perversions in Literature and Culture.* Ed.

Cindy Carlson, Robert Mazzola, and Susan Benardo. Aldershot, England: Ashgate, 2002. 167–88.

Thompson, Brock. *The Un-Natural State: Arkansas and the Queer South*. Fayetteville: University of Arkansas Press, 2010.

Tipton, Nathan. "Rope and Faggot: The Homoerotics of Lynching in William Faulkner's *Light in August*." *Mississippi Quarterly* 64.3–4 (2011): 369–91.

———. "What's Eating Anthony Burns? Dismembering the Bodies That Matter in Tennessee Williams's 'Desire and the Black Masseur.'" *Southern Literary Journal* 43.1 (2010): 39–58.

Trilling, Diana. "Fiction in Review." *Nation* 31 Jan. 1949: 133–34.

Turner, Alice. "Fall Preview: Rita Mae Brown." *New York* 18 Sept. 1978: 60.

Vespa, Mary. "Sued by Gore Vidal and Stung by Lee Radziwill, A Wounded Truman Capote Lashes Back at the Dastardly Duo." *People* 25 Jun. 1979: 34–36.

von Sacher-Masoch, Leopold. *Venus in Furs*. Deleuze, *Masochism* 141–293.

Voss, Ralph. *Truman Capote and the Legacy of* In Cold Blood. Tuscaloosa: University of Alabama Press, 2011.

Walker, Nancy. *A Very Serious Thing: Women's Humor and American Culture*. Minneapolis: University of Minnesota Press, 1988.

Walker, Nancy, and Zita Dresner, eds. *Redressing the Balance: American Women's Literary Humor from Colonial Times to the 1980s*. Jackson: University Press of Mississippi, 1988.

Warhol, Andy. "Sunday with Mister C.: An Audiodocumentary by Andy Warhol Starring Truman Capote." *Truman Capote: Conversations*. Ed. M. Thomas Inge. Jackson: University Press of Mississippi, 1987. 236–95.

Warren, Carol. *Madwives: Schizophrenic Women in the 1950s*. New Brunswick, NJ: Rutgers University Press, 1987.

Warren, Robert Penn, ed. *A Southern Harvest: Short Stories by Southern Writers*. Dunwoody, GA: Norman Berg, 1972.

Warren, Robert Penn, and Albert Erskine, eds. *A New Southern Harvest: An Anthology*. New York: Bantam, 1957.

Waters, Arthur B. "Tennessee Williams: Ten Years Later." *Theater Arts* July 1955: 72–73+.

Waters, John. *Role Models*. New York: Farrar, Straus, & Giroux, 2010.

White, E. B., and Katherine S. White, eds. *A Subtreasury of American Humor*. New York: Coward-McCann, 1941.

Whitlock, Reta Ugena, ed. *Queer South Rising: Voices of a Contested Place*. Charlotte: Information Age, 2013.

Whitmore, George. "George Whitmore Interviews Tennessee Williams." *Gay Sunshine Interviews*. Ed. Winston Leyland. Vol. 1. San Francisco: Gay Sunshine Press, 1978. 309–25.

Wiles, Mary. "The Fascination of the Lesbian Fetish: A Perverse Possibility across the Body of Dorothy Allison's *Bastard Out of Carolina*." Calvin Thomas 152–62.

Williams, Tennessee. *Collected Stories*. New York: New Directions, 1985.
———. *Memoirs*. 1972. New York: New Directions, 2006.
———. *Tennessee Williams: Plays*. Vol. 1, *1937–1955*. New York: Library of America, 2000.
———. *Tennessee Williams: Plays*. Vol. 2, *1957–1980*. New York: Library of America, 2000.
———. *Where I Live: Selected Essays*. Ed. Christine Day and Bob Woods. New York: New Directions, 1978.
Williford, Lex, and Michael Martone, eds. *Touchstone Anthology of Contemporary Creative Nonfiction: Work from 1970 to the Present*. New York: Touchstone, 2007.
Wilson, Angelia R. *Below the Belt: Sexuality, Religion, and the American South*. London: Cassell, 2000.
Winchell, Mark Royden. "Come Back to the Locker Room Ag'in, Brick Honey." *Mississippi Quarterly* 48.4 (1995): 701–12.
Windham, Donald. *Lost Friendships: A Memoir of Truman Capote, Tennessee Williams, and Others*. New York: Morrow, 1987.
Winn, Janet. "Capote, Mailer, and Miss Parker." *New Republic* 9 Feb. 1959: 27–28.
Woodhouse, Reed. *Unlimited Embrace: A Canon of Gay Fiction, 1945–1995*. Amherst: University of Massachusetts Press, 1998.
Woodward, C. Vann. "The Irony of Southern History." *Journal of Southern History* 19.1 (1953): 3–19.
Zieger, Robert H., ed. *Life and Labor in the New New South*. Gainesville: University Press of Florida, 2012.
———. *Organized Labor in the Twentieth-Century South*. Knoxville: University of Tennessee Press, 1991.
Žižek, Slavoj. *The Metastases of Enjoyment: Six Essays on Women and Causality*. 1994. London: Verso, 2005.
Zwagerman, Sean. *Wit's End: Women's Humor as Rhetorical and Performative Strategy*. Pittsburgh, PA: University of Pittsburgh Press, 2010.

Index